PROMISES TO KEEP

MY INSPIRED RUN FROM SYRACUSE TO DENVER TO THE HALL

Floyd Little with Tom Mackie

TRIUMPH
B O O K S

Library of Congress Cataloging-in-Publication Data

Little, Floyd, 1942–
   Promises to keep : my inspired run from Syracuse to Denver to the hall / by Floyd Little with Tom Mackie.
      p. cm.
   Includes bibliographical references and index.
   ISBN 978-1-60078-753-9
   1. Little, Floyd, 1942– 2. Football players—United States—Biography. 3. Denver Broncos (Football team)—History. I. Mackie, Tom, 1963– II. Title.
   GV939.L58A3 2012
   796.332092—dc23
   [B]
                                   2012020779

This book is available in quantity at special discounts for your group or organization. For further information, contact:

Triumph Books LLC
814 North Franklin Street
Chicago, Illinois 60610
Phone: (312) 337-0747
www.triumphbooks.com

Printed in U.S.A.

ISBN: 978-1-60078-753-9

Design by Amy Carter

Photos courtesy of AP Images unless otherwise indicated

For my parents, Lula Mae Little and Fredrick Douglas Little, and my brothers, Fredrick Jerome Little and Charles Howard Little. Your profound impact and everlasting love continue to shine down from above—inspiring me every day to leave a legacy that will make our family proud for generations to come.

—Floyd Little

For Luke, my sweet boy, my whole world, my reason for being.

—Tom Mackie

CONTENTS

FOREWORD

I will always remember the first time I ran into Floyd Little. Or, more accurately, the first time he ran into me.

It was 1964. Floyd was a sophomore, and I was a freshman at Syracuse University. Freshmen were then ineligible for varsity competition. We were the scout team, put on the field to help the sophomores, juniors, and seniors prepare for the season. There were 25 or 26 of us at one end of the field and approximately 80 of them on the other end. I lined up at left cornerback. On my very first snap, Gary Bugenhagen—who later became an All-American tackle—and big fullback Jim Nance charged right at me with Floyd carrying the ball behind them. I came roaring up to stop the play; I probably dove to try to take somebody out. But Floyd ran right over the top of me. That was my first experience as a college football player, getting stampeded on the practice field by Floyd Little.

Happily, I've come to know Floyd in a much different light since our first meeting, first as a teammate and now as a friend. And I can say with both candor and pride that I've never met anyone quite like Floyd, a successful and accomplished man who has always carried himself with dignity, humility, humor, and grace.

Floyd was a tremendous football player. He was elected to the College Football Hall of Fame in 1983 and the Pro Football Hall of Fame in 2010. Floyd was a three-time All-American who still holds the Orange career records for touchdowns (46) and punt return touchdowns (5). He was the first Syracuse back to rush for more than 1,000 yards in a season, and he finished fifth in the Heisman Trophy voting in both his junior and senior years.

I was privileged to witness Floyd's most memorable performances at Syracuse—his five-touchdown game in Archbold Stadium in 1964 against a Kansas team that featured Gale Sayers; scoring four touchdowns, including one on a 95-yard punt return, in a victory over Pittsburgh in Shea Stadium in 1965; his 216-yard rushing performance vs. Tennessee in the Gator Bowl on New Year's Day 1967. The list is long, as is his inventory of achievement with the Denver Broncos, his only pro team. When he completed his nine-year NFL career in 1975, Floyd had been selected to five Pro Bowls, led the AFC in rushing twice, the entire NFL in rushing in 1971, and was the seventh-leading rusher in league history.

Floyd had terrific speed and unquestioned toughness. He was a great player. It was an honor to play on the same team with Floyd. And during his senior year in 1966, Floyd and Larry Csonka formed one of the greatest backfields in college football history. I was honored to be part of that magical backfield as the starting wingback that season, something I will always cherish.

But as good as he was on the football field, Floyd was—and is—an even better person. He was, without a doubt, the most popular person on the Syracuse campus. Everybody loved him. He was a very positive person who never said anything negative about anybody. People loved to have him in class. Everybody wanted to be his friend.

Floyd had a bumpy climb before he reached his lofty standing. He overcame obstacles and earned everything he got. Floyd lost his father when he was six years old. His mother worked several jobs while raising a large family, and his older sisters helped bring him up. His brother was in trouble with the law. He was shy.

But Floyd would not be held back. He was elected class president at Hillhouse High School in Connecticut. Floyd later attended the Bordentown

Military Institute in New Jersey. After leaving Syracuse, he graduated from the University of Denver College of Law, became a successful businessman, and is now the special assistant to the athletics director at our alma mater.

How did he rise from his humble childhood to put together this impressive resume? I saw Floyd's drive when we were teammates at Syracuse. The number one thing about him was his exceptional attitude. It was infectious. The smile was always there. The attempt to bolster his teammates was always there. Everything he did was with regard to the team and creating better self-esteem for everybody on the team. He was highly respected and well-liked by everybody. I remember holding Floyd in tremendous regard when we were teammates at Syracuse.

Floyd's work ethic was always second to none. Nobody had an attitude like him. His attitude was more, not less. Some players, when they reach a certain status, would rather be recognized and taken care of. That was not Floyd. He led the way by always working harder. In practice, we would run from drill to drill. I would make it a point to sprint to be at the front of the line. But Floyd would always be first, and I would always be second.

Ben Schwartzwalder, our demanding coach, would have us run through a series of drills in full pads, helmet included. One of them was a rope climb. Most of us grabbed one rope with two hands, wrapped our feet around it, and pulled our way up. Not Floyd. He would take a rope in each hand and race to the top. And he was still the fastest climber.

Though Floyd was an intense competitor, he was and remains a man with an inherent kindness, an infectious positive attitude, and an innate insistence on treating everyone with respect and kindness. When he wasn't performing an amazing athletic feat, Floyd was a gregarious young man who was always smiling, laughing, and making those around him feel comfortable—all traits he retains today. Floyd can step through a doorway and instantly light up an entire room with his smile and benevolence. Everybody is his friend. He has a great knack for putting people at ease and letting them realize he puts his pants on one leg at a time like everybody else. He's great at that.

I cannot overemphasize the quality of football player—or person—he was in college. Everybody respected him. I've never heard one guy say one bad thing about Floyd Little as a teammate. He had tremendous respect for and from his teammates. He has always stayed very loyal to his team-mates, and he's very loyal to Syracuse. Nobody ever had anything but honest praise for Floyd because of the quality of person that he is.

The position Floyd currently holds at Syracuse as the special assistant to the athletic director is perfect for him. He loves his job. He loves to inspire and help young people. And he loves Syracuse University.

It was a privilege to play football with Floyd. Today, almost 50 years after he introduced himself by running over me on the practice field, it is a great honor to call him my friend.

—Tom Coughlin
Head Coach, New York Giants
Super Bowl XLII and XLVI Champions

PREFACE

I t was all an illusion, you see.

The explosion of sports cable networks and HDTV and NFL packages and MLB.com and talk radio and daily blogs deluded the sports fan into believing he was drawing ever nearer to his idols—when in truth they were receding further and further away.

No more Willie Mays jumping into your stickball game and belting one four sewers away. No more Baltimore Orioles or Colts dropping by your corner taproom for a cold one after a game.

The explosion that tricked the fan into a sense of intimacy was actually what made their heroes run for the hills, the bodyguards, and the gated communities.

So imagine my cocked eyebrow and quizzical squint at the handwritten letter that appeared in my mailbox a few years ago. It was from a stranger who happened to be from my hometown—Wilmington, Delaware—asking me to write a story for my magazine, *Sports Illustrated*. He wanted a fairy-tale–like story about him befriending his boyhood idol from back in the '60s, Denver Broncos running back Floyd Little, and ending up leading the crusade that fulfilled Floyd's one last big wish in life—entrance into the Pro Football Hall of Fame.

Sure, I was skeptical at first. I had to see the 44 thank-you notes that Floyd had written to Tom in the months that followed the culmination of Floyd's Hall of Fame dream. I had to run my hands across the orange Broncos jumpsuit that Floyd had sent for Tom's little boy and stare at the photos of Floyd that Tom had plastered on his bedroom walls and propped up on his piano for inspiration as he practiced when he was a little boy himself.

I had to fly to Seattle and listen to Floyd gush about this odd, insistent fan who'd flown to California to meet him for lunch—a 40th birthday gift arranged by the fan's wife—and who'd ended up Floyd's buddy, his cheerleader, his battering ram banging at the castle doors of the Hall of Fame in Canton year after year, laying siege to the selection committee even after Floyd, exhausted and frustrated by decades of rejection, had given up. His witness as Floyd collapsed to the floor beneath his family's hugs and tears and his own astonishment when the Hall finally called his name.

Yep, it was all true, the most genuine fan-hero tale you could conjure in an age when technology and obsession had wrung the humanity out of the relationship between the immortals and the masses.

And now, with this book, you can add one more noun to the list of roles that Tom Mackie has played in Floyd's storied life: buddy, cheerleader, ramrod—chronicler. You can be certain that it's a book chockfull of candor and anecdotes that Floyd wouldn't have spilled to anyone except a cherished friend. And it's certain that the cherished friend knows how to keep your eyes riveted to a page. Otherwise I would've crumpled and tossed that stranger's handwritten letter and gone right on disbelieving in fairy tales.

—Gary Smith

ACKNOWLEDGMENTS

I can't begin acknowledgments without first thanking Triumph Books for helping to make this book a reality.

Reflecting on my life and my career, I have been truly blessed to be surrounded by incredibly supportive family and friends. I am an intensely loyal person, and I gravitate toward people who share my simple values of passion, commitment, and integrity.

The people I would like to thank are the ones who live these values and who always have my back. First and foremost, I would like to thank my wife, DeBorah, and my three children, Marc, Christy, and Kyra. Without you, I would not be the person I am today. You are my whole life and my reason for being. I am so deeply proud of each of you. I love you all so much!

Also, love and affection to my children's families: Marc's wife, Tigre, and Christy's husband, Adrian. And love to all my nieces and nephews especially Mike Sturdivant, who is a second son to me. I would also like to give special hugs and kisses to each of my grandchildren: AJ, Skye, Blaze, and Hayes. Poppy loves you all very much. You are my proud legacy and you make my heart sing with joy.

I would also like to thank my sisters: Betty, Rosa, and Priscilla. You helped me grow up to be the man I am today. Without you, I would not have had the chance to realize my dreams. You were there from the beginning always believing in me. Thank you.

Second, I would like to thank my best friend, Billy Thompson. BT, you are a Hall of Famer—there is no question. Someday the people who vote on enshrinement for Canton will recognize that. Hopefully, sooner than the 30 years I had to wait. I love you, man!

I would also like to thank lifelong friends like Jerry Simmons, Rich Jackson, and all my Broncos teammates. Also, Dr. Nancy Cantor, Dr. Daryl Gross, a special thanks to Tom Coughlin, Jim Brown, Darrell Elliott, Hal Williams, and to my Syracuse teammates and my current colleagues. Also, thanks to my teammates at Bordentown Military Institute and Hillhouse High. I would also like to extend a heartfelt thanks to Gary Smith for his magical story in *Sports Illustrated* about the authors of this book. You are a true master storyteller, my friend.

Many of my family and friends have passed on, and I would be remiss not to thank them. My father, Frederick Douglas Little. Dad, I did my best to keep my promise to you, and I hope that I've made you proud. My mother, Lula, the most influential person in my life. I miss my brothers dearly, too, Ranger and Charles. I also miss the incomparable Ernie Davis and John Mackey—two men that had a tremendous impact on my life. Thanks to Val Pinchbeck, who made the trip from Syracuse to the Broncos with me, and to Ernie Barnes, one of the greatest artists of my generation.

It would also like to thank those in the media who have been instrumental in helping me reach my goals. The great Jim Gray, who I am humbled and privileged to know. I'm glad he chose me to be his hero growing up. My friend Jim Saccomano. Jeff Legwold for his incredible Hall of Fame presentation. Also, to Mike Klis of the *Denver Post* for all his support. And a special thanks to Roberto Marcantonio, a dedicated Broncos fan, photographer, and developer of an incredible web site www.littleinthehalloffame.com that I believe was instrumental in helping grow support for my Hall of Fame candidacy.

Finally, I would like to thank Tom Mackie. Many of you read the story about our friendship and quest for the Hall of Fame. I am deeply indebted to Tom for all he has done. His drive, determination, and passion for helping me get into Canton changed my life. He is my hero, just like I was his when he was growing up.

Since being elected to the Hall of Fame, I have been extremely busy. Tom and I still talk frequently by phone, but I have not had a chance to see him a lot. That changed last fall when I was invited to speak to an audience of young people in Stockton, California, funded by the San Joaquin County Office of Education. During the question and answer session, the moderator, asked me about Tom and what I would say to him if he were there. Before I could reply, Tom walked up on stage surprising the hell out of me. I blurted, "You gotta be kidding me, you dirty dog!" and gave him a huge bear hug! The people at the San Joaquin flew Tom out just to surprise me. Incredible.

This is our second book for Tom and me. We had a blast putting it together. We agreed to be totally honest about a lot of things that could have been neatly swept under the rug. I decided why write a book if you're not going to tell the truth? We figure we're too old to worry about what people think anyway. I've always believed in something Mark Twain once said: If you tell the truth, you never have to remember what you told someone.

—Floyd Little

This book would not be possible without the hard work and determination of Noah Amstadter of Triumph Books and the tremendous editing of Karen O'Brien.

This may well be the final autobiographic icing on the cake for the triumphant life of my idol, the great Floyd Little. There's no doubt that his current job as the special assistant to the athletic director at Syracuse University will be his final professional legacy, but *Promises to Keep* chronicles his magnificent life in a lasting keepsake for all his fans.

Looking back on the nearly decade-long friendship I've had with my childhood hero, I still can't believe I had the opportunity to actually meet Floyd, let alone help him reach his elusive dream of being immortalized in Canton. After Gary Smith's *Sports Illustrated* story about our friendship was published, I received hundreds of emails from Floyd Little's fans thanking me for what I did. Many asked how I was able to stay determined even when all seemed stacked against us. This is my opportunity to reveal those who inspired me and motivated me to never give up.

Back in 2003, after I spent that incredible day interviewing Floyd, I wrote a story for the *Denver Post*. Before meeting Floyd, I asked *Denver Post* sportswriter Jim Armstrong if the paper would be interested in a story. He said, "Yes, just be sure to make it sing." I did my best and felt it gave compelling reasons why Floyd deserved to be in the Hall of Fame. When my story was rejected for being too much of a fluff, pro-Floyd story, I asked Woody Paige, then a Hall of Fame voter, if he could write a column on why Floyd should be in the Hall of Fame. For me, it wasn't about getting a byline. It was telling Floyd's story. To my surprise, Paige rejected my request, saying, "I do not want to do a column, and there is nobody else writing a column in Denver who knows Floyd or cares. I only have good thoughts about Floyd, but he will never be considered." Then, before I had a chance to respond, he sent another email dissecting a rhetorical question Floyd raised in my story: "What more could I have done? I was never interested in stats." Paige said, "He could have played longer, done better, and been on a winning team in the NFL." What ensued after those insulting comments can best be described as an email pissing contest. I called him "apathetic," and he called me "bitter." Bottom line: I quickly got a sense of what a challenge I was facing in helping Floyd get to Canton.

My exchange with Paige provided instant motivation to prove him wrong, and it kept my fire burning through the years. Deep down, I knew Floyd was a Hall of Famer. His numbers and impact in keeping the Broncos in Denver were clear proof. But I needed to change the country's uniformed perception of his achievements with the Broncos and the NFL. It was a promise I made to myself and silently to my childhood hero, Floyd.

Whenever I felt like giving up, I would think of Floyd and my promise to get him into Canton. Then I would re-read Paige's ominous line, "he will never be considered." Adam Schefter, another *Denver Post* writer at the time who is now at ESPN, added to my motivation. As the Broncos' beat writer, he used to answer fan questions in his weekly Broncos mailbag (along with rating restaurants). One time a fan wrote in asking why Floyd Little wasn't in the Hall of Fame. To my utter disbelief, Schefter wrote that although Floyd was a great pro, "he's not a Hall of Famer" because "he doesn't have the numbers." This truly upset me because Schefter was the president of the Pro Football Writers of America, which gave him a Hall of Fame vote. I remember thinking back then, *Here are two Denver writers who have a Hall of Fame vote. But they have either given up on Floyd or do not believe he is a Hall of Famer. No wonder there are no Broncos in Canton.* I could only think of what the late Dick Connor, the legendary Denver Post writer who saw all of Floyd's games, would have thought about the Broncos' Hall of Fame voters.

Luckily for me, I had some powerful people on my side. First was Broncos PR guru, Jim Saccomano, to whom I first sent my 44 Reasons back in 2003 and continued to send yearly updates. Through the years Jim made sure the media always had access to these stats, and he was always there to give me encouragement. Another influential person was the great Val Pinchbeck. For those who don't know about Val, he was the former sports information director at Syracuse University who left to become the Broncos PR man the year before Floyd was drafted. It was Val who convinced Coach Lou Saban to draft Floyd. Floyd put me in touch with Val when I was hitting roadblocks with Denver sportswriters. Though I never met Val, I corresponded with him many times on the phone and through email. At the time, he was retired and living near Tampa but he knew all of the national sportswriters and he had great insight into the Hall of Fame process. His encouragement and advice were priceless. Val and I kept in close contact for an entire year. Then in

March 2004, I heard the shocking news that he had died of a heart attack while crossing a street in New York shortly after visiting NFL headquarters. He was 73. I'll never forget going to his funeral at Saint Bart's in New York with Floyd and Marc and the hundreds of VIPs like Paul Tagliabue, Frank Gifford, and writers like Dave Anderson.

Years later when Floyd was finally voted in, the first two people I thought of were Val and Dick.

Another person who inspired me was Larry Felser, a Hall of Fame writer for the *Buffalo News*. He told me stories about Floyd, and how whenever he was covering a Broncos game, a writer in the press box would shake their head and say something like, "Wow, if Little had some help he would be even greater!" That comment gave me the idea to ask Hall of Famers who played with Floyd if they thought he deserved to be in Canton. Writers who never saw Floyd play can only look at stats and some old highlight reels. But the people who know the truth about whether or not you were any good are the ones who played against you. I spoke to Hall of Famers like Willie Lanier, Jack Ham, Joe Greene, Mel Blount, and Nick Buoniconti. I compiled a list of the top 44 responses from Floyd's peers. The great thing about corresponding with these legends was that I discovered how down to the earth they were. When I spoke to Blount, my son, Luke, who was not quite two years old, was playing loudly in the room. Blount laughed and told me, "The greatest thing you can give your children is your time." I'll never forget that.

You also learn things you never knew before. Last year, I spoke with former Jets star Emerson Boozer for an article I was writing about Broncos legend Billy Thompson. I casually asked Boozer what he would have done if the Jets had drafted Floyd the year after he joined the Jets, which was the rumor. Boozer told me, "That was no rumor, it was their sincere intention." He explained, "I wore 44 in college and when I was drafted by the Jets in 1966, I asked for that number. The Jets told me, 'No, we're saving it for when we draft Floyd Little next year.'"

Another important inspiration for me was from a close family member, Ray Ciesinki Jr. His father, Ray Sr., had been a Delaware sports legend as a high school coach, helping to lead track, basketball, and football teams to state titles. His father also happened to be my mom's companion. My dad passed in 1996, and a few years later Ray Sr. became a father figure to me. Like Floyd, Ray had been overlooked for the Delaware Sports Hall of Fame for years. Just as I started working on Floyd's behalf, Ray Jr. put together an impressive list of compelling reasons why his father should be inducted and presented it to the committee. It worked. In 2003, Ray Sr. was inducted!

The list of others who inspired me includes my mom, Nellie Ray, and my father, James W. Mackie. My sisters, Maryde Mackie Hand and Blythe Anne Mackie Lundstrom. Also, my brother, Jeff. His sons, Brendan and Kevin Mackie, each served a tour of duty in Iraq. Now Brendan is serving another tour in Afghanistan while Kevin is becoming a Delaware police officer. They are both true heroes.

Another person who helped an incredible amount is Roberto Marcantonio. And of course, Jeff Legwold. Chris Garbarino, who penned the book *The Cookie That Did Not Crumble*, the Cookie Gilchrist story, is someone who has become a trusted friend. Everyone needs loyal friends, so I cannot thank my lifelong friends, Dave Apostolico and Gregg Marvel, enough.

I would also like to thank members of the Broncos alumni for making me feel so special when I joined them at the banquet and the golf outing in 2010. It was great to hang with Billy Thompson and chat with Rich Jackson and Charley Johnson—other Broncos legends who I worshipped. It was also cool to meet unsung Broncos like Fran Lynch, Rod Sherman, and Larry Brunson. They were incredibly nice and down to earth—a true thrill.

Of course, this list is incomplete without thanking the man himself, Floyd Little, and his family. What can I say except that Floyd is the most incredible person I ever met. Few idols ever live up to the hype. But few idols ever come as close to being as great a person as 44. I love you, man!

I would also like to thank Emily for all she has done over the years to put up with a football nut like me. She gave me the two of the greatest gifts of my life: Floyd and my son, Luke.

Luke is now my biggest inspiration and my reason for being. Thanks to the genius of my favorite writer, Gary Smith, I got to enjoy my 15 minutes of fame. The rest of my clock belongs to Luke. Now four years old, he woke me up one Sunday at 5:30 AM. I muttered that it was too early to get up. He softly head-butted me and said, "Daddy, if we don't get up now we're going to miss the day."

Talk about inspiration!

—Tom Mackie

INTRODUCTION

I am proudly my father's son. The first commandment in the Bible accompanied with a promise from God says, "Honor your father and your mother that your days may be long upon the land which the Lord your God is giving you." [Exodus 20:12 (NKJV)] Out of this commandment, I honor one of God's greatest gifts to me, my father, by writing these few opening words to an autobiography of a life well lived—the life of Floyd Little.

A highlight of Dad's life was his enshrinement to the Pro Football Hall of Fame. After Dad received the 42 votes that elected him into the Pro Football Hall of Fame, he drafted me to present him at the Enshrinement Ceremony. Giving me such a high honor was part of a promise he had made to me nearly 20 years earlier: if he ever went into the Hall of Fame, I would be there with him. When Dad was inducted in July 2010, the last words of my presentation speech were, "Now ladies and gentlemen, please join me in presenting to the Pro Football Hall of Fame, a giant of humanity, an uncommon man, my hero, my best friend, my dad, Floyd Little."

Although my presentation speech went over well with family and fans, the four-minute speech was very difficult to write. How can a son sum up his dad in four minutes for the world? So the final words of my presentation speech not only officially presented Dad to the Hall (my assignment), they also painted a picture of his attributes of which I am most proud. I called him, "A giant of humanity, an uncommon man, my hero, and best friend."

Now he honors me with the same challenge of how to present his autobiography in 1,000 words or less! Really? Impossible to do, but a task I am honored to have.

Dad's autobiography is not just a model for all to demonstrate how imperfect people can be giants, role models, and do extraordinary things, it is also an extension of his legacy for our family and the next generations to come. "A good man leaves an inheritance for his children's children." [Proverbs 13:22 (NKJV)] Floyd Little leaves a very rich inheritance for us all.

So I am profoundly aware that Dad's grandchildren, his great-grandchildren, and so on, will thumb through the words of his autobiography to glean an understanding of their own heritage. They will pour through the stories Dad tells and undoubtedly laugh and laugh and laugh because he is truly the funniest person I know. But of equal importance, they will see—as you will—Dad's development as a son, an athlete, a father, and a businessman and see the trials and the struggles throughout his life. These are the ingredients of Dad's success. Yes, there were many failures and disappointments. In fact, his teachers in elementary and high school believed he was incorrigible and unteachable. Few people encouraged Dad to pursue higher education, as is the case in so many urban centers even today. But he did graduate from college, and his college football career is now the stuff of legends.

This autobiography illuminates the perseverance and stubbornness Dad had throughout his life to never take "no" for an answer and highlights philosophies like, "If you haven't been turned down seven times, that only means you haven't asked enough." These philosophies charted his way to triumphs during trying times—and there were many.

His own father died when he was six. Raised by a single mother with five siblings, his older brother, Ranger, became his father figure, but the trajectory of Dad's life would change at an early age with a single moment. Dad vowed to be a success after finding himself and his family evicted on the sidewalk with their cherished belongings. He was born into poverty. There's no way to make that sound better. It is what it is.

But Dad often recounts in a jovial way how he often followed behind his mother (whom I affectionately called Grama Little) as they walked from the store. She often threw her purse in the sidewalk trash can as they walked home. And Dad, the dutiful son, would run and retrieve her purse from the trash can. Never understanding why she would always do such a thing, Dad once asked why. Her response, "It's empty. It's trash!" They had very little but that gave birth to one of his most famous sayings, "He who steals my purse steals trash." Poverty is simply the starting point of Dad's story, and that's what made him who he is. When you are so low that you have to look up to see down, defining moments can be created that burn a desire into you to never return to that dark scary place. You either stay where you are or you decide to harness whatever you have inside you and bring that will, thought, or otherwise intangible thing to bear on your circumstance. The intentional force of that thing is what makes a champion. That's what happened that day on the sidewalk. Dad decided, never again.

My father's autobiography is a collection of how he applied his will or that thing over the course of a very full life that makes him an American champion. It makes me so proud to be his son and it makes my sisters, Kyra DaCosta and Christy Jones, proud to be his daughters.

Something else also happened for Dad thanks to his meager beginnings. When you don't have a silver spoon in your mouth, you have to turn to each other in indescribable ways. Character is birthed out of rough upbringings but enriched when surrounded by family. All they had was each other. Dad's character was shaped early on. This is when he learned, "Your word is all you have."

Dad's character was displayed in the feature film *The Express*, the story of Syracuse football star Ernie Davis. The film rightly depicts that Ernie recruited Dad to play for Syracuse. Although Dad had many offers from other esteemed football programs, Dad gave Ernie his word he would attend Syracuse. Although the decision was not an easy one, particularly after Ernie died of leukemia while recruiting Dad, Dad honored his word and attended Syracuse, and the rest is history. Dad went on to be the final "44" in the historic trilogy of Jim Brown, Ernie Davis, and Floyd Little. His character has been a guiding force for our entire family.

Promises to Keep will inform generations to come of their heritage and will also inspire you to be a giant of humanity, an uncommon man or woman, a hero, or even a best friend. Because that's the impact Floyd Little has on everyone he meets.

My father's story is an American story; it's a story of what any American can do and become with hard work and determination. It's the story of an American champion. It's the story of Floyd Little, the wind beneath our wings, my dad.

—Marc Little

1

THE BEGINNING

This book isn't just about my life's journey to Canton and beyond. I also wanted to write this book in the hope of inspiring fans like you to go out and fulfill your own dreams. If you're not doing everything you can to live your dream, you have to ask yourself, "What am I waiting for?" Life is not a dress rehearsal. It's the only one you get. And while fulfilling your dreams is a thing of beauty, the commitment and sacrifice necessary can be daunting. I know. I'm not here to tell you how easy it is. I'm here to share with you how hard it can be. Life is hard. It's not easy. Dying is easy. Before you meet your Maker, make sure you've squeezed every last drop of life out of this world. When your time is up, you want to leave completely fulfilled, at peace, knowing your loved ones will carry on your proud legacy.

I was a 25-year-old rookie running back. A bowlegged, 5'10", 195 pounder soaking wet. Critics said I was too old and too small to make it in the NFL. When I was drafted by the Denver Broncos, a last-place AFL team, the so-called experts stacked the deck against me even more. They said I was just a scatback, a shifty little guy who might make it as a kick returner but definitely not an every-down back. So I went all-in against the naysayers.

I played with a fury for nine seasons, became an every-down back, a 1,000 rusher, a perennial Pro Bowl player, and I retired as the seventh-leading rusher in NFL history. That wasn't by accident. That was pure will. In 2010, I was elected to the Pro Football Hall of Fame. In a sense, being enshrined in Canton now gives me a sense of immortality. Did I fulfill my dream? Yes. Did I do it by myself? Hell, no. I needed a cadre of supportive family, friends, mentors, coaches, teammates, fans, competitors, *and* naysayers every step of the way. No one travels life's journey alone. The one thing I did have was an uncommon will—a non-stop drive to achieve everything people said I couldn't.

Here's the thing: God only gives you drive or talent. You don't get both. In the history of sports, God has only made two mistakes: Muhammad Ali and Sugar Ray Leonard. Somehow they were both given generous heaps of drive *and* talent.

Sometimes you don't know what you've been blessed with until something happens in your life and you discover it for the first time. For me, it happened when I was 14 and everything in my life seemed lost. A vision appeared that changed my life. After that, I made a promise that I never stopped striving to keep. A promise that drove me to achieve things that I never thought possible. Along my life's journey, I've been asked to keep more promises. I believe a promise is your word, your bond. That's what defines me, and that's all I have. This is where those promises begin.

My Family

My father, Frederick Douglas Little, died when I was six. He was named after the abolitionist Frederick Douglass. When he passed, my mom, Lula, was left to raise six kids in Waterbury, Connecticut. My mother was a saint. But at the same time she was a disciplinarian. You couldn't get anything past her. If you did something wrong, she would find out and you'd get a beating. She worked many jobs to support us. Because she was so busy, I was able to keep one secret from her for many years—my athletic talent on the football field. She thought I was too small to play football and didn't want me to get hurt. Consequently, my older sisters Betty, Rosa, and Priscilla helped me hide my secret gridiron life for years. They stitched up and cleaned my clothes when they were ripped to shreds. My mom didn't find out I was a pretty good football player until I got my scholarship at Syracuse. By then, what could she say?

I was the second youngest. Along with my three older sisters, I had a younger brother, Charles, known as "Jitty," and an older brother, Frederick, known as "Ranger." My father gave him the nickname from his favorite radio show, *The Lone Ranger*. Ranger got into trouble a lot. But our family always pulled together. We worked hard. I was shining shoes when I was six. And when I wasn't working, I was tagging along behind the skirt of my oldest sister, Betty. I was shy and self-conscious. My skin was darker than other black kids, and they called me Cheetah.

By the time I was 13, we had moved from the projects in Waterbury to a small apartment in New Haven. We had no choice but to move. Ranger got us evicted. Think about it—you have to be pretty bad to get evicted from the projects. Ranger was. He and some other boys got in trouble for continually beating up other kids. Our entire family got tossed to the curb because of it.

At first life didn't change much for us in New Haven. We continued to take odd jobs to bring in money. The pressure of constantly working and doing badly in school started to weigh on me. I was an angry young man. It took a watershed moment of pure frustration and angst for me to finally change my ways.

The Vision

By the time I was 14, school had become too much for me. I could barely read, and then one day I was asked to read aloud and mispronounced a word. All the kids laughed at me. I got mad and refused to read in front of people again. I was challenged every day because of it. I failed tests, and my homework was always wrong. Some older kids teased me that I was stupid. So I got in a lot of fights. Most kids, though, were afraid of me. They'd see me and cross to the other side of the hallway. By the time I got to the eighth grade, I was just going through the motions. We were on social security. We all had more than one job, and I was always tired. My clothes were shabby. My shoes had holes. My hair was uncombed.

Then one day I snapped. I beat the crap out of some kid for basically no reason. Then I punched a teacher. When the kid's parents showed up, I fought with them, too. I was just mad at everyone. Mad at my life. Mad that every day seemed worse than the day before. It's no surprise that I got tossed out of school that day. The principal threw me out. I was outside, sitting on a curb, sobbing, afraid to go home because my mom was going to beat me. Hyperventilating, I didn't know what I was going to do. I felt beyond helpless.

All sorts of terrible things entered my head. Should I just run out into the street or rob a store, just to get this miserable life over with? Those thoughts had never entered my mind before. I wasn't a depressed kid. I was just seething with anger and frustration.

Then in the midst of all these tears, I heard my father's voice and I looked up. There he was, standing before me. Because I was so young when he died, I didn't have many strong memories of my dad. I've been told he had been a promising baseball player in one of the Negro Leagues back in the 1930s. Then he met my mom, Lula, and got married. Later, he got hurt playing ball; he got kicked in his ear and lost hearing in it. A few years later he died of ear cancer and believed it was from the baseball accident. My memory of him was him either fighting someone or sequestered to the bedroom, too sick to come out. When I did see him, he had stained bandages wrapped around his head. Fluid and pus would seep through.

But in this vision, my father looked healthy. There were no bandages or torn clothes. His face was full, and his eyes were alive. I was shaken, couldn't take a breath. Totally transfixed, my dad pointed at me and said, "Floyd, I have chosen you to take my place. I want you to live the life that I didn't get to live. I'm counting on you to do the things I couldn't do and to finish the things I couldn't finish. I want you to become a leader. Promise me that you'll do something great with your life so you can protect our family."

Then he was gone. My dad had come back to tell me to change my life. He could see my future and wanted to tell me about the journey I couldn't see. Somehow his spirit saw that I was struggling and found a way to communicate with me. I was in shock. He had a half-dozen other kids, most of them older than me. Why did he choose me, the second youngest? I closed my eyes and soaked in the moment. I realized this was my wake-up call. My life was passing me by, and I needed to do something about it. My dad had come back to ask me to keep a promise to him—to do the things he couldn't do and finish the things he couldn't finish.

From then on, I began to change. I straightened the hell up. I went home after that, told my mom I was expelled from school, and took my beating, knowing that she would never beat me again.

The next day, I went back and pleaded to the principal to let me back in. He slammed the door in my face.

So the following day I tried again using a different approach.

Robert Schreck

Every student has a teacher they like. Even a kid like me who hated everyone. Robert Schreck was an English teacher who was also an assistant basketball coach. I was a lousy English student but good at hoops. Mr. Schreck was someone I could always count on. Somehow he understood me, understood my struggles. I went to him and begged him to ask the faculty and administrators to give me another chance. It wasn't easy. He was mad at me for getting kicked out. It was a very humbling experience for me to ask for help. I would rather be castrated than ask someone for help. I believed it was a sign of weakness. But after my surreal experience with my dad, I knew it was the only way to turn my life around. I needed help. I needed someone to care. I had proved time and again I wasn't making it on my own.

So I went to Mr. Schreck's class and begged. I was on my hands and knees. It was time to recognize my faults. I didn't care what the other students thought. I wasn't self-conscious or paranoid anymore. At first, Schreck looked through me and said he couldn't do anything for me. But I wasn't going to be denied. I came back day after day, every day on my hands and knees.

I knew I had to get back in school. It was the only way I could change my life. Deep down I knew I didn't deserve it. I had become a bad guy. People were genuinely afraid of me. But this was my life. Whether I deserved a second chance or not, I needed to get back into school.

After weeks of pleading my case, Mr. Schreck became convinced that I was genuine in my commitment to change. He decided to stick out his neck for me and went to the school administration and pleaded my case. I found out later, like me, he went several days in a row, probably pleading on his hands and knees. Whatever he did, it worked.

Weeks after getting kicked out, I was finally back in school thanks to Mr. Schreck. I owed him big time.

What's Football?

Sometimes you question why something is happening to you. You ask God or whatever higher power you believe in, "Why are you doing this?" or "Can't you stop this from happening?" That's how I felt when we got kicked out of the projects. We had been through so much, and now we had to move to another town and start over.

But that's the blessing of change. It usually means a new start. A short while after Mr. Schreck gave me a second chance and got my ass back into school, I discovered something that became my passion and ultimately changed my life—football.

A classmate of mine, Al "Tubby" Rogers, saw me hanging out near my home one day and came up to me. He said, "Kid, do you play football?" "Um, no. Never played," I replied. "Well, a bunch of us get together on Saturdays over at the park to play. We always need guys, why don't you stop by?"

Well, I had to deliver papers in the morning, but after my route, I thought, *Why not?*

I showed up and saw a bunch of kids, many of them older, flying around wearing shoulder pads and cleats. Some even wore helmets. I was sporting torn jeans, a ripped shirt, and shoes with barely any soles. I was the only one who had no equipment. But instead of feeling scared, I smiled. *Boyohboy, this is going to be fun!* I thought. *These guys are really hitting each other. Hard. This is right up my alley!*

At first they put me at guard. I said, "Okay, what's a guard do?" You push people out of the way so the guy with the ball can run, they told me. I grinned and absolutely loved it. I got rid of so much aggression that day, shoving people around and knocking people silly. I would hit a guy and see another guy 10 yards down the field and hit him, then I'd see another guy farther down and deck him. After a while one of the guys said, "Hey, you're fast. You're hitting guys and flying past the ball carrier down the field. Maybe we'll put you at receiver." "Okay, what's a receiver do?" They run down the field and catch the ball.

So they moved me from guard to receiver. I ran down the field so fast no one was near me. I waved my arms wildly. "I'm open, I'm open. Throw me the ball!" I cried. But no one could get me the ball. I ran down the field so fast I'd gone too far.

The next time I came out the guys put me at running back. "Okay," I said, "what's a running back do?" You carry the ball and try to score touchdowns. Well, the first time I got the ball I ran the whole way for a touchdown. I scored again the next time I carried the ball. In fact, I scored the first six times I touched the ball. It didn't matter that I was sliding all over the place with my treadless shoes. People were coming from all directions to get me. I was zigzagging all the way down the field. If I ran 80 yards for a touchdown, I was traversing at least 180 yards to get there. Funny thing is, that became my running style. Years later I would say, "I try not to run over anybody. I try to run around as many guys as I can."

After that day in the park, football became my favorite sport. I still loved basketball, but football was the perfect fit for me. It gave me the physical outlet I never had before. Where else can you hit someone full force and get a pat on the back instead of your ass thrown out of school?

Looking back, it was a blessing we got kicked out of the projects and had to move to New Haven. It was a blessing that I met Tubby Rogers and discovered football. If we had stayed in Waterbury, I may not have gotten into sports. I may have ended up in a gang or worse. My whole life began to change after we moved to New Haven.

My life changed each time I showed up at the park to play. Each time there were more and more people watching me play. One day a guy named Dan Casey came to watch me. He was the head football coach at Hillhouse High School. Meeting him put me on an athletic path that I would never look back on.

School Praise

Some kids may look at playing sports as a way to escape from the ghetto. I never saw it that way. I saw my athletic ability as a way to get an education. At the time the thought of making it in the NFL or the NBA was about as likely as winning the lottery. That's why, after the vision from my dad, I knew the first step was to get my ass back into school.

I realized that I needed to surround myself with good people if I ever wanted to be successful. I had to rid myself of the procrastinators and the naysayers and surround myself with the doers and people who were positive influences.

Think about it—your attitude is the one thing you have 100 percent control over. It's the person with the positive attitude who gets the opportunity, the raise, and the promotion. Just like it's the negative person who always feels like they're the victim, the one who should have gotten the raise, and the one who wished they had the promotion.

This old adage rings true—whether you think you can or you think you can't, you're right. It's your attitude that makes all the difference.

When I got back into school, I made a conscious decision to change, to surround myself with positive people. I didn't talk back to anyone. I didn't start trouble. I tried to be friendly to people I had been a jerk to before. I even did something few thought I was cable of doing—I ran for class president!

I'd like to think running for class president was my idea. Sorry, no. That's the last thing I thought about doing. I was committed to change. But running for class president? Bullshit. There was no way in hell I was going to do that.

Mr. Schreck, who had become my mentor, had other ideas. "Floyd," he said, "you've done a lot to change people's perceptions of you. But there are a lot of teachers and faculty who think you're full of shit. They don't think you've changed. They think you're trying to skate by. They think you're trying to say the right things, but don't believe a word you're saying. I know better. You've changed. Running for class president will make them believers. Better yet, I think you can win."

Believe me, running for class president was the last thing I wanted to do. I had changed a lot, coming back to school, being humble, showing I was honorable. But Mr. Schreck demanded I do more. He fought hard to get me back in school. He told me that trying to become a better student wasn't enough. As class president, I would have to be an outspoken advocate for the students. I would have to make speeches and support student causes. That wasn't me. I was shy, an introvert. But Mr. Schreck was my mentor. Not only did I believe in him, I felt like I owed him a debt of gratitude.

Despite my fear of being humiliated, I ran. What's more, I ended up running against this popular girl who was attractive, smart, and friendly. There was no doubt she would get all the votes. But I didn't care. Mr. Schreck convinced me this was an opportunity to stand out from the crowd. It was my chance to portray myself in a positive way. I had stood out negatively plenty of times. I was determined to change and become the leader my father wanted me to be.

For the first time, I began listening to the other students. I didn't go up to the other kids and say, "Hi, I'm Floyd Little and I'm running for class president." Instead I said, "Hey, how are you doing? What do you like about school? Or what would you like to see changed?" Then I sat and listened. I took notes. I wrote down their names and was able to remember them. I discovered that I had a photographic memory. I could take a mental picture and remember details like I was reading it from a book. It was a nice discovery. But when it came to trying to win the election, I had no agenda and no real expectations. I did, however, promise one thing—a Coca-Cola machine for the gymnasium. That was my only campaign promise.

Election Day came and something extraordinary happened. I received more votes than there were students. I had a crazy 50 to 1 winning ratio. They stopped counting after my votes exceeded the number of students. Who knows why I won. Maybe people really started to like me. Maybe they believed I could make a difference. Or perhaps everyone was just afraid of me. Maybe they believed if they didn't vote for me, I would beat them up. Whatever the reason, I didn't care. It was the first time I stood out in school in a positive light.

Of course, to be perfectly honest, I did prove to be a typical politician in terms of my one and only campaign promise—the Coke machine. I was never able to deliver on it. Even today, friends from my youth give me a hard time about it. They say, "Hey, Floyd. I'm thirsty. Where's that doggone Coke machine you promised?"

Chance to Make a Difference

Being elected class president changed me forever. It started my journey as a leader. One of my biggest responsibilities was leading school assemblies. Basically, I became speaker of the house. I had to announce administrators and faculty members. Although I had been elected class president, people knew I struggled academically. I was still a C student. I didn't suddenly become smarter. Public speaking is frightening for most people. It proved particularly difficult for me.

But as I learned throughout my life, practice and preparation became the foundations of my success. I developed an unflappable will to succeed. Even for a simple assembly, I spent hours rehearsing the names I would have to pronounce. I had come a long way to earn the respect of faculty and teachers. There was no way I was going to jeopardize it by mispronouncing a name and being subjected to ridicule. It may sound over the top. But I had been down for so long. I couldn't afford to take a step back.

Thanks to hours of practice, I became a proficient public speaker. I was far from a grand orator, but no one laughed or teased me. I had overcome a fear, a weakness, and I rose above people's expectations of me. I even carried myself differently. I made sure my clothes were clean and neat before school. My hair was combed and kept short. I dressed the best I could, considering we didn't have money.

But the real difference I made as class president had nothing to do with my so-called job description. I had been a troubled kid, and I challenged myself to change. Now I wanted to pay it forward. I began trolling the halls, looking for kids who were looking for trouble, like the way I used to. I'd go up to kids who were skipping class, kids who were hanging out in the bathroom. I'd walk right up to them and say, "What are you doing? You know better than this. Now get to class!" I had already beaten up the toughest guy in the school the year before. The class bully. Kids knew I wasn't to be messed with, and most of them scattered when they saw me coming.

Those weren't the kids who concerned me. The kids who weren't afraid of me, the ones who got in fights all the time and talked back to teachers—those were the ones I wanted to reach. I'd break up a fight and then pull the instigator aside, look at him face to face, and talk to him. "Fighting isn't going to help you accomplish anything. I used to be like you," I said. "I know you're frustrated, but this isn't the answer. This is only going to get your ass thrown out of school, then what will you do? Staying in school is the only way you're going to be successful. Next time, just walk away."

Some kids rolled their eyes. But some bought what I was saying. I wasn't talking down to them. I was relating to them because I had been in their shoes. I had their respect. More so than the respect they showed for teachers and administrators. I'd like to think I was able to help save some of those troubled kids.

Hillhouse Days

My mother never wanted me to play football. I was small, and she was afraid I'd get hurt. My sisters and I kept it a secret from her for years. Whenever I tore my clothes, my sisters would sew them up. We played on a rocky field with glass everywhere, and my clothes were perpetually stained with blood. My sisters had a tough time keeping me looking like the Tide poster boy.

High school football coaches would come watch us play. One of them was Hillhouse High coach Dan Casey. I'd heard great things about Hillhouse and was thrilled to go there. When I went out for the football team, I thought I'd be the starter. But I discovered early that life is all about overcoming obstacles. Not only didn't I start, I was fourth string.

Our first home game was against Warren G. Harding High School. We were down 14–0 in the first quarter. So I went up and asked the coach to put me in. "Go sit down at the end of the bench," he yelled. I persisted. "Just one play, one play!" He shook his head in disbelief. By the second quarter both first- and second-string backs were hurt, and we were down 21–0. I knew if I could get in that I could make a difference.

"Tell you what," the coach finally sighed, "go in and block and tell the quarterback to give it to [Bill] McCoy." Since I had just one play, I went in and said, "Coach wants me to carry the ball." I took a pitchout and raced 48 yards for a touchdown. I handed the ball to the official and sat back down at the end of the bench.

Coach Casey walked over and told me to go in the next series. I said, "That's okay, I just wanted one play." He was flabbergasted. When we got the ball back, he ordered me in. Again, I raced another 60-something yards for a touchdown. At this point all of the other halfbacks were feeling better, but it was too late. I scored five touchdowns that game and never sat the bench again.

After that, I had the confidence I needed to play the game. Teammates noticed that I had written "All-State" on my duffel bag next to my name. People may have thought I was being arrogant, but I did it for myself. That became one of my first athletic goals. I wrote that so I could see it every day and know the hard work and sacrifice I needed to invest to make it happen. Another goal was for our team to win the state title. When I left Hillhouse, we had accomplished both.

Ranger

It's true that you never compete harder against someone than against your brother. My older brother, Ranger, was my biggest inspiration during my early years. I like to interpret it as reverse psychology. Ranger was a troubled kid. Just two years older, he spent his days smoking, drinking, and hanging out with friends, usually at Beaver Pond Park, the sandlot where I played sports every day. I ran around that park before every game to get fired up, and they would sit on bleachers high as rockets and heckle me. "Why are you running so much? You ain't going anywhere," he'd say. "I can still whip your ass."

Ranger was a heck of an athlete, much better than me. He was a great basketball player and could have gotten a scholarship. But he was never willing to sacrifice hanging out with his friends and getting into trouble in order to take his future to the next level. It was the opposite for me.

As I mentioned earlier, God only gives you talent or drive. He gave Ranger talent, but my brother could never muster the drive. My talent was average, but I made up for it with 100 percent drive. By the time I was 18, I could finally beat Ranger in a race. It was then I decided to go all out all the time. I had three gears—fast, sprinter, and off-the-charts. I convinced myself to run as if I was stuck in third gear with the switch broken. Thanks to my brother's reverse psychology, my determination to make something of my life became boundless.

Jock of All Trades

When I began playing football, I was pretty confident. I didn't want to wear a lot of gear. Things like knee pads and thigh pads slowed me down too much. I also didn't think it was necessary to wear a jock strap. That is, until someone stepped right on my nuts in the middle of a pile. That's the most pain I'd ever felt. My unit was in pretty bad shape. I had to be helped off the field. After that my jock was the first thing I put on. I even wore it in the shower. I never played without it again.

No Guidance

After my first big varsity high school game, I didn't think anything could stop me. I made All-State as a junior, and people all over recognized my jersey No. 33. I was eager for a spectacular senior season—until I was informed I was too old to play. I had been held back a year as a youngster because of an illness, and now I was 19. On top of that, despite my dedication to do well in school, I was still a below-C student. My guidance counselor told me to forget about college. I hoped to get a football scholarship, but no one would take a chance on me. I even tried to get a job as a janitor, but I couldn't even fill out the application. I still had trouble reading, which made understanding content and directions difficult.

Looking back, it still angers me that this guidance counselor was so negative. I mean, her title was "guidance counselor." Two words that describe a person who helps someone. Sometimes in life you come across people who you hope can help you. When they don't, then it's up to you to decide where to go next. I could have said, "Yeah, she's right. I'm not college material. Maybe I'll go hang out with my older brother and just try to get by." But I didn't. I said, "To hell with her. She just uttered my least favorite phrase, 'I can't.' I will do whatever it takes to prove her wrong." Those words became my new inspiration to make a liar out of her.

2

PREP SCHOOL

Bordentown Military Institute

At a crossroads in my life, I needed someone to believe in me. I wasn't going to take this on all by myself. So I did the smart thing, I asked for help. I talked to Coach Casey about wanting to go to college. He put his hands on my shoulders and said he would do whatever he could. For weeks, I didn't hear from coach. Then one day I got a letter from Bordentown Military Institute, a college prep school in Bordentown, New Jersey, not far from Trenton. Coach Casey apparently had written to Notre Dame and asked if they'd take a chance on me. Instead, Notre Dame suggested that he try enrolling me at Bordentown to get my grades up.

The timing could not have been better. The headmaster at Bordentown, Dr. Harold Morrison Smith, wanted to integrate his school and thought I was mature enough to be the first African American to attend. He also knew I could help the football team. It was 1961, and BMI was one of many schools above the Mason-Dixon Line that didn't have any African Americans. I thought, *Sure, no big deal.* Besides, there were no second options.

Before I knew it I was heading to New Jersey. Suddenly, I was petrified. Imagine being the only black person at a school—in 1961!

15

Me and Red Grange

It took me awhile to get acclimated to Bordentown. The place was packed with military officers who were tough as dirt. I had to stand up straight, salute people, fire weapons, and take orders. I looked forward to football, but I found out that football at BMI was really boot camp with equipment. We did pushups, climbed rope, and crawled in mud.

My coach at Bordentown was a tough son-of-a-bitch named Al Verdel. He was like Vince Lombardi with an even worse haircut. I remember the first day of practice he gave me No. 77. I told him, "77? I'm a halfback, not a lineman." He stared at me like I pissed on his cornflakes. "Son," he whispered, "we run the Single Wing here. All backs wear numbers in the 70s. If you want to play, you'll wear this number."

From then on I thought wearing 77 was cool. That was Red Grange's number. For people not familiar with the Single Wing, the quarterback is actually a blocking back. The halfback is the guy who takes the snap from center. I was happy to touch the ball on every play, and we had a great team. We never lost in the two years I was there. In one season I scored 24 touchdowns in seven games.

Most of the guys went on to be captains of their college teams: Joe Novogratz captained Pittsburgh; Joe Plumeri captained William & Mary; and Phil Sheridan captained the 1965 Notre Dame team.

Clashes with Classmates

It was a difficult transition being the first African American at BMI. Most of the guys just stared at me, and very few said a word at first. My first roommate actually thought I grew a tail at midnight and turned into some kind of animal. I quickly became a practical joker and decided to mess with this guy.

One night while my roommate was sleeping, I crept slowly to his bed and sat at the edge and yelled, "Aaaggghhh!!!" It scared the shit out of him. His eyes bugged out, and he howled like the world was coming to an end. "What the hell are you doing?" he screamed. "It's midnight," I said, "I want to show you my tail!"

It wasn't long before I had a new roommate, Herb Stecker. We both went on to Syracuse where he remained my roommate and became co-captain with me senior year.

Sugar High

Just like Hillhouse, I held several jobs at Bordentown to help pay for my scholarship. One job was working at the cafeteria. A guard on our team, Fred Jackson, worked there, too, and he hated my guts. The reason? Basically, I was black and he was from Georgia. I tried to be friends, but he just wanted to fight.

One day I was cleaning tables after dinner, and there were a bunch of strawberry shortcakes that hadn't been touched. I put one on top of the refrigerator and dabbed some extra whip cream on it so I could identify it later. At the end of the shift, I sat and ate my dessert and Jackson just stared at me. The next day he came up to me and said, "You switched desserts yesterday. You took my strawberry shortcake and ate it in front of me." I told him he was mistaken. He didn't believe me and took my corn-flakes and poured them on my uniform. After weeks of this abuse, I lost it. I said, "Let's go." We went down to the train tracks and started swinging at each other. I had heard he was a boxer, so I waited for his best punch. He swung wildly and missed. I floored him with a right hook.

At that point six months of hostility poured out of me. I started punching him so hard that I broke my knuckles. He had to be taken to the infirmary. We got in trouble and had to go meet the Commandant, Colonel Roosma. We walked into his office and the colonel got up and positioned himself inches from our faces. "I understand you had a fight without permission," he said. "Yes," we agreed. Back then, if you had a fight you had to actually sign something and have supervision. Obviously we hadn't done that.

He gave us 100 demerits each. Then right before he opened the door he asked, "Who won?" I had to bite my lip. Jackson looked like he had fallen 500' off an ugly tree and hit every branch on the way down. I looked like I was plucked from the pages of the Montgomery Ward catalog. "Sir, I won," I said. And the commandant just nodded.

Shhh, Fight Quietly

Another fight I got into was while working at the school library. This one co-worker used to give me wet willies, when you lick your finger and stick it in someone's ear. He did it a million times before I finally flattened him.

I thought that was it for me and went back to my dorm room and started packing my bags.

I got this knock on my door, and it was Colonel Roosma. He came to scream at me. He went on for 10 minutes before I pushed him up against the wall. I told him, "It won't matter if I deck you. I'm already out of here."

I told him everything that had happened, and I think my intensity scared him. After he left I just sat on my bunk, waiting for the military police to kick my ass out of school. By some miracle it didn't happen. I was confined to my quarters the rest of the semester, except for practice and classes. But they let me stay. When I came back my second year, no one bothered me. I played basketball and ran track, as well. While playing basketball, I was given No. 44 for the first time. Little did I know it would become my favorite.

Photographic Memory

While at Bordentown I had to take the SATs. The first time I got 200. You get 200 for signing your name. I thought, *This is crazy. I'm never going to suddenly become smart enough to pass.* So I learned how to memorize questions. Math problems, vocabulary words, everything. I took the SATs again and this time got 280. But I didn't give up. A few of us formed a study group and hit the books every night for weeks.

I concentrated on taking a mental picture of every word and, amazingly, it worked. I learned to memorize each word and the meaning on each page. I went over each question with my professors until I knew the answers. I studied for weeks. Luckily, the third time I took the test I was given the exact same version as the first. I knew the questions on page six as well as pages 68 and the ones in between. My score went from a 280 to 1,280.

A year later, after I was at Syracuse, I got called to the Dean's office. I walked in and a half dozen administration people stood behind a long desk. They accused me of cheating on my SATs, saying someone else must have taken the test.

I was outraged. So I sat there and gave them examples of how I passed. "On page 58, from top left to right, the text reads…" and I recited the page. Then I did it for two more pages. The dean was dumbfounded. The faculty couldn't believe it. They immediately dropped the charges. From that day on, my photographic memory has served me well. I've been able to remember a lot of things, even poems, because of this unknown gift of taking mental pictures.

Recruiting Wars

The longer I was at Bordentown, the more I started thinking about a military career. I thought the next logical step would be to go to Army at West Point. Many Bordentown graduates went to West Point, as well as Notre Dame and other fine schools.

One day Army's coach Paul Dietzel made a visit to Bordentown specifically to meet me. I spoke to our headmaster, Dr. Smith, about whether it was ethical to talk with Coach Dietzel about going to Army when Notre Dame was the reason I was here. Dr. Smith assured me that Notre Dame hadn't paid my way. "I'm the one who wanted you here," he told me. "No one else is responsible for you being here except me." That was the first time I had heard that, and it gave me such a feeling of independence.

Meeting General MacArthur

A few weeks later I was invited to meet the man himself—General Douglas MacArthur, the military legend. A limousine picked me up and brought me into Manhattan to the Waldorf Astoria Hotel. General MacArthur had a suite there, and even though he was up in years, he was as impressive as ever.

When I walked through those doors it felt like I was meeting the president of the United States. To say I was excited is like asking a priest if he enjoyed hanging with the pope. General MacArthur shook my hand and talked to me about the value of education, about being a leader. On top of General MacArthur, there was a slew of New York Yankees and Brooklyn-L.A. Dodgers in the suite all committed to getting me to go to Army. It was a veritable who's who, including Elston Howard, Roy Campanella, Branch Rickey, and a few others.

I was told that if I went to Army I could become the first black general. General MacArthur told me how the military needed more African Americans. "There are opportunities," he told me, "to be a high-ranking officer." I could be a role model for other minorities. Of course,

I knew the game. It was all to get me to play football. But it was still impressive.

All told, I had 47 football scholarships. Funny, two years earlier I wasn't college material. Because of the great influence that Army had at BMI and the tremendous impression that General MacArthur left on me, I was leaning toward Army. But all that was put on hold after a snowy night in December 1962.

3

SYRACUSE UNIVERSITY

Ernie Davis

In the movie *The Express*, just before Ernie Davis walks out of the tunnel and onto the football field for the last time as a member of the Cleveland Browns, Ben Schwartzwalder walks up to Davis and says, "Ernie, I don't know what you said to Floyd Little, but he's coming to Syracuse." It was an emotional conclusion to a great movie. When you watch the film you can see why they scripted it that way. But in real life it happened differently.

I was on winter break from Bordentown on a snowy night in December 1962. I had just returned to my home in Connecticut after taking the Army's strenuous endurance test at West Point. Another recruit, Dave Rivers, who eventually became Army's captain, and I were put through a series of endless physical endurance tests that included pull-ups, sit ups, rope climbing, sprints, and long-distance running. We were so drained by the end that I could barely stand, and Dave was practically out cold. I felt like it was going to take me a year to recover. Somehow I managed to break all the endurance records set years before by Doc Blanchard and Glenn Davis, the original Mr. Inside and Mr. Outside.

I wasn't home for more than an hour when the doorbell rang. A blanket of snow had covered the region, and the darkness was barely illuminated by the pristine snow. I opened the door and there stood a short white man with gray hair and glasses, Syracuse football coach Ben Schwartzwalder. Next to him were two assistants. The three men parted like Secret Service agents, and standing behind them was this tall handsome man wearing a fine camel-haired coat. He was stacked up better than dirty laundry. Ernie Davis. My sisters were practically pawing at him through the door. "Who is that?" they kept whispering behind me. It was as if as Elvis Presley was at our doorstep.

You can't imagine people like that coming to our neighborhood at that time of night. It seemed as if Ernie was more like their escort.

The four men introduced themselves and asked me if I wanted to go to dinner. Well, in my house, a free dinner was like hitting the lottery. On top of being exhausted, I was starving. So they took me to Jocko Sullivan's, a nice bar and grill restaurant on the campus of Yale University. It wasn't every day that I was chauffeured to a fine restaurant, so I kept pinching myself underneath my coat.

At the restaurant my main concern wasn't talking football, it was eating. I had already finished reading the entire menu from front to back. I didn't know what steak or lobster looked like. So I was going to order one of each. Then right after we ordered, Ernie tapped me on the shoulder and said, "Let me talk to you for a minute." And I'm thinking to myself, *Before I eat?* So I got up and followed him. Of all places we head into the men's room. He goes in and puts one foot up on the urinal and looks at me. Well, I always wanted to be like Ernie, so I put one foot up on the urinal just like him. We looked like we were holding fort at the OK Corral. We sat and talked for about 45 minutes, right there in the men's room.

He said to me, "I hear you're a real good football player." I said, 'Well, I'm not a bad player." He said, "I hear you've got a lot of scholarship offers." I said, "Yeah, 47 of them." He said, "Let me tell you a little bit about Syracuse." I'm all ears. I mean, here's Ernie Davis, the first African American to win the Heisman Trophy, who just signed a contract with the Cleveland Browns for big money, like $100,000. He also just signed another $100,000 contract with Pepsi. And here I used to cash my checks at the 7–Eleven.

Ernie told me, "They got a football coach up there who likes to run the football. He doesn't like to pass. His philosophy is that three things happen when you pass the ball and two of them are bad. They can catch it and you can drop it. Not good. At Syracuse you'll be running the ball. But more important, they care about your education. They want you to go to class. They're concerned if you miss class because they want you to graduate. Even if you decide you don't want to play football anymore, you'll still keep your scholarship. That's one of the most important things about Syracuse."

So I started thinking about all those scholarships I was offered—football scholarships. This was more like an academic scholarship. I didn't know how smart I was, but with the help of Syracuse, the faculty, and all their support, they could help me through this all. I said, "Ernie, this sounds good. I'll go to Syracuse." I told him I would go, but I was still leaning toward Army and Notre Dame. For one thing I hadn't eaten yet, and I could always claim light-headedness.

Months passed and I still hadn't decided. Then I got this phone call from someone who told me Ernie Davis had died. I said, "Ernie Davis, the Heisman Trophy winner?" He told me, "Yes." I was like, "How could he die, he's only 23 years old?" He told me Ernie had some rare blood disease called leukemia. I was shocked. I started thinking, *My God. I promised him I would go to Syracuse.* I hung up the phone and sat there as this incredible flow of emotion poured out of me. I couldn't believe such an incredible man with such a bright future was gone. I had given Ernie my word that I would go to Syracuse. To me, my word is my bond. It defines who I am. I couldn't go back on my word. Right then, I knew what I had to do. I picked up the phone and called Ben Schwartzwalder. "Coach," I said, "I'm coming to Syracuse."

Ernie Davis had that kind of effect on so many people. I wanted to continue that legacy. I wanted to go to Syracuse to be the kind of player he was and the kind of player he could have been in the pros. More importantly, I aspired to be the kind of man Ernie was off the field—to carry on the tradition that Ernie had asked me to fulfill. He wanted me to wear 44 like he had and Jim Brown before him. He told me Jim did okay there, he did fine, and so would I.

When I got to Syracuse and was given 44, the same number worn by Ernie and Jim Brown, I was determined to live up to their legacy. I was a huge Jim Brown fan. But Ernie is the person I wanted to pattern myself after. He never had a chance to fulfill his dream and live a long life. So I tried to be the man Ernie didn't get the chance to be. I wanted to live the life Ernie should have been given. If they associated me with the kind of person Ernie was, that was a good thing.

When I put on the No. 44 jersey for the first time, I didn't set out to rush for more yards than Jim and Ernie. Just being part of that legacy was good enough for me. What a tremendous honor! Jim Brown is the greatest player to ever step onto the football field. Ernie Davis was a trailblazer, the first African American to win the Heisman Trophy. Because of those two men, I always played as hard as I could in college. Of course, that was my mentality on every level. But in college, I played as hard as I could because I wanted to continually honor the No. 44.

The Legend of 44

Although Ernie Davis had promised me number 44, it wasn't guaranteed. Unlike today where freshman are eligible to play varsity, I spent my first year at Syracuse in 1963 playing on the freshman team. I must have made an impression on the coaching staff because when I showed up at my first varsity practice in 1964, I was given No. 44. To wear the number and follow in the footsteps of the great Jim Brown, my idol growing up, and the incomparable Ernie Davis well, it was beyond a dream come true. I instantly became part of football history.

In 2005, during Syracuse's Homecoming game against South Florida, Syracuse finally retired No. 44. It now sits in the rafters of the Carrier Dome. I was there for that unforgettable weekend culminating in the halftime retirement ceremony where Jim Brown, Ernie Davis's mother, Marie Fleming, and other great players including Bill Schoonover, Michael Owens, Rob Konrad, and I were each given a replica No. 44 jersey and helmet from our playing days. My family and friends were there, including my grandson, Blaze Kennedy Jones, to whom I gave my jersey and helmet. I've been told that the university may un-retire the jersey for special occasions. One of them will be when Blaze goes to Syracuse and plays tailback for the Orange. He'll wear his Poppy's number proud. I'm 70 years old, but I'm eating right and staying in shape in hopes that I'll be around to see Blaze wear No. 44.

Another Guy Named Floyd

My coach at Syracuse was a living legend. Floyd "Ben" Schwartzwalder coached the Orangemen from 1949–73, went 153–91–3, and won four Lambert Trophies and a National Championship in 1959. But you'd never know it by meeting him. He grew up in the coal mines of West Virginia and was a football star for the Mountaineers in the 1930s. He joined the army in 1941 as a paratrooper and attained the rank of Major. He fought valiantly in World War II, fighting in many battles, including on D-Day, and he earned the Purple Heart among other awards.

At only 5'8", Ben didn't look like a former player or a decorated war hero. He was short, wore thick glasses, and had this deep southern drawl. But he was one of the toughest guys I've ever known. He played center at West Virginia at the imposing weight of 148 pounds. He was an intense man who always clenched his fist and tightened his jaw when he spoke. Unlike my coach at Bordentown, Ben wasn't a yeller. Instead he would pull you by the jersey and say, "C'mon, you're better than that."

He was part psychologist, part father figure. He was successful not just because of his football acumen. He knew how to reach your heart. Ben grew up dirt poor. He understood his players no matter their socio-economic background. He treated us like family, always encouraging. He built our trust, and we ran through walls for him.

Divine Advantage

My first varsity game was as a sophomore against Boston College. I didn't start but played a little offense and defense. I knew right away that Division I football was a good deal tougher than anything I had faced. BC beat us up pretty good, losing 21–14.

At the end of the game the team chaplain, Father Charles, came up and put his arm on my shoulder and said, "Floyd, it's going to be okay. You're going to be okay." Now, BC is a Jesuit school. They have rows of priests sitting there at every game. This one was no exception. I looked up at Father Charles and said, "I don't know, Father. Just look at all the priests they've got. We've only got you!"

Kansas Comet Meets the Kid?

With one varsity game under my belt, I continued to work hard in practice. I was running with the second and third teams and often took plays the distance. I never thought much of it because I wasn't with the first group.

We were playing Kansas that week, and the whole nation was talking about their star, Gale Sayers. This guy was as smooth as Al Green and seemed to glide through the air when he ran. I was looking forward to the game. I kept thinking, "If they put me in on defense, maybe I'll get to tackle him." I never got the chance. Minutes before the game, Coach Schwartzwalder came up to Jim Nance, our powerful senior fullback, and said, "Jim, I'm starting you at fullback and the Kid at tailback." I sat there thinking, *Who's the Kid?* Then guys started tapping me on the shoulder saying, "Have a good game. Make number 44 proud."

I was so nervous it reminded me of my first day at Bordentown. After that initial hit, though, I was in it to win it. I scored five touchdowns on runs of two, three, 15, 19, and 55 yards, totaling 159 yards on just 16 carries. We smoked them 38–8. After the game the first thing reporters asked me was, "Who are you?" I was just happy we won, and I performed well enough that people at school believed I deserved to wear No. 44.

Gale Winds

I got to know Gale later that year when we both made the 1964 Look All-America Team. It was quite an honor since I was the only sophomore chosen. They held the banquet at the Waldorf Astoria Hotel in New York, the same place where I had met General MacArthur.

Gale and I went out in the city afterwards. He had just signed with the Bears and insisted on paying. We went to a bar and grill and had a good time. When it came time to pay, Gale took out this wad of cash so big it looked like a head of lettuce. He had trouble folding it back into his pocket. I freaked. My mom told me to never take money out in public, especially in New York. I only had a few bills, but I hid them all over my body—in my left sock, right sock, inside my jacket, my pants pockets, behind my ears.

"Gale, don't flash that money around. Someone is going to rob us," I warned. "Let's get back to the hotel right away." We both started looking around the room, and the paranoia crept over us. We left the bar so fast it looked like we were late for the subway. Once we hit the street we took off running faster than the wind. I started thinking, *Two black guys running in the streets of New York at midnight probably doesn't look too good to cops*. Before we knew it we were back in the hotel, laughing our asses off.

Penn State Pinkos

For decades Syracuse's archrival has been Penn State. Coach Schwartzwalder hated to lose to anyone, but he especially despised Penn State. In 1964, my first varsity year, we were playing Penn State and held our final meeting the night before. Five minutes into it, Schwartzwalder stopped talking and started peering around the room. Then he began looking behind pictures, under the desk. "Shhh, quiet everyone," he whispered. "This room is bugged. Follow me." He quickly ushered us down the hall to another room and immediately locked the door behind us.

"I have to tell you something," he said, looking serious as a judge. "People who go to Penn State are Communists. The coach, Rip Engle [yes, there was someone before Joe Paterno], is best friends with Nikita Khrushchev." We were like school children listening to tales of the big bad wolf. You have to remember, this wasn't that long after the Cuban Missile Crisis. The Communist scare was real. I was thinking, *Oh, boy, oh boy. This is bad*.

We were so scared we went out and had one of our best games of the season. I didn't want to be touched by a bunch of Communists, so I tried to score every time I touched the ball, and did on a 71-yard punt return in a 21–14 win. My junior year I scored three touchdowns, including a 91-yard punt return and a 28–21 victory. Someone told me I even outran the film crew on that run. I tried to play that way all the time but especially against Penn State.

Later when I was with the Broncos, I was invited back to speak at a Syracuse banquet. When I got up to the podium I looked down and there in the front row was Rip Engle, the former Penn State coach. I started thinking, *Oh, my God. What's he doing here?* I started to hyperventilate and kept glancing over at him. I started changing my speech, watching what I was saying. After I finished, I downed a glass of water. I pulled Ben aside. "Did you see him, Coach?" I said anxiously. "Rip Engle! What the hell is that Communist doing here?" Well, Ben cracked this sheepish grin and looked down at the ground. "Floyd," he muttered, "Rip is, well—he's one of my best friends. He's not a Communist. I just made up that stuff to get you guys fired up. I guess it worked." I was shocked. I laughed initially out of embarrassment. But boy, I was pissed. I was still very impressionable back then about the world. We all fell for it.

Passing the Test

When I was at Syracuse, Ben had maybe five assistants. Today, there are assistants for every position plus quality control guys who basically assist the assistants. So we used to joke that one of Ben's assistants was his dog.

He had this big poodle named Casey that had a perpetual digestion problem. The dog would fart in meetings all the time. While Ben gave his fire-and-brimstone pregame speeches, his dog would be farting along, stinking up the joint. Sometimes he ripped the silent-but-deadly kind. Other times the farts sounded like a clogged pipe fighting for air. Once in a while the dog seemed to time it so he let loose a Doozie at the end of Ben's speech—almost like an exclamation point for dramatic effect. The dog only did it while Ben was speaking, which didn't help our confidence in the game plan.

Tech Knockout

As an African American player in the early 1960s, I experienced a fair share of prejudice. My first taste of it in Division I football was a 1964 game vs. Virginia Tech. Most of the southern schools had all-white teams, and Tech was no exception. But to the surprise of some, Tech apparently had no African Americans in their entire school. Days before the game, one of our political science professors asked the African American players to protest by not playing. I felt if anything, we would make a better statement by playing.

So we played and happened to win in the last minute 20–15. I rushed for 155 yards and a touchdown, but it was a slugfest. Those guys beat the shit out of us. There was intense hitting on every play and plenty of pushing and shoving after the whistle. It was one of the most physical games of my college career and the first time during a game that I felt like someone hated me because of my skin color.

Racial Tensions at the Sugar Bowl

While the Virginia Tech experience was one game, the 1965 Sugar Bowl was a whole week of racial tension. We faced LSU, and although Congress had just passed the Civil Rights Act, there was a long way to go toward equality. Following my days at BMI, I thought I was used to being judged differently. But that week in the Big Un-Easy hurt me deeply.

There was only a handful of African Americans on our team. So we pretty much stuck together. We tried to get a cab one night and none would stop. Finally, we saw a cab idling on a back street. We got in and the driver just sat there and read his newspaper. Finally, he looked up and said, "Don't you boys know this cab's for Whites only? Get out!" We were infuriated.

Later, Charlie Brown, an All-American defensive back, and I were walking down Canal Street and went into a Walgreens for a soda. Instead of serving us at the counter, the store clerk poured the soda into paper cups and told us we had to drink outside. Another store wouldn't let us use the water fountain.

Everywhere we turned we were judged by our color. So we practiced in Pensacola, Florida, at the Naval Base. We were ready, and I thought we were going to run the ball down LSU's throat. But for some reason right before the game, Ben announced we'd surprise them by passing the ball. I ran the ball just eight times.

All I can say is it backfired terribly. We lost 13–10. I don't know if it was the treatment some of us experienced that week, but we certainly didn't play with the same intensity that we had during the season. I felt emotionally drained by the time the game was over. It opened my eyes to the many injustices we African Americans were facing.

The Big Return in the Big Apple

When I finished my playing career at Syracuse I had broken many of the rushing records set by Jim Brown and Ernie Davis. I rushed for 2,704 yards and scored 46 touchdowns. Yet the thing I became most known for was my punt returning. I returned a record five punts for touchdowns; three were more than 90 yards.

When it came to returning punts, coaches told me never handle a punt beyond the 10-yard line. The problem was I always believed I could take it the distance, no matter how far it sailed. I know coach Schwartzwalder didn't always approve, but a few times it paid off.

One example was against Pittsburgh at Shea Stadium in New York. It was my junior year, and the game had special meaning because my mother was there. I scored four touchdowns, including a 95-yard punt return. I found out later that Weeb Ewbank, the coach of the Jets, and owner Sonny Werblin attended the game and were blown away by my performance.

Sometimes there are plays in your life that make such an impact you can remember every cut, juke, slash, and dash. This was one of them. I can still hear coaches yelling at me to get away from it and let the ball go in the end zone. But I gambled and caught the ball at the 5-yard line. I started thinking, *Shit, now look what I've done!*

I started upfield and dodged three players and cut back against the grain to the other side. It felt like crossing six lanes of traffic. Then I saw a tiny gap and dashed through the middle until the hole closed. I cut back to the right at midfield and noticed there were two guys to beat. I turned on the afterburner and started eyeing the end zone. They had an angle on me, but I was able to gain some separation. I started thinking of my mother watching me and how I wanted to make her proud. Somehow I was able to make it the final 50 yards for a wild 95-yard touchdown. As I crossed the goal line I felt nauseated and dizzy. I turned around and there were guys strewn all over the field. The stands were going bonkers, and I felt a great deal of pride—and relief. The first thing I thought was, *Thank God, Ben's not going to kill me.*

Plays like that helped me become the nation's yardage leader with an average of 199 per game. Afterward I sought out my mother in the stands and posed for a picture that appeared in the papers the next day. It's the one moment that stands out most during my Syracuse career because my mother was there to share it.

Almost Quitting

Midway through my senior year in a game against Navy, my bright outlook changed when I severely sprained my ankle. Even though I was supposed to miss a few games, I had my ankle taped up like a Popeye forearm and kept playing.

Unfortunately, I couldn't cut like before, and my yardage plummeted. By the third game fans started to boo me. They yelled, "What kind of All-American are you?" Some even called me at home to complain. I felt I had let the university down.

Aside from the injury, my weight dropped from 195 to 183. I went for blood tests, and the doctor kept having me come back for more. I was convinced I had leukemia like Ernie Davis. Finally, the doctor told me I had a massive iron deficiency. They started pumping me with vitamins, and my weight quickly returned to normal.

Still, I was depressed at my sub-par performance and decided to quit. I know this wasn't what I promised my father, or Ernie Davis, but I was a confused young man at a crossroads. I made my way to Ben's office and told him. I was ready for him to tell me I was crazy to quit. Instead, he sat back in his chair with his chin on his chest, eyes looking at me above his glasses.

"Floyd," he began, "I understand if you want to quit. There won't be any shame in it. You have contributed more to the team than any player we've ever had. You don't owe this university a thing. But I want to tell you something. Of all the players I've coached, I think you're the best."

I got emotional, and the tears started to flow. Ben wasn't the type to just throw out compliments. For him to say these things took me by surprise. "You've done enough for this university that you no longer need to play or come to games or anything. But I'd like you to stay at Syracuse because I made a promise to your mother that I'd make sure you graduated. I'd like to keep that promise."

Then coach did something that to this day still opens the floodgates. Before I got up to leave, he reached in his drawer and took out his paratrooper wings, the ones he had earned parachuting on D-Day. He said, "I want you to have my wings. Please take them as a token of my appreciation for everything you've done at Syracuse." I was beyond speechless. I was a slobbering baby. I gave Ben a hug and practically crawled out his office.

I went back to my dorm and thought about the past four years. All the games, the All-America honors, being captain, and the exhausting struggles I had endured. Then I thought about my father, how I had promised him I would make something of myself. I thought of Ernie Davis and the commitment I had made to him. Then I thought about Coach Schwartzwalder and the man he was. I thought about my teammates and how proud I was to be part of the tradition at Syracuse. So I started thinking about finishing up the season and seeing what the future brought. There was just one home game left against Florida State. We were fighting for a bowl berth. I went into Ben's office and told him I wanted to play. He looked at me for a few seconds then said, "Go suit up."

I went out and had one of the best days of my career. I rushed for 193 yards, scored three touchdowns, and we beat the Seminoles 37–21. I had bigger days before that, like 196 yards and four touchdowns vs. West Virginia. But this meant more. As I jogged off the field at Archbold Stadium for the final time, I saw a bed sheet draped over the visiting locker room entrance. It read, "Booth III thanks Floyd Little." Booth III was my freshman dormitory. That simple tableau almost dropped me to my knees. To know guys from my freshman year wanted to pay tribute in my last home game. It was an incredible ending to a memorable career and a difficult few weeks.

To this day, I get choked up thinking about that day in Ben's office. How he gave me those wings that meant so much to him. But then I have to laugh. I mean, Ben was a master motivator. Part of me believes he had a box of those wings in his desk that he handed out to players whenever they felt like quitting!

John Mackey

A lot of people know Ernie Davis was sent to my New Haven home on a blustery snow-swept night to recruit me. But what fans don't know is that later when I visited Syracuse to try and weigh in on my 47 scholarship offers, it was John Mackey who showed me around.

As much as I worshipped Davis, I knew John was now the team's biggest star. It meant so much that Ben Schwartzwalder sent his big gun to impress me. John was friendly and personable. He really listened, and he didn't act like some hotshot All-American. He had this quiet strength about him. I found out later he was a very confident young man.

After touring campus, John told me he was setting me up that evening with the most beautiful woman on campus. He didn't lie. He introduced me to this stunning coed named Sylvia. She was model tall with long dark flowing hair. Sylvia had this infectious smile. I thought I hit the jackpot. John joined us with his own date, and the four of us enjoyed a great dinner. All night I was mesmerized with Sylvia like I was escorting Miss America. To be honest, I didn't talk a whole lot to John during our meal, but I was blown away by his match-making skills.

I floated back home with this school-boy crush. Months later after Ernie died and I had made the commitment to go to Syracuse, I showed up on campus thinking about giving Sylvia a call. I mentioned her to a classmate. He looked at me like I was crazy and spit out his coke laughing.

"What's so funny?" I asked. "Sylvia, you're going to call Sylvia? Man, she just got married—to John Mackey. They've been going out forever."

I looked at him in disbelief. "That dirty dog," I muttered. John had set me up with his beautiful girlfriend just to impress me to come to Syracuse.

Now that's a confident man. In fact I recently talked to Dave Bing, the Hall of Fame basketball player for the Pistons, who's now the mayor of Detroit. He told me that John had set him up with Sylvia, too, when he was recruited to play basketball at Syracuse.

What can you say about Sylvia—she's an incredible sport!

A Hall of a Career

John went on to enjoy a Hall of Fame career, playing tight end with the Baltimore Colts. He was Johnny Unitas' go-to guy for many seasons. He retired with more than 5,200 yards receiving during an era where you could climb all over the guy. That's more yards than fellow Hall of Famer Dave Casper, who played a decade later. John had more yards with around 50 fewer catches than Dave.

I was fortunate enough to play against John a few times, especially when he played for the Chargers late in his career. He still stretched the field and could do it all—block, catch, and run like a power forward. No one could stop him in an open field. Who could forget that 75-yard touchdown pass he caught in Super Bowl V? I can still see the ball being tipped and John reaching up to snag it and outracing everyone to the end zone.

Despite his incredible career, it took 20 years for John to get to Canton. That's unbelievable. Now when today's players feel personally slighted if they're not first- or second-ballot Hall of Famers, I have to laugh at their arrogance. They made John Mackey, the greatest tight end in NFL history, wait two decades. I have news for the young guys. If you don't get elected to the Hall of Fame on your first few ballots, deal with it. You're not better than John Mackey.

After retiring, John did so much for NFL players. He became president of the NFL Players Association after the AFL-NFL merger. As president, John fought to improve players' pension benefits and access to free agency. He filed and won an antitrust lawsuit against the NFL, eliminating the so-called Rozelle Rule, named for then-commissioner Pete Rozelle, that mandated equal compensation for teams that lost free agents and had the effect of limiting free-agent signings. John's lawsuit eventually led to the players' union achieving full free agency. Needless to say, John was a true ambassador to the league and a pioneer for players' rights. He was a great player, teammate, leader, father, husband, and humanitarian.

John's dementia eventually forced him into an assisted-living facility. The cost of his care well exceeded his pension of less than $2,500 a month.

His plight led the NFL and the players' union to establish the "88 Plan"—his uniform number—which provided nursing-home care for retired players suffering from dementia or Alzheimer's disease.

Even with all the incredible things he did for others, John never lost his sense of humor. When I was still playing he used to tease me that I could only be half as good as he was. "Why is that?" I'd ask. "Because you wear 44. That's half of my number, 88!" That dirty dog.

John's Courageous Fight

I saw John a lot at Syracuse events over the years. We became close. John's dementia started in his early fifties when he first experienced memory lapses. We would talk about the effects of playing in the NFL.

I had five concussions that team doctors told me about, and John had his share, too. But we could have had more because we played in an era where if you got your bell rung, the trainer would ask you how many fingers he was holding up. You always answered two. It was the same when I was in high school, prep school, college, and the pros.

The answer was always two. It never changed. We all joked how team doctors and trainers never caught on. They always held up two fingers. Sometimes I wouldn't even look. I'd say "two" before the trainer even held up his hand. I would grab my helmet and run onto the field before he replied, "Okay, you can play."

Back then, we didn't recognize that our brains were shaken like coconuts from all those hits. When you consider the reckless abandon with which John played, he must have taken more shots than he realized.

A few years after he was diagnosed with dementia, I saw John at a Syracuse event. I said, "Hey, John!" He looked puzzled. "Where do I know you from?" he asked innocently. He didn't even recognize Jim Brown. It got worse for him later. One time while going through airport security, John got confused. He saw a line of people being held back by security, so he burst through the gate. Two TSA guys tried to grab him, and John beat them up. After that he was on the no-fly list and had to be driven or take a train everywhere.

Although he had periods of amnesia, he still could be lucid and recall details of his past. In 1996, after I had been passed over for the Hall of Fame for the 15th time, John wrote a letter to then–Hall of Fame voter John Steadman of the *Baltimore Sun*. He wrote, "If there is no room for Floyd Little in the Hall of Fame, please take me out and put him in. He deserves it that much."

I gave that letter to Tom Mackie back in 2003, and he used that quote as one of his "44 Hall of Famers on 44 Floyd Little" presentation. Of all the quotes that Tom compiled from Hall of Famers, I knew that quote would have a huge impact on voters. I was right. When I finally did get elected to the Hall of Fame, voter John McClain included John's quote in his story about me the following day.

I am eternally grateful to John for doing that for me. I get choked up just thinking about it. I know it came straight from the heart. But there is one other thing that John did for me that's even more precious than that quote. It was John and a friend of mine, Charles Davis, who introduced me to my wife, DeBorah, at a Syracuse function in 2000.

And Sylvia, my one-time date? She and John were married for more than 50 beautiful years.

Larry Csonka

After Jim Nance left for the pros, Larry Csonka became the fullback during my junior and senior years. Of course, everyone knows about Larry's exploits in the NFL. The immovable force of those great Miami Super Bowl teams in the 1970s. Larry was one of those naturally strong guys. He grew up on a farm in Ohio and had the biggest arms, shoulders, and head you ever saw. His helmet was the size of a milk bucket. Larry also had a big butt. Whenever we ran out of the I formation, all I could see was Larry's ass. Opponents couldn't always see me behind Larry. Then again, I could never see what was going on behind those huge cheeks.

Our offense was pretty simple. We ran an unbalanced line with four linemen on one side and two on the other. Our All-American tackle, Gary Bugenhagen, was usually the lead guy. We'd break the huddle and opponents would yell, "Run, run!" even if it was third-and-forever. Before we'd get down in our stances, Larry would ask, "Floyd, who do I have?" "Number 68." And he'd say, "That guy?" and point right at him. The defender, realizing the play was going right over him, would mutter, "Oh, shit!"

Larry probably doesn't know this, but I'm the guy who got Ben to switch Larry to fullback. When our starting fullback, Ron Oyer, went down in 1965, Ben said, "What are we going to do? We have no fullback." I suggested moving Larry from linebacker to fullback. I said, "How about Pigeon?" which was Larry's nickname because he walked with his knees knocking like a pigeon. "I'll tell him what to do until he learns the plays." Well, the first few games Larry mostly blocked. He carried the ball maybe three times. After he got comfortable, he wanted to carry the ball more. I wasn't really in favor of that because that meant I was in front of him blocking!

Larry and I got along great. I was a serious guy even in college. Larry was more laidback. He watched the way I handled myself and told me later he decided that if he wanted to make it to the pros, he'd better start mirroring his life like mine and become more dedicated. Of course, we shared plenty of jokes, too. He used to tell me, "Floyd, if I didn't like you, I'd fart in your face before every play."

We got to play against each other a few times in the pros. His rookie season, the Dolphins came to Mile High and we teased about who would outrush the other. The competition was pretty close. There was no scoring in the first half. Then in the third quarter, Larry scored. But moments later, I scored and we won 21–14. I rushed for 126 yards, and Larry had a great game, too, rushing for 97. We played again in 1969 and in the half-loaf game in '71.

Larry continues to be a great friend. When Tom Mackie called Larry a few years back to ask him if he thought I deserved to be in Canton, Larry said something that still chokes me up today: "There are people who are competitors that earn the right to go into the Hall of Fame. Then there are people that ride in on the laurels of others. Floyd Little earned every yard he ever gained in the NFL. He not only retired as the seventh leading rusher in NFL history, he earned every step of it."

I saw Larry shortly after the Hall of Fame selection at an autograph show in Houston. We were both signing near each other. Right before I was finished, I felt this arm around me. It was Larry giving me a big bear hug!

Tom Coughlin

Back in 2006 when I wrote my first book, few fans knew the secret past of Tom Coughlin. I revealed this smallish, wiry coach had played Division I football at Syracuse. Not only that but he played in the same backfield as two members of the Pro Football Hall of Fame: Larry Csonka and me.

Indeed. Tom was our starting wingback my senior year. Even then he was like a coach on the field. Guys who didn't know him well thought he was a know-it-all. Truth is, we needed someone like him. He not only knew all the plays, he memorized all the assignments of every player. If someone was unclear of an assignment, Tom wouldn't hesitate to tell him what he needed to do.

Tom wasn't the most talented player, but he worked incredibly hard. To be honest, he probably didn't have the raw talent to play Division I football. But he made up for any deficiency in talent with enormous drive and determination. It's not surprising to me that Tom became a successful NFL head coach. He's used the same drive and determination to win two Super Bowls, both over the highly favored Patriots. He's been a student of the game since his playing days.

He's also been a proven winner, although the New York media still calls for him to be fired whenever he loses a couple games. He won as an assistant under Bill Parcells. Then he won as head coach at Boston College and with the Jacksonville Jaguars. There are players in the NFL who say they wouldn't want to play for Tom. Well, they probably don't have the drive and work ethic that Tom has. His style may not be for everyone. But Tom was an overachiever as a player and just wants to give guys the opportunity to be the best they can be. His intentions are completely honorable. You always hear there's no substitute for hard work. Tom is the patron saint of hard work. Some say he's had an up-and-down coaching tenure with the Giants. Well, when you're coaching today's players, you have to be willing to change. And Tom had the foresight to change.

As much as I admire Vince Lombardi, I'm not sure he would be as successful in today's NFL as he was during the 1960s. Tom, who was an assistant under Bill Parcells, was a lot like Lombardi during his days in Jacksonville. Tom was rigid, a strict militaristic guy, and he carried that over during his first couple years with the Giants. He was considered a control freak. He actually put a big digital clock in the locker room, and things ran on Coughlin Time. If a meeting was at 10:00 AM, players had to show up at 9:45 to be on time. If they showed up at 10:00, Coughlin flagged them for being 15 minutes late. Although he did it to instill discipline, many players perceived it as a mind-fuck. It wasn't until 2007, his fourth year with the Giants, that Coughlin removed the clocks and began dealing with players on a more personal level. His players responded by putting together an incredible late-season surge that culminated in the second-biggest upset in NFL history—the Giants' 17–14 Super Bowl XLII victory over the 18–0 Patriots.

Even after that incredible world championship in 2007, the media was trying to fire him three years later when the Giants lost to the Eagles on a last-second punt return. I can't think of another coach that the media calls for his pink slip more than Tom. He continues to be the most "fired" coach in the NFL.

This past season was like déjà vu all over again for Tom Coughlin. But to me it was even better than his first Super Bowl victory. I've known Tom for a long time, and I don't think I've ever seen him get emotional. That's why his speech before the NFC Championship Game vs. the 49ers was so incredible. Guys said his eyes were like a sprinkler. He brought in three former Giants greats—Mark Bavaro, Rich Seubert, and Michael Strahan—guys who had all won Super Bowls with New York.

Tom told his players, "All three of those guys would give anything to be playing in this game. But their time was then. Their time has passed. Your time is now." That's powerful stuff. It reminds me of the scene in the movie *Dead Poets Society* when Robin Williams' character, John Keating, brings his English students to the school's hallway. He stands them in front of pictures of students who attended the school 100 years ago. He tells them, "Look at their faces. They're just like you, full of hope and dreams. Except they've already lived their lives. They're now worm food. But you have your whole lives in front of you." He's trying to get his students to realize the same thing Coughlin did. Their time is now. *Carpe diem*, "Seize the day."

Tom's speech before Super Bowl XLVI was even more incredible. He used a word that I don't think he ever used in a speech before and one I never heard him utter: love. After losing to the Eagles on a last-second punt return the season before, Tom's message the entire season had been "finish." Play a full 60 minutes. Finish the game. In this speech he touched on "finish" and "belief" because the Giants, after starting 6–2, dropped four in a row and were at 7–7 with two games to play. They went on to win the next four and were sitting there, one game away from being world champions, as Tom said, because of their "belief in one another."

The players thought his speech was over. A typical Tom speech but very well delivered. As players began to get up, Tom paused and looked straight at them. He said, "Championships are won by teams that love each other. I know this team does. But I want you to know something. I want you to know how much I love you guys, each and every one of you."

The players were shocked. They stood up and went crazy. I was taken aback, too, when I heard about it. But I am so incredibly proud of Tom. Just think how far he's come from his "my way or the highway" days. He took a team that was about to be eliminated from playoff contention and got his players to believe in one another. They went on to beat the Cowboys twice in three weeks, then they outplayed the 15–1 Packers in Green Bay, followed by the tough, resilient 49ers in overtime. Then they knocked off the favored Patriots again in the Super Bowl.

Coughlin's incredible coaching record plus his two Super Bowls wins over the supposed genius of Bill Belichick should put Tom in Canton. If he gets inducted someday, he'll be the third Pro Football Hall of Famer from that 1966 Syracuse backfield.

Incredible stuff.

44 Scissors

If you ever want to get Tom Coughlin started, ask him about Syracuse's 44 Scissors play. It was a staple play for the Orangeman back in the day—a misdirection, inside handoff to the wingback. Tom, of course, played wingback, also known as flanker. He loved that play and always performed well in practice. But in the games, Coach Schwartzwalder always asked me to run it. Tom would get so upset, and I don't blame him.

But you could see Schwartzwalder's predicament. He had two All-American backs in Larry Csonka and me. Why would he let someone else carry the ball? You can bet Larry and I used to tease Tom about it. "Tom, you're never going to carry the ball. Get used to it," we'd say. Still, Tom held out hope whenever the play was called during a game.

The play would come in and quarterback Rick Cassata would say, "44 Scissors Play," and Tom's eyes would light up. Then he'd add, "Tailback switch." And poor Tommy would be crestfallen. I felt bad for him, but damn that play always worked. Jim Brown and Ernie Davis ran it to perfection before me. So naturally I was called on to run it a lot. It was a great misdirection play. As soon as you got the ball, all you had to do was hit the hole fast and boom—you had only the safety to beat. We still laugh about that play today.

216 Yards, Not Enough

We played Tennessee in the 1966 Gator Bowl in my last game for Syracuse. We were determined to win and approached the game very seriously. This time Ben assured us that we would be running the ball. A lot. Larry and I had developed into a solid one-two attack.

Tennessee had a very good team. They were solid on defense, holding teams to less than 10 points a game. Although we ran well against the Vols, we found ourselves down 18–0 at halftime. Tennessee's passing game was killing us. Larry and I scored in the second half to make it 18–12. But when we got down close to the goal line near the end of the game, Ben called for Oley Allen to carry the ball. Oley fumbled, and that was that.

I was devastated we lost. It wasn't just Oley's fumble. We had several turnovers. But when you compile more than 340 yards rushing and lose, something is wrong. I left everything on the field—I rushed for 216 yards, my highest total ever. Csonka added another 100-plus yards. My jersey was so shredded it looked like a soiled rag. After the game a teammate, Joseph Radivoy, asked to keep it as a memento. I said, "Sure," and handed him the jersey. I never thought about it again. Then in 2005 at the Syracuse 44 retirement ceremony, Joe told me he still had the jersey and wanted to give it back. He mailed it to my oldest daughter, Christy, and when she got it she called me crying. She said it still had the grass stains on it and had been well preserved in a plastic bag. I was amazed. I thought, *Boy, I bet it smells pretty bad!*

Three Times a Charm

I really enjoyed my time at Syracuse. Everything I attained in life really started there. I met an attractive girl, Joyce Green, who I married, and we had two beautiful daughters. When we went out we usually went to the Varsity, a fabulous eatery where Jim Brown and Ernie Davis used to hang out. It's still there like it's been for more than 50 years. Whenever I go back to Syracuse, I always stop by the Varsity.

Every time I go back I get to meet some of the current crop of student athletes and catch up with other Syracuse alumni who carried on the tradition after me. Guys like Art Monk, Joe Morris, Rob Konrad, and youngsters like Marvin Harrison, Donovan McNabb, and Dwight Freeney.

Perhaps the thing I'm most proud of from those days is that we always had a winning team. We upheld the fine tradition that Ben Schwartzwalder set out when he arrived in 1949. I loved my teammates because they never gave up in any game. Their dedication and commitment were instrumental in my success. I am grateful for everything they did to help me become the player I was. Because of them, I became college football's first three-time All-American since Doak Walker and a top candidate for the Heisman Trophy each year. We've gotten together numerous times over the years, and we enjoy sharing old stories and reliving all those games. They are a tremendous group of guys. I know I was a pretty intense teammate, but none of them ever seemed to hold it against me. I think they respected me.

One time Myron Cope, a terrific writer who later became the radio announcer for the Pittsburgh Steelers, asked me if there was a special ritual I performed before a game to play so focused and intense. "Sure," I said, "I drink a half glass of fresh blood on Saturday morning, sleep in a dark cage, and eat raw meat. Then when it is game time I'm so excited to be free no one can catch me."

4

WELCOME TO THE BRONCOS!

Pre-Draft Rumors

The 1967 NFL Draft was unique because of the impending merger between the AFL and NFL. The AFL had become very popular. It was a wide-open league that starred exciting players like quarterback Joe Namath of the Jets and Lance Alworth of the Chargers. It wasn't a three-yards-and-a-cloud-of-dust league like some people viewed the NFL. Before Namath signed that incredible $400,000 contract in 1965, the AFL usually missed out on the top college players. Players were drafted by teams from both leagues, and then a bidding war would ensue to see who could offer the most money. Since the AFL didn't have the money or the prestige, 99 times out of 100 the top players jumped to the NFL.

That all changed the year I was drafted in 1967. For the first time the draft operated a common draft, like it does today. Only one team could draft you, and that team had first rights to sign you. With no bidding war, none of us were going to be rich like Namath. Still, I was told by Jets coach Weeb Ewbank and owner Sonny Werblin that I was going to be Joe's teammate. They had been at Shea Stadium to watch my four-touchdown game against Pittsburgh and told everyone, "He's the best. We want him." It was exciting to think about playing for one of the AFL's brightest teams—especially since it was close to Syracuse and my family in Connecticut.

I felt pretty good about my future. Then right before the draft, an article in *Sports Illustrated* came out that all but rejected me as a top pro prospect. As so-called experts, I suppose they felt the need to set the record straight. One concern was my age. At 25, I was ancient for a running back. Then there was my size, or lack of it: 5'10", 195 pounds. They said I was too small. I remember a reporter teasing me, "You're just a 'Little' guy, aren't you?" He seemed amused by his bad pun, as if he was the first guy to ever tell me that. I said, "My heart is as big as any man out there."

Most backs in the NFL were 6'2", 215 pounds. So they ranked me behind bigger prospects like Clint Jones from Michigan State; Mel Farr, UCLA; Willie Ellison, Texas Southern; Harry Jones, Arkansas; and Ray McDonald, Idaho. They all were about 4" and 20 pounds bigger. I took it personally.

I thought, *How dare they tell me what I can or cannot do. I'll show them. I'll go to the Jets with the 12th pick and enjoy a great career in the country's biggest market.* Deep down, though, I started thinking that if pro teams seriously bought into the article, I might still be around in the last round. My sophomore year Wake Forest's Brian Piccolo led the nation in rushing and scoring and went undrafted. And he was bigger than me.

On draft day, I had no idea what my future would be. The first few picks were predictable. Bubba Smith, Michigan State's mammoth defensive end, was chosen No. 1 by the Baltimore Colts. How Baltimore, an elite team, ended up with the top pick I still scratch my head over. Turns out they traded with the New Orleans Saints. The Vikings selected next, running back Clint Jones, Bubba's Spartans teammate. Then two quarterbacks: Heisman Trophy winner Steve Spurrier from Florida went to the 49ers, and Purdue's Bob Griese went to the Dolphins. With the fifth pick the Houston Oilers chose linebacker George Webster, another Spartan.

Now the Denver Broncos were on the clock with the sixth pick. The draft obviously wasn't televised. You sat by the phone waiting, hoping that someone, anyone would pick you. There were 17 rounds, so you could burn through a few pairs of pants just waiting. At this point the Jets were the frontrunner. I'd even talked to the great Vince Lombardi about the Packers, who held the ninth pick. Little did I know something was brewing in Denver that would forever change my life.

The Broncos had made it clear among their brass that they were drafting Gene Upshaw from Texas A&I, now known as Texas A&M–Kingsville. But right before their pick, Coach Lou Saban turned to Broncos PR Director Val Pinchbeck, who just happened to be Syracuse's former PR man, and asked, "Val, what kind of player is Floyd Little?" "Why Floyd is a great player," Val said. "He's a consensus All-American and a terrific runner." Then Lou asked, "What kind of person is he? Is he someone you can build a team around?" Val nodded, "Absolutely. Floyd is a great person. He was captain and an outstanding leader." Lou stood silently for a moment. Val said, "Why are you asking? You said you're drafting Upshaw." Lou looked back and smiled, "We're not drafting Gene Upshaw. We're going to draft Floyd Little."

When the phone rang, I expected to hear Coach Ewbank's voice on the other end. Instead I heard the booming voice of Lou Saban. "Floyd," he said, "this is Coach Lou Saban. Welcome to the Denver Broncos."

That's how I became a Bronco.

Where's Denver?

My first reaction to being drafted by the Broncos was shock. I wasn't even sure where Denver was. I was an easterner and thought it was some cow town in the middle of nowhere. And because I never heard of them, I thought, *Maybe they're not very good.*

I checked their record, and I was right. Denver had been one of the AFL's worst teams for years. They never had a winning record and often finished in last place. They had a couple of good players—receiver Lionel Taylor and defensive back Austin "Goose" Gonsoulin—but by the time I got there, they were gone. People had made fun of their uniforms for years. Their "barnyard brown" colors with hideous vertically striped socks were the only things writers talked about. Later when they switched to orange and blue uniforms, the media made fun of the funny orange helmets with a cartoon horse that looked like a giant inkblot.

The first thing I thought was, *I'm not going to last too long there. I'll get killed.*

So I went out to Denver with my agent, Andy Marciano, and we expected the worst. Instead I fell in love with the place. It was a friendly town surrounded by the most beautiful mountains I've ever seen. Most of all, I really liked Coach Saban. He was a no-nonsense guy who had coached the Buffalo Bills to back-to-back AFL championships a couple years earlier before going back to the college ranks to coach the University of Maryland for a year, a school that Syracuse played often.

"We're going to build a team around you," Lou told me in our first meeting. That made me feel good. *We'll be pioneers and be credited for building a great team,* I thought. But it was bad. The Broncos organization was in disarray, and the owners—Gerald and Allan Phipps—had threatened to move the team several times to places like Atlanta and Chicago. Now they were intent on moving the Broncos to Birmingham, Alabama. I wasn't too keen on the South at that point, so I was hoping we stayed in Denver. The point of contention was the Broncos' stadium. Denver played in an old minor league baseball park called Bears Stadium. It looked like a giant erector set. One of the requirements of the AFL-NFL merger was that each stadium had to seat at least 50,000 people. Bears Stadium probably seated half that much. And just before I got there, a $250,000 stadium bond issue to upgrade the stadium was rejected by the folks of Denver.

The Broncos were headed to Birmingham unless something drastic was done. The team felt that the first step to keeping the team in Denver was to sign their top pick—me. The Broncos had never signed their No. 1 pick before. In the past they had drafted several future Hall of Famers, such as Merlin Olsen, Dick Butkus, Paul Krause, tackles Bob Brown and Bob Hayes; plus great pros like Ray Mansfield and Marv Fleming. All of them scoffed at playing for Denver and high-tailed it to the NFL.

So I waited for Steve Spurrier to sign with the 49ers and then asked for 50 cents more. Literally. I just wanted to make a few pennies more than the Heisman Trophy winner. The combination of my signing and the addition of a great coach like Lou Saban began to pique the interest of Broncos fans.

Still, the city needed to raise about $2 million to keep the Broncos in Denver. A group of Broncos supporters helped raise the necessary funds. Corporations started giving money, the Phipps' matched the contributions, and the players went door-to-door to raise money. We rode in motorcades with the tops down so fans could meet us. We walked down crowded streets shaking hands. We got on buses and made goodwill trips throughout Colorado, Wyoming, Nebraska, the Dakotas—all over Broncoland. It was amazing—a true grassroots effort to keep the city's beloved Broncos in Denver. I was already being recognized as a savior. People were buying up tickets because I was the first pick to sign. Our PR staff coined us "The *New* Broncos." Finally, the money was raised and the stadium began undergoing expansion. When it was finished a few years later, the name was changed to Mile High Stadium.

I had become part of something special in a town that, just a few months earlier, I didn't know existed.

The Packers vs. The College All-Stars

I began my professional career playing in a number of All-Star Games. The first game, you could say, offered a bit of a challenge. It was against football's greatest dynasty—the world champion Green Bay Packers in the annual College All-Star Game in Chicago. Up until 1976, before high salaries and the fear of injuries halted the contest, the top college seniors played an annual exhibition game against the NFL Champions. Being 1967, of course, it was the Packers. They had just walloped the Kansas City Chiefs 35–10 in Super Bowl I. Now we baby-faced college kids were the next team up. Sounds fair, huh?

During the All-Star week I got to meet a number of fellow rookies and new Broncos teammates: guard George Goeddeke and defensive tackle Pete Duranko from Notre Dame; Mike Current from Ohio State; and tight end Tom Beer from Houston. I also got to know the guy the Broncos initially wanted to draft: Gene Upshaw, who became a Raider. We got along great and Gene gave me the nickname "Wheels," because he said my bowlegs were round like wheels. During the next nine years Gene and I faced each other many times in those Broncos-Raiders games. Until his passing, Gene still called me Wheels.

We "All-Stars" lost 27–0 to the Packers, but it might as well have been 127–0. All I remember is getting my ass handed to me on every play. Our quarterbacks were Steve Spurrier and Bob Griese, and all of us were being tossed around like pint-sized rodeo clowns. I learned very quickly that the

NFL was full of great players. I also realized why the Packers kept calling us "All-Stars," because that's all my aching head could see.

It's a Long Walk Back Home, Alex Karras

While I was away playing in the All-Star Games, the Broncos made history by becoming the first AFL team to beat an NFL team. It was an exhibition game in Denver against the Detroit Lions. During the coin flip, Alex Karras, the Lions' defensive tackle, looked around the stadium and said to Dave Costa, "If we lose, I'll walk to Detroit."

We took a 10–0 lead and beat the Lions 13–7. More than 40 years later, I guess Alex is finally crawling up his driveway.

NFL Meet Mr. Gilchrist

The next week we beat another NFL team, the Minnesota Vikings. I started at halfback with the great Cookie Gilchrist at fullback. Carlton "Cookie" Gilchrist was an awesome specimen. He was the first to gain 1,000 yards in the AFL and was the league MVP in 1962. As big as Jim Nance and Larry Csonka were, Cookie was even bigger. He stood 6'3" and was listed at 250 pounds. But I'm telling you, he was more like 270. He was all muscle, too. Cookie once got into a fight with then-heavyweight champion Sonny Liston over a woman and whipped his ass. A few years earlier Cookie had played on the first of Lou's back-to-back AFL championship Bills teams before going to Denver and Miami. Now, in the last year of his career, he was back with the Broncos. But, boy, he could still play.

We ran a lot of sweeps, and Cookie just destroyed the Vikings' two defensive ends, Jim Marshall and rookie Alan Page. So much so that by halftime, Page, now a Hall of Famer and a Supreme Court Judge in Minnesota, was moved inside to tackle where he remained and blossomed the rest of his career.

Cookie and I each scored touchdowns, and we beat the Vikings 14–9. Before I met Cookie I considered myself a pretty tough guy. But he was the toughest football player I knew. He didn't think much about his appearance when he was on the field, which made him even more intimidating.

Sometimes he didn't wear a jockstrap or chinstrap in games. In practice he wore street socks. It was almost like he crawled out of bed, grabbed his helmet, and calmly went about the business of kicking someone's ass each day.

Farewell to One Tough Cookie

A week after that Vikings game, we flew to Nebraska for my first away game as a professional. Nebraska was celebrating its centennial, so the AFL decided to host a game there between the Broncos and Raiders. I guess the organizers wanted two teams that hated each other.

We won 21–17 and Cookie dominated another defensive end, big Ben Davidson. Davidson was afraid of Cookie. Every time we ran a sweep, Cookie buried him. After a half-dozen sweeps, Davidson looked like he was just trying to get out of Cookie's way.

Besides Cookie's performance, the thing I remember most about that game was flying out of Nebraska. We were in a small plane and after take-off I noticed we were circling the airport, slowly trying to rise higher with each go round. Finally, the pilot told us that due to the weight of the passengers, the plane was trying to gain momentum to pull itself over the Rocky Mountains. For someone like me who's afraid of flying, this did not bode well. I was looking around for a few guys to throw off the plane to make it lighter. After we got over the mountains, the pilot asked for the bigger players to move to the front to keep the nose down. I started thinking, "Yup, the AFL definitely is the poorer league."

Cookie taught me a lot about not being afraid of anyone and never backing down. I was lucky and honored to have played with the great Cookie Gilchrist. He passed away at the age of 75 of cancer in January 2011. He was posthumously diagnosed with stage four chronic traumatic encephalopathy (CTE), which is a type of dementia resulting from head injuries. What we call in football as "concussions." No doubt Cookie gave more concussions than he received, but in the end he paid the ultimate price.

After he passed, Cookie's son, Scott, found files upon files of journals, letters, and notes that Cookie had kept over the years. Scott and a friend of theirs, retired police officer Chris Garbarino, pieced together his life story in a wonderful book, *The Cookie That Didn't Crumble*. I urge anyone who loves football and wants to know the behind-the-scenes truth about the game and one of its great legends to read this book.

5

THE LOU SABAN YEARS

The Man and the Mayhem

You've probably seen clips of Lou Saban on NFL Films with those intense, memorable sound bites. I can tell you he wasn't mugging for the camera. That was Lou. He hated losing, despised mistakes, and would get so caught up in a moment that he would fire you and everyone associated with you for almost anything, even if the sun cast a wrong shadow on you. He could be warm, caring, and soft-spoken one minute and the Tasmanian Devil the next. I remember Lou fired our receivers' coach, Sam Rutigliano, who later became the Browns' coach, during Sam's first game with the Broncos.

Sam was up in the press box on the phone with Lou during a crucial fourth-down play. There was a miscommunication, and the play failed. Lou yelled up to Sam that he was fired and should go pack his bags. The rest of the game Sam wondered what he was going to tell his wife since they had just arrived in Denver and had barely unpacked. We came back to win the game, 26–21, and Lou pretended it never happened.

Lou was the epitome of the irrational and irascible football coach. He had been a heck of a football player for the Cleveland Browns in the 1940s with Coach Paul Brown and quarterback Otto Graham. They were part of the All-American Football Conference then, which later merged with the NFL. During the four years that Lou played linebacker and fullback, the Browns won the AAFC Championship each year. After his playing days, Lou went into coaching and had great success, especially those two AFL crowns with the Bills. So, like me, he wasn't accustomed to losing.

Pulling a Saban

You recall the 1999 NFL Draft when Iron Mike Ditka, then the Saints coach, traded all his draft picks so he could move up to nab Ricky Williams, the Heisman winner from Texas. Since then, anytime an NFL team makes a bad deal, people call it, "Pulling a Ditka."

Well, I like to think of it as "Pulling a Saban." In 1967, my first year with the Broncos, Lou decided we needed a top-flight quarterback. He had promised to build a team around me so I thought he was going to either draft a great quarterback or make a trade for a proven veteran. He did neither. Instead, he jeopardized the Broncos' future by giving away two first-round draft picks—our 1968 and '69 picks—for Steve Tensi, a Chargers backup. Steve had attempted only 52 passes in his short career. Evidently Lou wasn't impressed with the stable of quarterbacks from the year before that combined for 28 interceptions and just 12 touchdown passes.

Still, we all gave Steve the benefit of the doubt. He was tall, about 6'5", rail thin, and had long sideburns. He often slicked back his hair and loved to sing Elvis tunes. He was also a bit of a lady's man, and I wondered if he actually thought he was the King. Well, this Elvis sang a lot of blues because he got hurt a lot. Our pass protection was abysmal during those early years, and our quarterbacks got smacked around a lot. I liked Steve. He had a good arm and was pretty tough. Everyone agreed, though, that he wasn't worth those two number ones. By 1970, bruised and battered, Steve had hung 'em up.

Rookie Roundup

During my first year with the Broncos, we had 26 rookies on the team. That's not a misprint—26! I still think that must be an NFL record. Lou liked to bring in new kids all the time. There were plenty of days where I was at my locker changing into my uniform, and next to me was a new guy I had never seen before. The following day the guy would be gone and there was someone else in his place. This was the norm.

One time we actually signed a guard an hour before the game. I didn't meet him until we were in the huddle. Someone introduced us before our first play: "Number 61, meet Floyd Little. Floyd, this is Number 61. He's going to be blocking for you today." I looked at the guy in disbelief. "Does he even know the plays?" I found out the answer quickly. On the first play he pulled one way, and our left guard the other. Wham, right into each other. I thought: *Yeah, this happens all the time on the Packers.*

You're Killing Me!

If there's one phrase that sticks out in my mind from my days with Lou, it was his exasperated phrase, "You're killing me!" Lou said it all the time. Because we lost so much, that phrase chimed in your head like a clock stuck on midnight. Everyone heard it, even coaches.

The first time he said it to me was in practice. "You're killing me, rookie. You're killing me!" I still heard it after I became one of the top backs in the league. By then, he changed it up a bit. "Floyd, come here. Son, you're killing me."

Despite his claim, Lou must have had the life expectancy of 50 cats because he seemed to have numerous coaching lives. After Denver he went back to the Bills, then coached college and high school teams into his eighties. No matter how tortured and aggravated he seemed, Lou loved coaching. It was his life. I saw a story about him a few years ago on ESPN. He was coaching a high school team and was telling those kids the same thing. "You're killing me!" he screamed.

You Hit Like a Grandmother

There's no debating this—Lou had one of the toughest grandmothers in history. I never met her, but evidently she was better than anyone on our team. Lou told us so. Often.

"My grandmother is better than you," he'd yell. "My grandmother hits harder than you."

The guy who probably heard it the most was Chip Myrtle, a linebacker who played for us for six seasons. Chip was a good pro, a solid player. But whenever the defense gave up a big play, he'd seek out Chip and make him the scapegoat. "Chip, my grandmother is tougher than you," Lou screamed.

One time Chip stretched in vain for a tackle and landed in mud. When he got up he had a big chunk wedged between his helmet and face-mask. The clod stuck out like a mutant boil. Lou, of course, ignored the effort and got after him again with the grandmother shtick. "Geez, Chip. My grandmother—" But Chip ignored him. He refused to turn around. Even during a timeout he wouldn't acknowledge Lou's rants. Finally Lou screamed, "Hey Chip. At least get that goddamn dirt off your helmet. You look ridiculous!"

Poor Chip. The thing is he had heard it all before coming to the Broncos. Chip played for Lou at Maryland before Saban signed him as a free agent in 1967. Talk about walking a mile to get your feelings hurt. Chip traveled 2,000 miles from the east just to hear Lou taunt him as a pro.

Nine Straight Losses

After beating the Patriots in our first game, I was upbeat about the season and happily looked forward to facing the Raiders again. This time, however, it was in Oakland and we didn't have Cookie. He had been hurt against Boston and didn't carry the ball the rest of the season.

To say we lost to the Raiders was to say that Custer lost at Little Big Horn. We were crushed and embarrassed 51–0. Nothing worked for us. I ran the ball seven times, and our quarterback, Steve Tensi, passed for 17 yards. Every time I looked up, the Raiders were scoring. After that ass-whipping, I think we were so stunned we went on to lose another eight games. That's nine straight. I had never experienced anything like it.

There were a lot of reasons we lost. Our offense was young, and Lou kept changing the lineup every week in hopes of finding the right mix. We had no cohesion, and I had nowhere to run. I was bloody and bruised so much my body felt like it was in a car accident each game. And Lou just got madder and madder at everyone. During film sessions, no one wanted to sit in the front row because they knew Lou would scream at them. The projector would be humming along, and Lou would yell names in the dark. He'd ask a player to speak up, but few of us did. Some guys tried throwing their voices, and Lou would start hollering at a spot in the room where no one was sitting. He looked like a man who had gone crazy. But deep inside we knew it was no laughing matter. We needed a win bad.

No Oranges for You!

In the midst of our nine-game losing streak that first year, we played the Oilers at old Rice Stadium. This was before the Oilers moved to the Astrodome. Lou was fed up with everyone in that game, especially the kicking game. He had become unglued because the punt and kick coverage teams each allowed long returns that set up easy field goals. By halftime Lou was his usual boiling-pot self.

As we entered the locker room, Lou kicked over our halftime snack—a table of oranges. The fruit bounced all over the place, under benches, into the shower. "No oranges for you!" he snapped, like he was the Soup Nazi from *Seinfeld*. He asked for all the kickoff and punt coverage players to raise their hands. Slowly, each one did. "Go stand over in that corner," he declared. "Now get dressed. You're all fired."

The special-team guys didn't believe him. When halftime was over they tried to get back onto the field, but Lou wouldn't let them. We were stunned. He made them sit and stew in the locker room the rest of the game. We lost pathetically 10–6. When we returned to the locker room we found oranges splattered all over the place by the special team players.

I believe that was the first reference to Orange Crush.

Go Take a Cold Shower

One of the cities we hated playing in was Buffalo. It wasn't so much the weather, although it was usually horrible. It was the "amenities." The Bills played in aptly named War Memorial Stadium. Heck, its nickname was "The Rockpile." It was a haunting mass of rusting steel. The visiting locker room looked like a dungeon, and the ceiling was always dripping stuff that wasn't water. If you want an idea of what the stadium was like, watch *The Natural*. That's where the movie was filmed, and I'm sure they cleaned it up a bit for Robert Redford. Worse were the showers. The hot water lasted for only a few seconds before it turned into winter at Niagara Falls.

We were 0–9 in our last nine games when we flew to Buffalo to face the Bills. It was a predictable rainy day with more wet stuff in the forecast. We were determined to get a win that day for Lou, especially since, as the former Bills coach, he hated losing to them. He kept saying, "Don't embarrass me today."

The game turned out to be a muddy mess. I scored from about 10 yards out in the first quarter, and we built a 21–7 lead. That was the good part. Then the weather got really nasty, and the rain turned into a deluge. By the fourth quarter a few players were hurt, so Lou started enlisting people to go in on the kickoff team. The downpour was so bad no one wanted to go in. Instead, we all huddled on the benches with our ponchos hanging over our heads so he couldn't tell who we were. Lou was screaming, "Hey you. Show me your face. What's your name? Go in on the kickoff team." But some guys just slumped lower inside their ponchos. Lou even started wrestling with one guy trying to unveil his identity. I didn't want him doing that to me, so I jumped up and ran onto the field like a wet rat.

Luckily, we held on to win. Buffalo closed the gap, but we prevailed 21–20. When the gun sounded we didn't even shake hands. We pushed each other out of the way in a mad dash for the locker room. We wanted to be the first to enjoy those precious seconds of hot water. After the water turned cold, most of us decided to skip the shower. We flew home covered in mud, but happy.

Blocking the Big Cat

One of our linemen during those early years was tackle Tom Cichowski, a good player and one of the many guys Lou had coached at Maryland. Tom had good size and could match up pretty well with almost anyone. Well, sort of.

During a game against the Kansas City Chiefs, Tom was having a tough time against behemoth defensive end, Ernie Ladd. At 6'9", 300-pounds, Ernie was the biggest player I'd ever seen. He was an All-Star earlier with the Chargers and was finishing his career with the Chiefs. Of course, his nickname was "The Big Cat."

Our line coach, Whitey Dovell, had a pretty simple blocking scheme back then. He'd either call his linemen to block "down," "out," or "fan-it," which meant big man on big man, little man on little man. So if the defensive end was across from the tackle, he would get the end and I would be responsible for blocking the outside linebacker, the "little" man, which against the Chiefs was future Hall of Famer Bobby Bell. Frankly, I didn't want to block either of those guys. Bobby was a great player, and Ernie, well, was as big as a Ford Explorer.

Ernie was overpowering Tom play after play. It got so bad that by the third quarter he begged me to block Ernie for one play. I said, "Are you crazy? He's 6'9". I'm 5'10". Do the math." I kept refusing him. Then on one play I was lined up in the backfield a few yards behind Tom and heard him say, "Down, down," meaning he was going to block the tackle, which meant Ernie was uncovered for me to block.

"Son of a bitch," I murmured under my breath. As the ball snapped I saw Ernie barreling straight at me. I was the only thing between him and the quarterback. I ran and hit him as hard as I could. I aimed for his stomach, but due to the size differential I hit him much lower—in the nuts. I could hear him cursing me like a warden. He was mad as hell. He pushed me back like a folding chair, but I was able to slow him down long enough for our quarterback to get the pass off. He got up, and I apologized profusely. "Sorry. I didn't mean it," I said. "Goddamn it, kid," he yelled and stumbled back to the huddle, holding his package. Meanwhile my helmet was sideways. I was looking out my ear hole and had mud all over my face. My neck felt like I got slugged by a two-by-four during a hurricane. "T-t-thanks, Floyd," Tom's voice quivered. "I just needed a break."

Who Wants a Piece of Me?

With six preseason games a season, we played a few at neutral sites. Now erase your mind of the glamour spots that teams travel to today, like Japan or Mexico City. We played in Nebraska my rookie year, and this season we upgraded to Utah.

We flew to Salt Lake City to play a night game against the Patriots. It was at Utes Stadium, and the humidity was so bad you'd sweat in a pool. The Patriots were the designated home team. But we didn't find that out until we were warming up in our home uniforms. Our equipment manager had made a mistake. Lou said, "No big deal. We'll both wear home jerseys." The officials refused. They said our jerseys were too similar to Boston's red ones. I guess they were right. But jeez, it was a preseason game and the stadium was practically empty.

So we borrowed the Utes' white jerseys. Of course, they were too tight. We looked like a semi-pro team out there, wearing these shrunken jerseys. We played like a semi-pro team, too. By halftime, we were losing 8–3.

Lou wasn't cutting us any slack because of the crappy uniforms, either. "You guys are the worst team I've ever coached," he cried. "You're all a bunch of gutless thieves. You're stealing money. But it's not your fault; it's my fault. I thought you could play this game. But I was wrong. Don't worry. When we get back I'll get some people to replace you, and you won't have to feel bad about yourselves anymore."

Then the heat must have gotten to him because Lou challenged a few guys to fight him. "I can kick anyone's ass on this team, and I'm 104. C'mon, who wants a piece of me? Let's go." Right then, defensive tackle Rex Mirich, who was 6'5", got up and walked towards him. Lou wheeled around, looking like he was confronting Bigfoot. He regained his courage and knocked over a table of juice. "Let's go, Rex. You think you can take me? Well, I'm not afraid of you," he said, both fists shaking noticeably. "Relax Coach," he said. "I'm just getting some water."

Everyone broke into laughter, and Lou even appeared to lighten up. We went out and won that meaningless game 16–14.

Bulimic Bob?

One of the more interesting guys I ever played with was guard Bob Young. He was a short, powerful guy from Texas, 6'1", 270 pounds, and one of the strongest guys I ever knew. Bob joined Denver as a rookie in 1966 and played with us for five years before going on to Houston and then to the St. Louis Cardinals where he was part of that great offensive line in the 1970s with Dan Dierdorf and Conrad Dobler.

Bob was a big eater. He loved to scarf down food all the time. He didn't seem to care what he ate. Our pregame meal was usually steak and potatoes. But sometimes we had shrimp, which was a big mistake because Bob loved shrimp. Anytime we saw shrimp, we knew Bob was going to have a long day.

One game Bob had loaded up on so much shrimp that he was puking on almost every play. He was as green as Ireland and kept throwing up in the huddle. So we just moved the huddle a few yards to the left or right after each upchuck. Toward the end of the game it started looking like a well-choreographed dance move. Bob would get sick, and we'd move the huddle in unison, "Step 1–2–3" to the right or "1–2–3" to the left. Bob also had this high-pitched voice, which was peculiar for such a big man. That whole game he'd say, "Sorry guys," after each barf, sounding like Kermit the Frog.

Bob was a great pro who passed away at the young age of 52. I consider him one of the strongest offensive linemen I've ever known.

Mr. Biggs

The first time we played the Jets at Shea Stadium, one of our tackles, Sam Brunelli, was having a tough time against Verlon Biggs.

Biggs was an All-Star, and he was beating the crap out of young Sam. Unlike Tom Cichowski, who had left me out on an island blocking Ernie Ladd, Sam asked me to help double-team Biggs.

In the huddle Sam said, "Floyd, this bastard is beating me to the inside. If you can slow him down inside, then I can keep him from rolling outside."

When the ball snapped, Biggs barreled his way to the inside as Sam predicted. Just as he planted his foot, I hit him low to the inside. "Motherfucker," Biggs howled, "my knee!" He rolled on the ground before teammates helped him. "I'm going to get you, rookie," he roared as he limped to the sideline. I apologized several times. The last thing I wanted to be known as was a dirty player, especially as a rookie.

Later Biggs was back on the field. We had built a 26–0 lead, and he was staring at me like I was the last pork chop at a family picnic. I got the ball on a sweep, and Biggs was bearing down. As I neared the sideline and planted to cut up field, Biggs launched himself, spearing me in the shoulder. I fell sideways to the ground; I knew it was separated. Biggs stood over me and snarled, "That's payback, motherfucker."

We won 33–24 at Shea, the same place I scored that long punt return against Pitt. This time I returned a punt 72 yards for a touchdown. But the biggest impression made on me that day—the NFL is full of paybacks. The worst thing you could do is hurt a guy because he'll do all he can to even the score.

Trying to Do It All

My first couple of years with the Broncos were incredibly frustrating. We had a young team with an assortment of players from everywhere. Defensively, we had a good line, but we couldn't stop the pass.

Offensively, though, we weren't very good. We couldn't pass or run. As the No. 1 pick, I thought I could carry the team. But teams crowded the line, and the holes weren't there. Val Pinchbeck, the Broncos PR director, told me that some of my best runs were just getting back to the line of scrimmage. Years later my ability to get positive yards after being hit behind the line of scrimmage is something that Jeff Legwold charted and discussed at my Hall of Fame presentation.

That left one area where I could really help the club: the kicking game. My experience returning punts and kickoffs in college allowed me to excel right away in the pros.

As a rookie in 1967, I led the AFL in punt returns with a 16.9 yard average, which is still a Broncos record. I also led the league in combined yards two years in a row from 1967–68, and I was the only player to return a punt for a touchdown both years.

Still, there was little solace because we weren't winning. I felt the fans deserved better.

Captains Kaminski and Cichowski?

Rookies are usually never chosen team captain. But with 26 rookies on our team and a lot of inexperienced guys from other clubs, Lou made the voting open to everyone. As a 25-year-old rookie, I guess I was more mature than others. For whatever reason, I was honored to be chosen the Broncos captain as a rookie and for all nine seasons I played with the Broncos.

Maybe one of the reasons I was voted captain had to do with the shortness of my name. We had a lot of guys with long names. I think it was much easier to jot down "Little" than to try spelling "Kaminski" or "Cichowski."

You're Fired! (The Buffalo Game)

There was nothing Lou Saban enjoyed more than beating his old team, the Buffalo Bills.

After sneaking out a victory in soggy Buffalo my rookie year, we were happy to play them at home the next year in 1968.

Our quarterback that day was rookie Marlin Briscoe, the AFL's first starting black quarterback. Marlin was small at 5'11", 178 pounds, but he was more like 5'10". He could roll out, run, and throw with velocity. We drafted him in the 14th round that season from tiny Nebraska-Omaha. He played quarterback there, but we first tried him at defensive back and flanker.

Steve Tensi had hurt himself again, this time by heaving a ball to some kid 80 yards away near the practice field. Lou couldn't believe it. So he continued playing musical quarterbacks. John McCormick, a veteran guy from Massachusetts, played some. Jim LeClair started a couple games. He even put rookie Joe DiVito in—our punter.

Midway through the season Lou decided what the hell and gave Marlin a shot. Almost instantly our whole team seemed to step it up a notch. Teams could no longer focus solely on me. They had to account for Marlin's scrambling, which allowed receivers like Eric Crabtree, Al Denson, and tight end Tom Beer more time to get open. We nicknamed Briscoe "Marlin the Magician."

Marlin threw two touchdown passes early on to stake us to a 14–0 lead against Buffalo. The Bills came back to make it 14–7. Then right before halftime, Marlin called a screen pass. I caught the ball, broke a tackle, gave a head fake, and outraced everyone down the sideline for a 66-yard touchdown and a 21–7 halftime lead.

By the fourth quarter it was 28–14, and we were feeling pretty good about things. I was having a good game with 70 yards rushing and more than 100 receiving. That all changed in seconds.

Ahead 31–22 with two minutes left, we were set to punt when a Bills player broke through, blocked Joe DiVito's kick, and ran it back to the 3-yard line. They scored, and suddenly it was 31–29 with a 1:30 left. Lou was livid. We recovered the onsides kick and coach grabbed me by the shoulder pads and snarled, "Protect the ball and don't go out of bounds." I thought *No sweat*. I had done this many times at Syracuse. Of course, today the rules allow you to kneel four times; back then we had to run plays.

I took the handoff and started running left. I don't know what happened, but I tripped on a clump of sod and began losing my balance. To keep from going out of bounds, I began waving my arms and the ball just fell out. It seemed like it happened in slow motion. No one hit me. The ball trickled out of my hands, and I lunged for it as I hit the ground. The Bills' George Saimes picked it up and headed for the goal line. I managed to drag him down at the 10. The Bills wasted no time and kicked a field goal to take the lead 32–31 with just 30 seconds left.

Buffalo was beyond ecstatic. They were hugging each other, rolling around on the ground. They probably would have made snow angels if there was snow. And Lou, well, he was angrier than I had ever seen him. He was volcanic red. I went back to receive the kickoff, but he stormed out on the field. "Get the hell out of here. You're fired." I was shocked. He said, "I'm serious. You're fired. Highway 25 runs north and south, 70 east and west. Take your pick out of town." I said, "Screw you," and began walking off the field toward the locker room in the south end zone.

Everything had turned so quickly. I was furious at myself for fumbling but even angrier at Lou for embarrassing me in front of my teammates. I thought, *I'm done. I don't need this shit. I've given everything I've had to this team.* Then halfway up the tunnel I changed my mind. "There is no way I'm going to be run out of town this way," I muttered. "Not by that fat bastard."

So I turned around and ran back onto the field. By now Fran Lynch, my roommate and backup, had replaced me in the lineup. I went into the huddle and yelled at Fran to get out. He said, "Coach told me to go in for you." I said, "I don't give a shit. I'm not leaving. Someone better get out or we'll get called for 12 men in the huddle."

Saban saw me and started shouting, "I fired you, Little. Get the hell out you son of a bitch." I yelled back, "Fuck you, I'm staying in." Now all the guys are getting upset, especially Fran. He didn't know what to do. Then the referee came over and demanded that one of us leave. I refused to budge. Finally, Fran threw up his arms and ran off the field. Lou started screaming at Fran for disobeying him, and the guys in the huddle started yelling at me for pushing out Fran.

I pleaded with Marlin. "You have to do this for me. I don't care how far you throw the ball. I'm headed for the flag. Just throw it as far as you can, and I'll get it."

Down to only 25 seconds standing on our 31-yard line, we were out of options. So Marlin looked at me and the rest of the team and said, "Okay, let's give it a shot."

Marlin took the snap and rolled out. I was split right and ran a fly pattern. I noticed right away that there were two guys on me. George Saimes, an All-Star safety, and Booker Edgerson—both became Broncos later on. Marlin waited to the last second before uncorking an arching beauty. It sailed about 65 yards in the air. Sandwiched between these two guys, I knew I'd have to leap high to grab it. I waited until the ball was above my head and jumped as high as I could. I plucked the precious pigskin out of the air and felt the defenders grabbing at the ball and pulling my facemask the whole way down. When I landed, Edgerson had fallen to the ground and I tried to maneuver away from Saimes only to be gang tackled by him and linebacker Harry Jacobs. The play had gone for 59 yards. An official threw a facemask penalty and suddenly we were in field-goal range with just a few seconds left.

Our kicker, Bobby Howfield, who was from Bushey, England, came trotting out to kick the game winner. I grabbed him and said, "Please, please kick this for me." He smiled and said, "Don't worry about it, Mate. I got this one," and he kicked it straight through.

The whole stadium went crazy. I guess it was the first big comeback at the miracle mansion later called Mile High Stadium. People were congratulating me, but I barely acknowledged them. I sat there on the bench bawling, knowing this was my last game. Then out of the corner of my eye I saw Lou pointing at me to come over. I said, "F-U!" and walked toward the tunnel. He stared at me with those blistering eyes and ordered me to come over. So I walked over. "What the hell do you want?" I said. He looked at me and pointed his index finger a few inches from my face. "I'm giving you one more week," he smiled.

Later I found out I had racked up 295 yards in that game, a record that stood for more than 25 years. I also heard that before the kick, Lou grabbed Howfield and said, "See that little space next to the door of the dressing room? You can squeeze through it to get to Colfax Avenue. If you miss this kick, use that exit to get out of here. Don't bother going to the dressing room!"

Now there's a vote of confidence.

The Test, Part I

I always had a lot of respect for Lou as a coach. He didn't always act rationally, but in the heat of the battle, real competitors never do. Lou and I were similar in a lot of ways, but it took Lou's annual psychological test for both of us to realize it.

The purpose of Lou's test was to determine your personality and what position you were best suited to play in the professional ranks. I was a little nervous about taking the test. Unlike the SATs, there was no way to prepare or study for this. I was afraid he'd think I wasn't smart enough or patient enough to make it in the pros. I tossed and turned the night before.

The next morning I went in and took the test in a corner of the room. The whole time I kept thinking, *I can't screw this up.* Of course, my competitive juices started flowing, and my mindset changed. "Screw him. I'll take this test honestly," I decided. "He'll find out what kind of wild man he drafted," and I answered all the questions candidly.

A few days later, I got a call from one of his assistants. "Coach Saban wants to see you." "About what?" I asked. "Come to his office, please." And the assistant hung up. My body froze. "Oh boy, oh boy," my mouth grew dry. "This is it."

I went and Lou promptly invited me in and shut the door. I sat there nervous for a few minutes, and he just stared at me from across the table like we were in a poker game with all the chips in.

"Floyd, I got your test results back and," he paused, "I've got to say I'm a little shocked." I could feel my palms begin to ooze sweat. "Son, it says here you're a homicidal maniac."

My eyes bugged out. I couldn't think of a response, so I tried to look puzzled. "Is that, um, bad?" I asked.

Suddenly his cold gaze disappeared, as if he had just solved the energy crisis. "No, son, that's great! You're like me. I'm a homicidal maniac, too!"

I thought he was joking. But he was serious. "No wonder we've been at each other's throats," he continued. "We're crazy. We're competitive S.O.B.s who'd rather be strapped to the front of a torpedo than lose a game."

According to his test results, my personality was more suited to play linebacker. "They're daredevils," Lou said. "They love contact and crave competition. I was a linebacker and fullback when I played."

So I asked him, "What's a running back personality supposed to be like?" He laughed. "They're either very smart or a little crazy. Guess what you are?"

As strange as the conversation was, I felt a real connection with Lou, maybe for the first time. He told me that quarterbacks' personalities were similar to generals. "That's why they don't have any friends," he cracked. "Offensive linemen are the smartest. They're very neat and meticulous. Defensive linemen are just like animals. Now you know why we don't even give them playbooks. We just tell them to attack."

From that point on, I didn't worry about hiding who I was. If guys didn't want to win, they were going to incur my "manic" wrath.

Saban Comparisons

I've been asked a few times which of the modern NFL coaches most resembles Lou. That's tough to answer without playing for these coaches. But I'd say the coach that mirrors Lou's expressions and demeanor would have to be Bill Cowher, formerly of the Steelers. Bill was animated with that well-chiseled jaw and demanding presence, but you could tell his players loved him. That was Lou. He screamed, cussed you out, and kicked over his share of tables, but we loved playing for him. Winning made him so happy he became another person. Lou would have this huge shit-eating grin on his face, and he'd grab you by the neck and hug you. His whole life was coaching. He loved every minute of it.

The Half-Loaf Game

The end for Lou Saban as the Broncos coach came weeks before he would eventually resign. The fans had grown impatient. This was his fifth season as coach, and we still hadn't won more than five games. It was the first game of the 1971 season, and we were playing at home against the

Miami Dolphins. Miami, an expansion team created in 1966, was already putting together a team for the ages. They would appear in the next three Super Bowls, including an undefeated season in 1972.

We were on the opposite sides of the spectrum. With the retirement of Steve Tensi, Lou went out and traded for two unknown quarterbacks. He got rid of all our quarterbacks from the previous year and traded for backups Don Horn from the Packers and Steve Ramsey from the Saints.

It was another season with a new quarterback in the revolving Broncos organization. The only bright spot on offense was our running game. I led the NFL in rushing the first half of the 1969 season before a knee injury sidelined me for six games. Then I led the AFC in rushing in '70. The line was gaining confidence, and we felt like we could run on anyone. Billy Thompson nicknamed me "Folks," as in "Old Folks" and the line got excited whenever Folks's number was called.

We played the Dolphins tough that day. They were focused on stopping the run, but the line still managed to help me pound out 70 tough yards. Our defense played an exceptional game and kept us close. With 2:30 left in the fourth quarter, we were up 10–3 and Miami was running out of opportunities. Then on their final possession Bob Griese connected with receiver Paul Warfield for 31 yards and a 10–10 tie.

With more than 2:00 left were confident we could still win. We just needed a field goal. But Lou got conservative. He gave me the ball on a simple dive play, and I picked up three yards. On second down Don tripped, slipped, and fell to the grown for a bizarre nine-yard loss. Now it was third-and-16. Lou called another run that netted four yards, and we punted the ball back to them with 1:20 left. Dolphins safety Jake Scott ran back the punt 18 yards before our kicker, Jim Turner, hit him in the chest and caused a fumble. Our great fullback Bobby Anderson pounced on it, and just like that we were back in business.

We were jumping up and down. Mile High Stadium was rocking. We had the Dolphins where we wanted them. The clock showed 1:14—more than enough to drive for a winning field goal. But Lou didn't see it that way. He ran me three times, trying to run out the clock and secure a tie. The only thing was, on my third carry, I burst down the right sideline for 11 yards and a first down. Now near midfield, Lou decided to take a few chances. There were 27 seconds left. Don tossed a screen to Bobby for 12 yards. We could have kicked a long field goal then, but Lou wanted to get us closer. Unfortunately, on the next pass attempt, we were called for holding, and we were pushed back farther. With 15 seconds left, we were out of field-goal range. But it was only second down. There was time for some creative hitch-and-pitch play or a Hail Mary pass. Instead, Lou was content with a tie and called a simple dive play up the middle.

I was hit immediately at the line by a throng of Dolphins and could hear the boos cascade throughout the stadium. The last seconds ticked off, and the game ended 10–10.

The locker room was like a morgue. We played well enough to win and were upset about being denied the chance. Lou explained that a tie would give us confidence for the rest of the season, while a loss could devastate us before the season got underway. I didn't understand why we were only talking about "a tie or losing." Why wasn't winning an option?

When he met with the press, Lou was asked why he went for the tie. "Half a loaf is better than none," he told them. Well, the media had a field day, and the Broncos fans were angrier than I had ever seen them. We had lost 51–0 before, but nothing affected them like this tie.

The next few games fans threw half-loaves of bread at us. I think some bakery must have special ordered them, because they were extremely compact like little footballs. Some fans could throw them pretty far. I thought we should give a few of them tryouts. Just like that, Lou's nickname became "Half-Loaf Saban."

Lou Resigns

After four-and-a-half seasons as the Broncos coach, the losses affected Lou more than anyone. He had made a lot of trades, hired and fired a lot of players, and shuffled the starting lineup each week, but nothing seemed to work. Lou wasn't a patient guy, and the team probably suffered because of it. We needed cohesion. We needed to play with the same quarterback and the same offensive unit.

The owners, Gerald and Allan Phipps, were committed to Lou. But despite the owner's support, Lou and his family were bombarded by the fans' wrath. His wife and kids were harassed. Garbage was dumped on their lawn, the house was continuously egged and toilet papered. Lou's son, Tommy, got in a lot of fights at school. They were booed at restaurants. There was nowhere to hide from the disappointment.

Lou's last game as Broncos coach came in Week 9 of the 1971 season after an uninspiring 24–10 loss at home to the Bengals, in which Cincinnati compiled nearly 500 yards of offense. Our record was 2–6–1 at that point. For the first time, Lou didn't say much after the game. He left the locker room quieter than usual. Something was up. Monday when we came in for film session, we heard that Lou had resigned and had already left town. We were told he went back to Buffalo. It bothered me that he never said good-bye. I guess he had too much pride.

A Milestone Among the Muck

After Lou resigned, Jerry Smith, our offensive line coach, became interim head coach for the remaining five games of the 1971 season.

We finished 4–9–1, our worst record in four seasons. Somehow, in spite of all the losing, despite bringing in two new quarterbacks who combined for just eight touchdowns and 27 interceptions, despite Lou quitting with five games go, and despite the fans' vocal frustration, the offense helped me achieve some Broncos firsts. I led the entire NFL in rushing with 1,133 yards and became the first 1,000-yard back in Broncos history.

Even with a million distractions and even more reasons to quit, the offense banded together and made a statement to the entire NFL that the Broncos could run on anybody.

Winning the rushing crown was memorable. But I would have traded it for a trip to the playoffs.

Farewell to the Ultimate Old-School Coach

You've seen it before. A man becomes defined as a coach to such a degree that it becomes his name, Coach. And when he finally gives up his life-long passion, he dies shortly after. That happened with legendary Coach Paul "Bear" Bryant who famously said, "If I quit coaching, I'd croak in a week," then he died a month later. Recently, the same demise happened with Penn State's Joe Paterno, who passed away a couple months after coaching his last game.

Lou Saban was cut from the same cloth. After leaving the NFL in the mid-1970s, with two AFL Championships in his belt, he went back to college and coached until his eighties. He was the head coach of the University of Miami from 1977–78, where he recruited quarterback Jim Kelly. Then he coached at Army. After that, he took a hiatus from football and became the president of the New York Yankees to help out a friend named George Steinbrenner.

After somehow getting in an argument with Steinbrenner (who knew!), he took the head coaching job at Central Florida. Finally, he retired in 1985 to live in North Carolina. That lasted about two weeks. He got off his La-Z-Boy, and coached high school football for the next four years. Then he coached a semi-pro team for a short time before becoming the head coach at Peru State College in Nebraska in 1991 at age 70.

Lou even dabbled in coaching for the Arena Football League with the expansion Milwaukee Mustangs in 1994. Then he started a football program at Alfred State College in New York. From there he became head coach at SUNY Canton for four years, coaching the team until he was 80. Finally, he thought he had enough and retired again to live in South Carolina. That lasted a few months until he took the head coaching job at Chowan University.

When he died in 2009 at the age of 87, Lou Saban had coached for more than five decades and influenced thousands of kids. The impact this man had on football is immeasurable. We miss Coach.

6

JOHN RALSTON AND
THE RAH-RAH BRONCOS

The College Coach

When John Ralston became the Broncos seventh head coach in 1972, the team was in total disarray. John was completely different than Lou Saban. He was a college coach who came to the Broncos after leading Stanford to back-to-back Rose Bowl wins. John also was a professional motivational speaker trained by Dale Carnegie and seemed to be a walking video transcript of "How to Win Friends & Influence People." One of the first things he said when he got here was, "We're going to win the Super Bowl." He said that every year. It got old after five years when we couldn't even make the playoffs.

Football is a Game

John always had unusual pregame speeches. In one of his first games as coach we were playing the Redskins in Washington, and he must have thought we were a bunch of college freshman. "Gentleman, football is a game," he said, writing the words on a chalkboard. "Make no mistake, anything that ends in b-a-l-l is a game. You can be in the game of your life, but this is a game." Well, in the middle of Ralston's speech, John Rowser, a defensive back, raised his hand and said, "Coach, what about eyeball and meatball?"

John tried to ignore Rowser and kept talking. But the room exploded, and the meeting was over.

Trying to Catch our Breaths

Despite Ralston's "inspiring" speeches we weren't playing well. We were listless during games, and it was easy to point the blame. John's training regimen was to work the hell out of us in practices. He was like Dick Vermeil used to be. He held training camp at Cal Poly Pomona, which stands for California State Polytechnic University in Pomona, California, about 30 miles east of Los Angeles. I don't know why we held camp there. It attracted all the smog from L.A. The air quality felt like you were sitting in a garage with the car running. Sometimes it was 110 degrees in August. You hear of players getting heat stroke, I'm surprised someone didn't die every day.

Guys were working their asses off with sweltering two-a-days. And this was back when training camp was close to two months long. It got so bad that after the first week some players decided they were going to revolt. "Folks, he's a college coach, and he doesn't know what the hell he's doing," they told me.

My reaction was that of incredulousness. "Hey, what do you guys know about going to the Super Bowl?" I said. "None of us have ever been. We finished the season with four wins last year, and our coach was so disgusted he left. Now we've got this new guy, and he's won some Rose Bowls. Maybe he can turn it around. If this is what it takes to get to the Promised Land, I'm willing to do that. If you're not then you have to decide where you want to go because I'm going to do whatever it takes to win."

To me John Ralston deserved a chance. As a player I was running out of time. I was 30 years old. I had won two rushing titles, played in four Pro Bowls so far, but I had nothing team-wise to show for it. I had only a few years left and wanted to go out a winner.

We continued to go through Ralston's practices. But it quickly started affecting everyone—including me. He had these conditioning drills at the end of practice called Jingle-Jangles that included

running sprints up and down the field, touching different yard mark-
ers in progression like they do in basketball, except the field is 100
yards. Each day there were guys laid out throwing up. Some couldn't
even get up to go to the locker rooms. We had to hustle, too, or the
cafeteria would close. So I started to agree with the guys. This wasn't
going to make us better; it was going to kill us.

The next day I went to talk to the team but couldn't find them. I
looked all over the school and even drove into town. I finally found them
later in a small meeting room near the field. I burst into the meeting room
and said, "What's going on here?" They said, "Oh, damn. It's Folks. He's
found us!"

They said, "We didn't want to involve you, Folks, but we've had enough.
Either he goes, or we're all leaving." I told them, "You're not going anywhere. I'll talk to John today. I'll straighten it out. Do nothing until you
hear from me." They looked at me like I was a warden. So I pushed open
the door and freed them, "Now get the hell out of here!"

I have to say my teammates were a little afraid of me. I was a very
intense player, and they didn't think I was always playing with a full deck.
Sometimes that worked to my advantage. Guys scrambled out of the
meeting room like it was a police raid.

The Secret Plan

After the meeting I went over and knocked on John's door. He must
have just gotten out of the shower because when he opened the door he
was shirtless with a towel wrapped around his shoulders. He said, "Rrrr,
c'mon on in. Can I, rrr, get you a Coke or something?" John always spoke
from his diaphragm. When he wasn't addressing the team his words were
low monosyllabic sounds.

I cut right to the chase. "Coach," I began, "I have some concerns.
The team is not happy with all the conditioning. You're killing them out
there." He said, "Rrr, we have to get in shape. Guys are lazy and not willing to work hard." I said, "That's just a couple guys. Most of the guys you
have here are professionals. They know how to prepare for the season.
They know what it takes. Even after practice, they'll stay and work on
blocking and techniques. We can't do that if we can barely stand."

He wasn't convinced. So I said, "Do me a favor. If you want to see the guys who aren't willing to work, do away with the sprints at the end of one practice and tell the team, 'Those of you who want to stay and work with your position coaches can stay, and those who don't can head into the locker room.' You'll see the true professionals."

Ralston agreed. After practice he told us we could either hit the showers or stay and work with our coaches. Just as I anticipated, most of the guys stayed—the ones I knew would make the team better. But a dozen or so guys raced from the practice field like it was the last day of school. I stood next to Ralston and said, "Those are the guys you should be concerned with. Leave us alone and let us practice." By the end of training camp, none of those guys made the team.

Operator, I Really Need to Make a Call!

As a married guy with a baby girl, I called home at least once a day during camp. This was years before cell phones, so we had to use this crappy pay phone in the dorm. Sometimes for no reason this shitty phone would just disconnect. One time after a particularly long practice, I decided to call home before hitting the showers. Every time I put in money, the phone hummed then disconnected. So I called the operator and was cut off in mid-sentence. I got angry. After a three-hour practice sweat was pouring off me and I was beyond irate. I called one more time. "Operator, I really need to call home—the number is 303-" and I got cut off again.

I went nuts. I grabbed the pay phone and yanked the goddamn thing off the wall and tossed it to the ground. Wires and cables were hanging out of the wall. I looked around thinking, "Holy shit!" and quickly scooped up the payphone and threw it in a garbage bin. The next day Ralston was steaming. He announced that the "culprit" who "took" the payphone would be fined $10,000. I didn't utter a word. I mean, that was half my salary.

The Rookie Show

It wasn't all sweating and complaining at Ralston's training camp. There was always the annual Rookie Show that first-year guys performed near the end of camp. Unbeknownst to me, this time they had prepared a special skit. It started normal enough. A few guys came out dancing and singing. Then they parted and behind them was Glen Bailey, a rookie I still see at alumni events. He was wearing my 44 jersey and started making a phone call. He mimicked my entire tirade and ripped out a cardboard payphone and heaved it in the garbage. The whole team roared. People laughed for five minutes. I started thinking, *Damn, he just rolled me under the bus.* I pretended to look puzzled, but I was a nervous wreck. *Oh, boy, this is bad. Real bad.* I could feel Ralston's eyes burning a hole in the back of my head.

Incredibly, Ralston never said a word to me. I'm guessing he thought I was his only ally.

The Two Sides of Ralston

There were two sides to John. One was the guy who made us practice to the point of exhaustion with recited nuggets of his Dale Carnegie shtick, "Every day and every way, just a little bit better." The other was Rah-Rah John. That John wanted to be your friend. He wanted you to like him, and he became the team's favorite, albeit, ugliest cheerleader. Whenever I was in the open field ready to score, John would be running along with me waving his clipboard. On one side it was great to finally have a coach who was giving you the thumbs up instead of the finger, but it took a while to get used to it.

You know how coaches sometimes gather the kickoff or kick return teams for last-minute instructions before they head onto the field? John actually huddled them up in the middle of the field. The players hated him coming onto the field, and it drove the coaches on other teams crazy. We were playing the Bears once and Abe Gibron, a large-and-in-charge coach of the Bears, was complaining to the ref, Fred Wyant. "Fred, what's that f—ing coach doing on the field?" Abe yelled. "This ain't college!"

The Test, Part II

Early that first year of his coaching tenure, John gathered the troops and said, "Gentlemen, I want to find out a little more about you beyond your height, weight, and 40 time. We're going to be handing out questionnaires for you to answer as honestly as you can."

I said, "Oh, boy, oh, boy. This sure as hell sounds like a test. Not good."
Well, damn if it didn't turn out to be the same personality test that Lou
had given. Afterward, I got a call that Ralston wanted to see me. *He's
going to give me high marks for candor, just like Lou did,* I thought. *He'll be
glad he has such an intense dedicated captain leading his team!*

I got to his office and John opened the door looking whiter than a piece
of sheet rock. "Rrr, c'mon in Floyd, have a seat," he stammered. I began to
shut the door behind me when he stopped me. "Oh, p-please. K-keep the
door open," he hesitated. "Fresh air. I like to have fresh air." This from the
guy who had us practicing at Cal Poly.

"I, uh, got your test back," he said slowly, "and, well, it says here you're
a Homicidal Maniac."

"Yup," I nodded, sipping my Coke, "that sounds about right."

"Well, what does that mean?"

"I guess it means if someone fucks with me I have no problem com-
mitting some heinous crime and still be able to enjoy a nice dinner with
friends over a bottle of Chianti."

"Well, rrr, that's not normal. I mean, you're our captain. We can't have
a leader with, rrr, homicidal tendencies."

I laughed. "Relax, coach. It's just my persona on the football field.
Welcome to the National Football League."

For the next few years Ralston tiptoed around me, making sure not to
upset me. Whenever we met in his office, he'd quickly sit behind his desk
so there was some sort of obstruction in the way. Just in case.

Going Postal

Once in a while you get a guy on your team who is truly scary. Dwight
Harrison was such a guy. A receiver at 6'1", 187 pounds he wasn't at all
imposing. Lou drafted Dwight in 1971 in the second round, between our
first pick, tackle Marv Montgomery, and our third, Lyle Alzado. Lou liked
Dwight for one thing—his speed.

Against the Packers his rookie year, Dwight and I assumed some added
responsibility during the game. Quarterback Don Horn threw an incredible six interceptions. As two of the faster players on the team, we had to
run down most of the guys. After about the fifth pick, Dwight refused to

go back on the field. "I'm not playing receiver anymore today if he keeps throwing interceptions. I'm tired of making all these tackles." I said, "You can't quit on the team. You're going back in!" We got into a bit of a shoving match on the sideline until I finally convinced him to take the field.

A year later, Dwight got into a fight with Lyle Alzado right before practice. Lyle had teased Dwight about dropping passes, and Dwight told Lyle to shut up and worry about sacking the quarterback more. Well, Lyle whipped him pretty good. Dwight started telling everyone he was going to kill that "motherf—r" and wanted to borrow someone's car to get his gun. Of course, no one obliged him, and he skipped practice to hitchhike 20 miles home in his flip-flops.

When Dwight got back we were in the film room, and he kicked the door open and stood there wearing shorts, sunglasses, a Derby hat, and a 357 Magnum. He looked like a character out of *Pulp Fiction*. "Where's that motherf—r Alzado?! I'm going to kill him." Everyone hit the floor, except me. Like a fool I said, "Dwight, he's not here, and you're not going to kill anyone today." He pointed the gun at me and said, "Get out of my way, Floyd. I don't like you anyway because of the Packers game." I couldn't believe it. That was more than a year ago! Now I've never had a gun pointed at me before, but I can tell you it's quite an effective laxative.

Finally, John Ralston was able to coax Dwight into his office. He must have used all his Dale Carnegie powers of persuasion to get him to put his gun away. Dwight was in tears the whole time. He finally handed over his gun and was immediately traded to Buffalo to be reunited with Lou. In exchange, we got Haven Moses. Lou converted Dwight to defensive back and, incredibly, he played another nine seasons with a couple other teams.

As horrifying as it was, I'd have to say it was almost worth having a gun pointed at me for Haven Moses.

Better GM than Coach

Say what you want about John's coaching methods. The guy was a great personnel man. We never seemed to win the big games under his leadership, but boy, did he bring in some great talent.

During his tenure, John traded for Charley Johnson, Bobby Maples, Haven Moses, Joe Dawkins, Jon Keyworth, and Ray May. And he drafted

Riley Odoms, Otis Armstrong, Calvin Jones, Barney Chavous, Paul Howard, Tom Jackson, Randy Gradishar, Claudie Minor, Louis Wright, Rick Upchurch, Rubin Carter, and Steve Foley. Five of them became Ring of Famers, and a few more deserve to be. Many of them were guys Red Miller took to the Super Bowl in 1977.

For some reason John has been vilified since his dismissal in 1976. The fact is he became the first coach to turn the Broncos into a winner. His record of 34–33–3 is dramatically better than Lou's 20–42–3 record. And few people know this, but John's college coaching record of 97–81–4 and two back-to-back Rose Bowl victories got him inducted into the College Football Hall of Fame in 1992.

I got a chance to speak with John Ralston in 2011 on Martin Luther King's birthday. He's 85 now and the only head coach of mine who is still with us. He lost his wife not too long ago and doesn't drive anymore. Things are really challenging for him now. But John's always had a positive outlook on life, and I'm sure he will make the best of his situation. I learned a lot from John about positive thinking. When I started improving as a public speaker, I used to follow him all over the country at speaking events. John told me he always used to recommend me. He's a different guy, and I think he echoed those sentiments about me when he told me I was an "unusual person." I thought his word choice was interesting. He didn't say "unique" but unusual. Still, he told me how proud he was that I was enshrined in Canton. Then he said, "Floyd, it's a privilege to know you. I'm glad you were the leader on our team. You were a great leader and great player. I love you." I told him I loved him, too. I also made sure he knew I felt he never got the credit he deserved as the Broncos coach.

Think about it, Ralston put together a team that went to the Super Bowl.

The Dirty Dozen

After I retired in 1975, there was no one to act as a buffer between the team and Coach Ralston. Things changed quickly. Charley Johnson retired, meaning John turned to backup Steve Ramsey to lead the team. The players wanted John to go out and get an established quarterback. Steve became the starter and did an admirable job leading Denver to a

9–5 record, its best ever. But in the biggest game of the season, a show-down with the Patriots at Foxboro in which a win would almost assure the Broncos of their first playoff berth, the team got whipped 38–14, and both Ralston and Ramsey got most of the blame.

It was supposed to be this close, tough-as-nails contest. By halftime we were down 31–0. Ramsey completed only about a third of his passes and had three interceptions. As a result the team decided the coach needed to go at the end of the 1976 season. Lyle Alzado became the "inspirational" leader. They got more than 75 percent of the team to sign a petition, a document they casually left for the press to find.

Who was the Dirty Dozen? They were the team's biggest stars: Lyle, Billy Thompson, Tommy Jackson, Mike Current, Paul Smith, Haven Moses, Rick Upchurch, Billy Van Heusen, Tommy Lyons, Louis Wright, Otis Armstrong, and Riley Odoms.

The bottom line about Ralston, they said, was that he simply was not a good coach and couldn't win the big games. It became clear against New England and earlier versus Houston when offensive coordinator Max Coley was sick. John had to call the plays for the first time, and it was evident he didn't know what he was doing. He even tried to get Charley Johnson, who was retired and sitting in the stands, to help. "Our offense," Billy Thompson said famously, "was like a ballet—one-, two-, three-, kick!"

After five seasons the Broncos had become one of the better teams in the AFC, but the fans and the teams desperately wanted more. John's pos-itive spin had run out of yarn.

Stan the Man

We had one of the best defensive lines in the league when Lou was coach, and everyone knew why—Stan Jones, our defensive line coach. Stan was a Pro Bowl guard for the Chicago Bears for many years in the 1950s and '60s, playing the 1962 season both ways. In 1963, he became a fixture at defensive tackle for the next four years. He was elected to the Pro Football Hall of Fame in 1991 after a stellar career that also included one season with the Redskins.

Stan was a natural leader who was one of the first NFL players to lift weights on a consistent basis. He was known as the strongest player in the league during his career. So when he became a coach he made sure his guys threw the weights around. He didn't just have strong players on the d-line—Rich Jackson, Lyle Alzado, Paul Smith, Rex Mirich, Dave Costa, Pete Duranko, and Jerry Inman were specimens.

Stan had these guys living in the weight room. Somehow he made it fun. His linemen looked like they were on vacation. They adhered to a different code than the rest of us. They went to meetings with their shirt-tails hanging out. They didn't shave. Heck, they didn't even have play-books. In practice Stan would tell them to "Just hit the guy in front of you!" Lou didn't yell at them much because they were Stan's boys. Stan would just sit there, puffing on a cigar with his rottweiler that hated peo-ple, and implore his guys to lift everything.

We all wanted to be defensive linemen and play for Stan. Rex Mirich got me into lifting with the linemen. I felt connected with their battle-in-the-trenches mentality. After Lou resigned and Stan left to coach with him in Buffalo, I continued working out with linemen.

I got to see Stan every year at the Broncos Alumni Weekend gala. He was such a tremendous person. Tom Mackie interviewed Stan in 2009 about whether I deserved to be in the Hall of Fame. I heard Stan talked glowingly about me for 40 minutes. Here's a little bit of what he said:

"I've seen some great players during my 40 years in the NFL. I played with Gale Sayers, and I would put Floyd Little in the same class with Sayers. Floyd was one of the greatest players I've ever been associated with—and let me tell you, I saw a ton in 40 years—I played 13 years and coached for 27. Floyd was an all-time best.

"The thing that is so amazing about Floyd Little's career is it [the Broncos] wasn't a good football team. We didn't have much talent, so he didn't have much to work with. When he ran, he was pretty much on his own. We didn't have the offensive personnel that many teams have that have great running backs. So the fact that he was able to be so productive was unbelievable. He was just an amazing player."

I got a chance to thank Stan at the Broncos Alumni Event shortly after I was nominated. He had suffered a stroke and also had skin cancer. I'm glad he made it to see me finally get elected to the Hall of Fame. He died in May 2010 at age 78.

Sam Rutigliano

I loved Hunter Enis. He was a former Broncos quarterback and my backfield coach when Lou was here. But the one coach I always wanted to play for was Sam Rutigliano. He was the receivers coach and a real student of the game. He constantly talked about technique, and as a smaller guy I understood the importance of using it to your advantage. Sam used to say that football was "combat with a little finesse thrown in." I always liked that.

After retiring I became a TV analyst for NBC Sports. I was in Seattle doing a Browns game when Art Modell stopped by the booth and asked me what I thought about Sam as a possible head coach. I told him, "Let's put it this way. I'm retired. I have no desire to play. But if Sam were my coach, not only would I come back, I'd play for free." A couple nights later, I got a call at 2:00 AM, and I automatically figured someone had died. It was Sam, bawling. "I was just offered the Browns coaching position," he said. He thanked me for my endorsement and offered me any coaching job on the team. I graciously declined. Looking back, if I had taken the job, I'd probably be a head coach now.

Mad Max

Max Coley came by way of the Steelers and joined John Ralston's coaching staff in 1972. As the offensive coordinator and backfield coach, he brought with him Pittsburgh's trap-blocking schemes. We ran traps, fake traps, draws, and more screens than ever. The funny thing is we seemed to have the greatest success against the Steelers.

Pittsburgh's defensive ends hated it the most. Dwight White and L.C. Greenwood never knew where a block was coming. They might get hit by a guard, tight end, or fullback. Linebackers Jack Ham and Andy Russell despised playing us, too. Andy and I became great friends. I played in his golf tournament for Children's Hospital for more than two decades. Every year he'd say the same thing: "Boy, I hated playing you guys." I can see why. Despite having a far worse record, during the five times we played the Steelers in my career, we were 3–1–1 against them. Two of those wins were at Pittsburgh.

7

CAST OF CHARACTERS

Marlin the Magician

Of the dozens of quarterbacks who played for the Broncos during my nine-year career, none made a more lasting impact on professional football than Marlin Briscoe. On September 29, 1968, we were playing the Boston Patriots when Marlin came into the game in the fourth quarter to play quarterback. That simple substitution changed history, making Marlin the first African American to play quarterback in an AFL game.

Marlin was undersized for a quarterback. Yet his elusive, improvisational style and rocket arm earned him the nickname "Marlin the Magician." In his rookie season with the Broncos, he threw for 1,589 yards and a rookie team-record 14 touchdown passes. But if anyone knew Marlin was talented, it was Marlin. Following his rookie season, Marlin met with Lou Saban, who asked him to switch to receiver. Marlin refused. He wanted to stay at quarterback. He also wanted to become the highest-paid player on the team.

At the time, I was the Broncos' highest-paid player, making an extraordinary $26,000 a year. Lou tried to reason with Marlin, telling him, "You can't make more than Floyd. He's our No. 1 pick and he does everything: rushing, receiving, and returning punts and kickoffs."

Marlin's response? "Well, Floyd's a fool to do all that. I'm not going to play for less than him—pay me or trade me."

Saban did one better. He cut Marlin, who wound up in Buffalo. He never played quarterback again. The Bills converted him to receiver, just like Lou wanted to do, and Marlin made the Pro Bowl one year. Later he earned two Super Bowl rings with the Dolphins.

I'm convinced Marlin would have enjoyed a successful career at quarterback had he been given the opportunity to play more than that one season behind center.

Golf Anyone?

Billy Thompson is one of the all-time great Broncos. "BT" was the first Bronco to play 13 seasons, and he only missed three games. Now they've got guys who get hurt in practice. Frankly, I think he was the most versatile defensive back who ever played. A Pro Bowler, Billy excelled at both corner and safety and as a rookie in 1969 became the only player in pro football history to lead the league in both kickoff and punt returns. Oh yeah, he also had 40 interceptions. Before Billy joined the Broncos, our secondary was pretty suspect. Lou went out and drafted six defensive backs in '69—Billy was the only one who stuck. Later we traded for Leroy Mitchell, who added more stability. Billy's a Ring of Fame member and now the Broncos' director of alumni relations.

He's also a heck of a golfer who consistently shoots in the low 70s. But when he first joined the Broncos, Billy had never picked up a club. I had learned to play golf at Syracuse. So one day I took Billy and Nemiah Wilson to City Park to show them how to play. That first time we must have lost 12 dozen balls. The squirrels were very afraid. On one shot Billy hit the ball into some trees and it somehow bounced out onto the fairway. "You must have used your Tree-wood," I cracked.

Billy continued to get better. One rainy Christmas we were out playing for $1 a hole. The day started with drizzle and by the time we were on the back nine there was a downpour of cats and dogs all over the place. Of course, since there was *big* money involved, we kept playing. We were having a good time until Billy decided to use a wedge on this flooded green to putt his ball. I told him, "You're not allowed to use a wedge.

You'll leave a divot on the ground." He said, "I can putt with any club I want. I'm using my wedge." Well, we stood soaking wet in this deluge, two hard-headed idiots arguing for 20 minutes on that one hole. Nemiah thought we were nuts and left. I guess that's what happens when ultra-competitive Broncos face off against one another.

I consider Billy my best friend. We talk at least once a week if not more. I think it's a shame that he's not even in the conversation when it comes to Broncos deserving of the Hall of Fame. I implore Jeff Legwold, the Broncos Hall of Fame representative, to look at some of the stats that Tom Mackie has put together about Billy and to do some digging of his own. Not taking anything away from other safeties Denver has had over the years—and believe me, we've had some amazing ones—but none of them stack up to Billy. The guy was a fierce hitter and could cover like a blanket. If you look at safeties in Canton, either they were good cover guys or they were great hitters. Billy could do both. He's the most versatile and complete safety of our era.

We Don't Need No Stinkin' Rods

On days off when we weren't arguing on the golf course, Billy and I would head up to the mountains near a lake where I had a place with a boat and a few snowmobiles. One time after a particularly brutal game, we decided to go up and do some fishing. We must have been out there for hours without a single bite. Good thing we had plenty of beer.

After a few brews we got creative and thought of a better way to catch fish. We tossed our fishing rods aside and dumped a bottle of salmon eggs in the water. Basically, they were caviar for fish. In just a few minutes there were bass all around the boat. Without letting go of our precious beer, we began grabbing at the fish with our free hands. I guess it didn't occur to us to put down the beers. We spent the next hour flailing desperately at these fish, spilling beer and splashing water everywhere. Imagine two 200-pound guys jumping from side to side on a little motorboat, swaying back and forth on a lake. By the end of the day we were so tired and wet from not catching a single thing, we decided to scare the shit out of the fish by doing cannon balls off the side of the boat. Yup, we were the picture of maturity.

Laboratory Rats

I can't recall a time when there wasn't a Broncos receiver wearing No. 80. A few years ago, of course, it belonged to Rod Smith, a phenomenal player who is now in the Ring of Fame. Before him Mark Jackson wore it, one of the Three Amigos. And before Mark, it was Rick Upchurch, one of the most exciting Broncos ever. But the guy who wore No. 80 before Rick was a pretty good receiver in his own right—Jerry Simmons. At 6'1", 210 pounds, Jerry was a gifted, fluid receiver who played for the Broncos from 1970–74. He was our only receiving threat those first couple of years when we were playing musical quarterbacks. When Charley came on board in '72, we traded for Haven Moses from Buffalo, and Jerry and Haven gave us bookend receivers who could catch any pass, short or deep.

Jerry was not only a jokester, he had a Dr. Evil laboratory approach to it. He loved to instigate things as if his teammates were amusing science experiments. He liked to get two guys mad at each other, then sit back and watch what he had created like he was at a movie premiere. All he needed was a bag of popcorn.

He'd say things like, "Hey, Floyd. Haven says he can beat you in the 40 wearing loafers." And then turn around to Haven and say, "Floyd thinks you're one of the slowest receivers in the league. Alzado is faster." Next thing you know, Haven and I would be challenging each other to a race—in the locker room.

Jerry continues to be one of my best friends. He was an executive with Hyatt for many years before retiring recently. When I purchased a condominium in Chicago a few years ago, Jerry helped me find it. He was there in Canton when I was inducted, and he's always been there for me.

The Best Quarterback

Of all the quarterbacks I played with, Charley Johnson was the best. He's a real-life genius with a Ph.D. in Chemical Engineering. Today he's the head of the Chemical Engineering Department at New Mexico State, his alma mater.

On the field, Charley was a true field general who never got the national recognition he deserved. Broncos fans remember his achievements, and the organization certainly honored his contributions by electing him to the Ring of Fame in 1986. But when great quarterbacks of his era are mentioned by the media, they never utter Charley's name. I remember *Sports Illustrated*'s Peter King put out a book years back, ranking the 50 greatest quarterbacks of all time. He didn't even mention Charley. But what was more unbelievable was that he ranked one-year wonder Greg Cook as the 38th greatest quarterback of all time. I played against Greg once. He was a good rookie, but to say he was one of the greatest of all time is ludicrous. To me, that's a slap in the face of guys like Charley. Greg Cook threw just 15 career touchdowns. Charley played 15 years and ranked 13th all-time in passing yards and 15th in touchdowns when he retired in 1975.

He was one of the best quarterbacks in the league for two decades, and in my mind he was the toughest. He had horrible knees that he had painfully drained before each game. He once threw for 445 yards and six touchdowns in another game, led the NFL in passing yards in 1964, and appeared on the cover of *Sports Illustrated* twice while with the Cardinals. He played nine years with the Cardinals and two with the Oilers before coming to Denver in '72. When John Ralston took over, he didn't hesitate to send a third-round pick to Houston for Charley's services.

Charley brought instant credibility to the Broncos quarterback position. In my nine seasons we brought in 35 quarterbacks. He was a true Texan, and he didn't mince words, either. After all, he honed his craft in the mid-1960s when the Cardinals hired his idol, Bobby Layne, to tutor him.

Charley didn't simply execute plays coaches called like most of our quarterbacks did. A play would come in from the sideline and Charley would grimace. He'd say, "Forget that, here's what we're going to do," and he'd change the play right in the huddle. He'd draw it up from scratch saying, "Haven, instead of running a down and out, I want you to run a post and clear out the left side. Now, Folks, you're going to run a flare route to that side. The Will backer will be coming hard, so make sure you chip him before you go out or he'll be catching your pass." Then he'd look me in the eyes. "Folks, it's on you. Better catch that damn pass, or the coach is going to chew my ass for changing the play." Charley took control of a huddle, and we all believed in him.

But one time I dropped an easy pass over the middle with no defender in sight. Charley didn't even look at me. He huddled every one up and said, "Same play to the same asshole on two."

Ouch.

Bed-Check

Besides trading for Charley Johnson, Ralston also grabbed Charley's Houston sidekick, center Bobby "Mapes" Maples. The whole makeup of the team changed when they joined Denver. They were two Texans and two incredible leaders who gave our offense some swagger. The team quickly began to ascend to the next level when they signed. As intense and tough as they were on the field, both Mapes and Charley were laid-back jokers off it. The two roomed together and were inseparable. If Charley was playing a joke on someone, you can bet Mapes was his accomplice.

During training camp one year, Mapes and Charley decided to play up their inseparable reputation. One night during bed-check, a coach gave the customary one knock and opened their door and found Mapes under Charley's covers in bed. The coach stood there with his jaw to the floor as Bobby stuck his head out of bed and smiled, "Charley, you should have told me someone was coming in!"

After that the coach just bypassed their room.

The Hack and the Critters

Dale Hackbart and Ken Criter were two great special teams players. Dale played only one season for us but is credited for making one of the biggest all-time hits—although it cost him dearly. We were playing the Bengals and Boobie Clark, their 6'2", 230 pound monster fullback, was returning a kick. Dale really leveled Boobie, and both crumpled to the ground. While Boobie stayed on the ground, "The Hack" got up and walked to the sideline.

"I think I'm hurt," he said. "Where?" replied the trainer. "In my neck." "What does it feel like?" "It feels like something snapped." He was quickly taken in for X-rays. Sure enough, the Hack had broken his neck.

Ken Criter, on the other hand, was a mainstay special teams ace who played for us from 1969–74. He was always the first one down the field, making incredible hits and touchdown-saving tackles. In honor of his dedication, our special teams were nicknamed, "Criter's Critters."

"You, you," I mean "Me, me, not you!"

There are a number of Broncos I believe are worthy of the team's Ring of Fame. One player I think is grossly overdue is Rick Upchurch. He's the only Bronco to make not one but *two* All-Decade teams, and he continues to be snubbed for the Ring of Fame. That is simply horrible.

I only got to play with Rick one season, but I was blown away by his talent. He quickly became one of the most dangerous playmakers in the league. During his nine-year career, he returned eight punts for touchdowns—an NFL record—and was voted to four Pro Bowls.

Rick showed the NFL that he was something special in his very first game in the 1975 season opener. We were playing the Chiefs at home, and Rick didn't even have his decals placed on his helmet yet. He and I were returning kicks that game. Yup, at 33, I was still back there, "being a fool" as Marlin Briscoe put it.

While awaiting the first kickoff, I told Rick my scientific approach to returning kicks. "Rick, if the ball is coming toward you, I'll say, 'You, you' meaning you return it. If it looks like it's coming to me, I'll say, 'Me, me' and I'll take it.'"

This seemed simple enough. Well, the first kickoff, the ball sailed clearly toward Rick, so I yelled, "You, you." He caught the ball and returned it 25 yards. Then, on the second kickoff, I noticed the ball was kicked pretty far. I said, "You, you. No, no. Down it in the end zone." Rick got confused and ran back five yards deep into the end zone, caught the ball, and returned it 25 yards." Being the intense veteran I was, I scolded him, "Never return a kick that deep. Just down it!" He looked at me with those glassy rookie eyes and apologized.

Late in the game, KC kicked off and the ball was heading toward Rick. I screamed, "You, you." Then it started sailing deeper. "No, no." Then, the wind shifted and the ball came straight back over my head. "Oh, shit, oh, shit!" I cried. Against my own rules, I fielded the ball deep in the end zone and, instead of downing it, I returned it 25 yards. Rick just glared at me. I had a shit-eating grin as I jogged off the field.

Rick had an incredible NFL debut, piling up 284 combined yards, including a record 90-yard touchdown catch from Charley Johnson. We won in a 37–33 thriller, but by the end of the day I could tell he didn't want to return kicks with me anymore. I had totally confused the kid.

My Paranoid Roomie

Fran Lynch was not only my dependable backup for all nine seasons; he was my roommate at summer camp and road games. He was a tough kid from Connecticut, like me, who was drafted the same year in the fifth round.

Fran was considered a long shot, but he became the epitome of a team player. He was hardworking, disciplined, unselfish, and a true professional. To give you an idea of his dedication and resiliency, he became the first player to suit up for the Broncos for 10 years.

Fran, however, did have one fear—getting cut. Each camp he would torture himself, thinking that this was the year. It went on for 10 seasons. Fran would hole up in his room and become a nervous wreck near the end of each camp. Every time the phone rang, he was afraid to answer it.

One time, Charley Johnson and I decided to play a joke on Fran. The phone rang 7:00 AM one morning—Turk time. I answered the phone. "Hello? Oh, hi Coach…. Fran, yes, he's here. What? You want him to come to your office and bring his playbook? Okay, I'll tell him." Meanwhile, Charley was on the other end laughing hysterically. I got off the phone and turned to Fran, who was 10 shades whiter than a loaf of Wonder Bread. "Coach wants to see you." "Shit, this is it!" he shook. "Don't worry, Fran. I'll go with you. Just don't forget your playbook." As Fran slowly walked down the steps to the lobby, he looked up and saw Charley and Bobby Maples, those Texas side splitters, clutching their stomachs and stomping the ground with their feet. Fran's ghost-white body turned Tabasco. "You bastards!" he screamed, and he threw his playbook at them. "C'mon Fran," Bobby crooned, "We're late for breakfast."

Naked Dreams

The one thing I noticed early on about Fran was his utter lack of self-consciousness about his body. He used to walk around naked all the time in the room. "Floyd, you're not bothered by this, right?" he'd presume. I'd laugh awkwardly because I didn't know how to respond.

He'd sleep naked, too. The night before games he would spread out buck naked on his bed and ask me if it was okay to drink a couple beers—like I was his coach. It was almost like a ritual. He'd say, "Do you think it's okay if I have a couple beers?" I'd say, "Fran, let me ask you, did you play last week?" "No," he'd answer. "Did you play the week before?" "No." "So it really doesn't matter how much you drink." He'd laugh, crack a few beers, and pass out naked. Not a good sight. Around that time, Dave Kopay, a former 49ers running back, had shocked the NFL by admitting he was gay and announcing there were gay players on every NFL team. So one time I decided to have a little fun at Fran's expense.

The night before a game I sat there and waited for him to drink his beer and get to the brink of passing out. Waited for his eyes to start to close. Then I quietly took off my pants and underwear and snuck around the other side of his bed and nudged my foot on his back.

Fran awoke startled and his eyes bugged out. "W-what are you doing?!?" "Huh?" I said. "Oh, I thought you were asleep." "What the hell!" he blurted. "Are you serious?" I just got up, nonchalantly put on my clothes and climbed back into my bed. For the first time Fran hurriedly put on his underwear, pants, shirt, and pulled up his covers to his chin. He stayed up the whole night staring at me. I had to think of drowning kittens to keep from laughing. But it worked. He never walked around naked again. For the next several years he'd sidle up to me once in awhile and whisper, "Were you serious?"

Sometimes you have to go to extreme measures to get your point across.

Wild Lyle

When Lyle Alzado joined the Broncos as a fourth-round pick from tiny Yankton College (South Dakota) in 1971, I was given the challenging job of being one of his mentors. He was a tough, hyper kid from Long Island. I was assigned as his traveling partner. It was my job to sit with him on planes and bus rides and act as a calming influence. For some reason, he listened to me.

While Rich Jackson and Paul Smith took him under their wings to make him a better player, I tried to make him a better professional. Lyle was a tremendous guy to know. He had a huge heart and a natural affinity for children. He became a fixture in Denver and started joining me for charity events.

Away from the public, Lyle was moody and easily irritated. Sometimes he was out of control with his emotions, which I could relate to since I had a short fuse. Some guys were afraid of Lyle, and it wasn't uncommon to see him sitting by himself struggling with his own thoughts. He so much wanted to be a great player that he used to always ask me, "What do I need to do to be a Pro Bowler?" I told him that he needed to establish the mindset that every play is your last play. "Imagine you have an imaginary switch under your arm," I'd tell him, "low, medium, and high. You turn it on high and pretend someone breaks it off so your only speed is all out."

Lyle began to heed my advice while learning techniques from Rich and Paul. Soon he was turning heads. Unfortunately, early on he developed some narcissistic tendencies. He loved hearing his name on the public address announcement and would sometimes jump offside on purpose. Just so he could hear his name. A few times he'd jump offside on third-and-5 and piss off his defensive mates. "C'mon Lyle, that's another four downs!" they'd yell. Guys would come up to me and say, "Folks, you gotta get him to stop that." I'd pull Lyle aside and tell him, "Lyle, a player's reputation is what defines him. You don't want to be known as a sloppy player. You want to be known as someone who never takes off a play. That's a true professional."

Lyle stopped purposely jumping offside and became extremely dedicated. After I retired in 1975, Lyle became a Pro Bowl end and the leader of the Orange Crush defense that propelled Denver to its first Super Bowl in '77. After a contract dispute he was traded to the Cleveland Browns in '79 and four years later won a Super Bowl with the Los Angeles Raiders. He finally became the national celebrity he always wanted to be and tragically changed a lot of people's perceptions about professional football.

Muhammad Comes to the Mountains

When you asked Lyle who his hero was, he never hesitated. "Muhammad Ali," he'd say. As a youngster Lyle was a Golden Gloves boxing champion.

He was a born street fighter, and I think he looked at Ali as the type of fighter he wanted to be—graceful, tough, and a popular showman.

On July 14, 1979, Lyle's lifelong dream came true and he fought Ali at Mile High Stadium for charity. The Broncos had been to the Super Bowl the year before, and Ali had retired for the time being. Lyle had asked me to be one of his seconds for the fight. The second is the person who assists the trainer, rinses the mouthpiece, gives water, and so on. His other second was the beautiful actress Susan St. James, who later married Dick Ebersol, the president of NBC Sports, the network hosting the event.

Lyle trained for weeks. "It's four rounds," he kept telling me. "I've got to last four rounds. I can't let him knock me out." Lyle was confident until a few hours before the fight when one of the promoters came in and announced the fight had been switched from a four-rounder to a six-round bout. Lyle freaked. "Are they shitting me?" he exploded. "I trained for four rounds, I can't go six." Then he was told to start drinking a lot of liquids because it was 90 degrees outside. "I won't last. I'll die out there," he shook. We spent the next few hours trying to calm Lyle. But, boy, he was nervous.

Lyle came out, saw a crowd of 40,000 people cheering him, and his whole demeanor changed. He not only went all six rounds against the greatest fighter in the world, he dished out some punishment, too. He fought Ali, the temperature, and the altitude with tremendous courage. I have to say I was so proud of Lyle that day. I probably wasn't the best second, either. I was in awe of being so close to Ali that sometimes I forgot to bring Lyle water. He kept saying, "Where's the water, Floyd? Where's the damn water?"

The End

I've been asked a lot about Lyle's use of steroids. As someone who never took pain killers, I'm probably not the best person to ask. I never saw any evidence when I played with him. Sure he was moody. But Lyle was that way the first time I met him. He never changed. Physically, though, I saw quite a change after he joined the Raiders. He had always been incredibly sweet and nice to my daughters. We were neighbors, and my kids would go over to Lyle's house for Halloween. He had this big dog, a husky named Bronco that my daughters loved.

One time during the 1980s, the Raiders were playing the Broncos in Los Angeles, and I took my daughters to the game. "Can we see Lyle?" my girls pleaded. So we went down on the field, and Lyle came over and picked them up just like when they were little. I looked at Lyle, and he seemed like a different guy. He was a lot bigger than when I played with him. He was at least 30 pounds heavier and cut like a washboard.

He finally won a Super Bowl with the Raiders. When he got the brain tumor and blamed it on steroids, I think he was embarrassed. He told people he didn't want me to see him deteriorating. He said that Howie Long and I were the two friends he respected the most. I really miss Lyle. Looking back I guess there were probably more guys on steroids than I thought. That's not why he admitted using steroids though. Even in the end, Lyle cared most about kids who looked up to him. He wanted them to know that they shouldn't do as he had done.

Pistol Pete

One of the true pros I played with was Pete Duranko. He was a mainstay on our formidable defensive line for eight seasons and was loved by everyone. He also had a great sense of humor that could get even the toughest audience—Lou Saban—to lighten up.

One time during a meeting, Lou was ranting about how he wanted to really get after a team. It had been a rather intense week, and Pete decided it was time for some levity. He put a laughing box in back of the room, and every time Lou spoke, the gizmo started this infectious giggle. Lou kept saying, "Who's laughing? Why, I'm going to fire your ass!" He quickly realized that no one was laughing; it was a machine. After a couple minutes even Lou couldn't contain himself.

There are only a few guys who could get Lou to laugh at himself. Pete was one of them. Tragically, Pete was afflicted with Lou Gehrig's Disease in 2000 and fought bravely for many years. Even though he was suffering badly himself, he made it a point to visit people who were suffering from the same disease to give them encouragement. It takes a tremendously humble and caring person to do that. But that was Pete. He passed away in July 2011 at the age of 67. It was an honor to play with him.

Unsung Heroes

Of all the Broncos from my era, the offensive linemen never got the credit they deserved. Think about it. During my career, 1967–75, only three of them, guard George Goeddeke, tackle Mike Current, and center Larry Kaminski, played in an AFL All-Star Game during the 1960s. When the leagues merged in 1970, none were ever voted to the Pro Bowl. That's incredible when you consider that I led the AFC in rushing two years straight, won the NFL rushing crown in '71, led the NFL in rushing touchdowns in '73, and during a six-year period from 1968–73 had more yards rushing and more yards from scrimmage than anyone. I mean, someone was blocking for me, right?

Without the line's incredible work ethic and dedication, I wouldn't have won a rushing crown, played in two AFL All-Star Games and three Pro Bowls, and retired as the NFL's seventh all-time rusher. Sure it took a few seasons to get some experience and stability on the line. But when they finally gelled in my fourth season, in my mind, they were among the finest in the league.

When Charley was quarterback, he would call plays only after getting input from the line. A play would come in for me to run through, for example, the six hole and Charley would say, "Let's forget about the six. Where can we pick up three yards?" "Run it behind me," Larron Jackson would yell. "No, I own my guy," Mike Current would chime in. "Run behind me." Charley would listen and call the play based on their feedback. When I ran the ball, my line would get all excited. "Folks is running the ball," they'd smile. "Let's do it for Folks!"

Maples

Center Bobby Maples may have been our quickest lineman. He was like center Tom Nalen. He wasn't big, but he was a great technician, an aggressive player who always had a hat on someone. He was a leader and played all out 'til the whistle blew. If you look at any photos of me running, you'll probably see Bobby on the ground after laying some wood.

He was a tough guy who even played linebacker early on in his career with the Houston Oilers. But center is where he excelled. In my last game at Mile High, I went off tackle and turned the corner downfield. Bobby got off his first block and ran past me to make another one. On the way back to the huddle, he said, "Floyd, when I can make a block and pass you to hit someone else, it's time for you to retire." I looked at him and smiled, "You dirty bastard!"

Bobby died of a heart attack in 1991 at the young age of 48. We talk about him a lot whenever we get together during Alumni Weekend. Now 20 years later, he is still missed dearly. I think a great epitaph would have been, "He always had a hat on someone."

Big Buddha

Larron "Big Buddha" Jackson joined the Broncos in a trade with Houston in 1971. At 6'3", 270 pounds he was a huge guard for that era. We decided that about 60 percent of Larron's weight, though, came from his butt. He had the biggest backside of anyone in the league. That's how he got the nickname, "Big Buddha." It just fit. Some of my best runs came from following his blocks on sweeps. Hiding behind his big ass gave me an extra half-second to make my cut and head upfield.

Larron has been a minister for years. When I see him at alumni events, I tease him, "Larron, your butt is so big that if you ever want to haul ass, you'd have to make two trips!"

Bruno

Sam Brunelli played six years for the Broncos, 1966–71, and he was a tough, strong-as-hell guard and tackle. We nicknamed him "Blowfish" because he had these huge Popeye forearms and used to pretend he was pumping them up by blowing into his thumbs.

Sam also wore three different numbers during his Broncos career—64, 68, and 72. I used to tease him that they were based on his three highest IQ scores. He'd say, "I'm smarter than I look." I'd reply, "I sure hope so!"

The Brawl

On every level of my football career, there was an episode where guys on my team found out exactly how intense I was about football. The biggest confrontation I had as a Bronco was with tackle Mike Current.

It was our rookie season, and we were playing the Raiders and, as usual, they were handing our asses to us. I was getting the shit beat out of me, and at halftime I heard Mike complaining that he couldn't block Oakland's defensive end, Ike Lassiter. Our line coach, Whitey Dovell, was imploring Mike to get tough. But Mike kept sulking. "I can't," he said. "I just can't block him!"

Well, I couldn't believe this was coming from a pro. I snapped. I jumped up, grabbed Mike, and body slammed him to the ground. He was in shock. The whole team couldn't believe it. Guys were trying to peel me off, but I wouldn't let go. I told Mike he didn't deserve to play professional football. "How are you going to beat Lassiter when you can't even beat my ass?" I screamed. "You've already quit and there's still a half to play. You might as well get the hell out of here."

Mike was so mad he stared at me in the huddle the rest of game. He didn't utter a word but his whole attitude changed. He dominated Lassiter the rest of the game. As Mike walked off the field afterwards, I said, "Mike, whatever happened at halftime I did it because I felt it needed to be done. If you want to go at it with me after we get out of the locker room, I'll meet you back here and give you that opportunity. No one needs to know but us."

He didn't saying anything and never met me afterward. Mike became a great player, but that episode kept us from becoming close friends.

Then a couple years after I retired, I was covering a Buccaneers game as a TV analyst. Mike had just joined Tampa Bay and left a message at my hotel room saying he wanted to meet me. When I got the message I thought, "Oh, damn. He finally wants to take me up on that fight now that I'm retired." I didn't know what to think. But I've always been a man of my word, and I agreed to meet Mike for dinner.

After an uncomfortable hello, Mike finally broke the silence. "I know it's been years, but I just wanted to thank you for what happened in that locker room our rookie year," he said. "I was mad for a long time. But that fight made me a better player. You helped me live up to that potential and allowed me to play in the NFL all these years. So thanks, Floyd."

I tried to act like I expected such a response. But I'm pretty sure my jaw was flapping on the table. I said, "I'm sorry it happened the way it did. I shouldn't have grabbed you. You're a grown man and didn't deserve to be treated that way. I just knew you were a better player than that."

Mike played 13 seasons and retired in 1979 as a Miami Dolphin blocking for my good friend Larry Csonka. I consider Mike one of the finest players I ever lined up with.

There are many other linemen I want to thank including George Goeddeke, Larry Kaminski, Tom Cichowski, Marv Montgomery, Mike Schnitker, Tom Lyons, Claudie Minor, Paul Howard, Bob Young, and Roger Shoals.

As many fans might remember, Mike passed away in January 2012 after allegedly shooting himself in the head with a shotgun. Reports say he was facing nearly 30 years of possible prison time for molesting children. I don't know how a guy changes like that. I don't even want to begin to speculate. Mike obviously dealt with some tough times. But I think the way he ended his life shows that he didn't like the person he had become and had a lot of remorse.

All I know is the guy I played with was not the guy I saw in the police shots that were printed in his obituary. I didn't recognize that guy.

Penny-Pincher?

Randy Gradishar was our top pick in 1974 from Ohio State. He joined the Broncos toward the end of my career and instantly upgraded our defense. At 6'3", 235 pounds, Randy was the first big linebacker the Broncos had. He was an intense young man and worked hard from day one. When he retired in 1983, Randy was a seven-time Pro Bowler and one of the leaders of the Broncos Orange Crush defense.

Randy also was a prankster. If something was missing from your locker, there was a good chance Randy was behind it. He could also be a bit of a goof. During one preseason game he saw a quarter lying on the field and called a timeout just so he could pick it up. The rest of the season, guys would walk by his locker and pretend they needed to make a phone call. "Randy, you got a quarter I can borrow?" we asked.

I know a lot of people are upset that Randy is not in the Hall of Fame. He is certainly deserving. He was a finalist a few times before he became a seniors candidate. I can attest that the road is much tougher as a seniors candidate. But I think if some fresh eyes at the Hall of Fame review Randy's impressive career, I feel strongly that he will make it someday.

Wholly Moses

After John Ralston traded for him in 1972, Haven Moses played nine incredible seasons for the Broncos. Who can forget his 168-yard, two-touchdown performance in the AFC Championship Game against the Raiders on New Year's Day 1978?

Haven suffered a stroke a few years back but thankfully is near full recovery. I'm not surprised about his resiliency. He took one of the toughest hits we've ever seen. One game against the Chiefs, he got hit in the helmet and completely shattered his facemask. It was just dust. Most people would be toe-tagged right there. But Haven got up and had only a cut on his lip. "What's wrong?" he asked as we painfully heaved a collective gasp.

Even after his stroke, Haven is still a great golfer. Of course, we don't want him to think he's Tiger Woods, so we tease him a lot. A couple of years ago during our Alumni golf outing, Haven was playing in the group ahead of us on a long par 3. We waited what seemed like forever as he lined up a putt. So BT said, "Screw this," and teed up his ball and knocked a shot right on the green—startling Haven and missing his ankle by a couple feet. Haven looked at us like, "What the f—!" We laughed and said, "Hurry the hell up!"

Ba-Ba-Barney

One of the great unsung players in Broncos history is defensive end Barney Chavous. Barney was a second-round pick in 1973 from South Carolina State and played 13 seasons for us. Only John Elway, Tom Jackson, and Dennis Smith played longer.

Barney had a southern drawl that was so thick you could pour it on hotcakes. He also had a stutter. If you think kids can be cruel, spend time around an NFL locker room. Everyone had a nickname, and Barney's was perhaps the meanest. "Ba-Ba-Barney." He was the one who laughed last. Barney was surprisingly quick and could rush the passer as easily as he could stop the run. One time against the Raiders, he knocked Ken Stabler for a bone-crushing sack. Barney got up and nonchalantly tapped him on the helmet for good measure. Stabler got mad and tried to go after him. But Stabler's own linemen held him back. They knew Barney wasn't the vindictive type. He just walked back to the huddle giggling.

The Broncos had an up and down history of how they've treated players. Back during my era they didn't always handle letting players go with dignity. Barney found out he was cut while watching the 6:00 news. After 13 seasons, that's how the organization let him go. The team got some bad press about Barney's callous release, and the brass hired him back as the strength and conditioning coach. I think that made Barney feel a little better, but the damage had been done.

Last I heard Barney was coaching high school football. He definitely never got the press he deserved as a player.

Tanked

The same thing happened to Jim "Tank" Turner. He learned he was cut from a news report in '79. Jim deserved better. Here was someone who was one of the game's greatest kickers. He accounted for 10 of the Jets 16 points in Super Bowl III—including three field goals—in the biggest upset in NFL history. Jim retired as one of the NFL's all-time scorers. He won a lot of games for the Broncos with those high-top boots. The Broncos later elected him to the Ring of Fame, but he's never forgiven the Phipps regime for using the local media to cut him instead of telling him face-to-face. He still lives in Denver and does a lot of charity work, but he hasn't been involved in many Broncos functions.

Tombstone

Lou Saban blew a few trades in his tenure. But trading for Rich Jackson was not one of them. In 1967 he sent Lionel Taylor, who wanted to exercise a clause in his contract to be traded, and another player to the Raiders in exchange for three players that included Rich, who was a backup linebacker at the time. Lou moved Rich to defensive end, and during the next five seasons Rich became the most feared lineman in the league. He not only dominated offensive tackles and anyone else who tried to stop him, he annihilated them. The head slap was still legal then, and he devastated guys with it.

He earned the nickname "Tombstone" because that's where he sent quarterbacks. Rich loved playing against his old team, the Raiders. Whenever we played Oakland, he went toe-to-toe with behemoth tackle Bob

Brown. It was like Godzilla against King Kong. We crowded the sideline to see them go at it. They hit, shoved, slapped, spit, kicked, and gouged. Hell, they did everything that would garner a personal foul today. It was like watching two bears fighting over a lunch basket.

During the '71 season I think we had the most formidable defensive line in the league with Rich, Paul Smith, Dave Costa, and Lyle Alzado. We also had Pete Duranko, Jerry Inman, and Tom Domres in there. All good, tough players. I don't know where our defense ranked, but I think we were near the top against the run and quarterback pressures. Rich was battling bad knees, and Lyle was a rookie. But Lyle adored Rich and worked hard to impress him. And ol' Tombstone loved having a protégé, of sorts, to teach. That all changed in '72 when John Ralston took over as coach. He made Rich practice every day on his bad knees. Rich's knees got worse, and John shipped him to Cleveland for a third-round pick. He also traded Dave Costa. I don't think Lyle ever forgave John.

Rich and I remain good friends. He lives in New Orleans and has been a school educator for years. We talk a few times a year, and I see him nearly every year at the Broncos Alumni weekend. He also came to my Hall of Fame induction. I think one of the great oversights in professional football is that this man is not in Canton. The argument is that he only played seven seasons. But if Gale Sayers gets a Hall of Fame pass for playing only seven seasons because of bad knees, then so should Rich for the same reason. He was a difference-maker, an impact player, and for most of his career he was the best defensive lineman in the game.

Super Dave

Dave Costa may not have been a household name, but he was a super player for us. He was a tough guy with a tremendous motor. He was a true character who probably would have fit in well with the Hells Angels. He wore leather jackets, rode a bike, and loved to go out and have fun. He had a perpetual smile that was evident even when he was mad. When *Monday Night Football* was born in 1970, the Broncos were still a good three years away from appearing in front of a national audience. It became a point of contention. But Dave made it a social event. He'd gather a few of us at a pub for dinner to enjoy the game over a couple of beers. He was a true entertainer who was always cracking jokes. Word got out that he was hosting a *Monday Night Football* party, and more guys showed up every week. Thanks to Dave we became a closer group, and that friendship continues each year during our Alumni weekend.

Shhh, Mr. Smith

Perhaps the most consistent player we ever had was Paul Smith. He was a quiet guy who was fundamentally sound. Paul wasn't a big talker or a big weightlifter for that matter. But he studied film and perfected techniques that allowed him to become a good pass rusher and an effective tackler.

No one ever graded out more consistently than Paul. He'd quietly be among the leaders in tackles and quarterback pressures each game. He's a Ring of Famer who played for the Broncos for 11 years before being traded to the Redskins. He passed away in 2000, and we all miss him. Very few offensive linemen were able to get the best of Paul. He was just too damn good. He influenced a lot of young linemen, including Lyle Alzado, John Grant, and Rubin Carter.

Quarterback Carousel

Fans and media look back at those Broncos teams during my day and wonder why we didn't win more. After all, we always had a pretty good defense, and we were able to run the ball effectively. I think when you lose there's enough blame to go around for everyone. Although I contributed in a lot of areas, I was my own toughest critic. When you walk off the field after a loss, you have to look at your own performance first before you can start judging anyone else's. Still, few teams ever win consistently if there is inconsistency in the quarterback position. And that was a glaring problem. Until Charley Johnson arrived in 1972, quarterback was Denver's Achilles' heel. All you have to do is look at how many we had. From 1967–71, Lou brought in 27 quarterbacks.

Lou was an impulsive coach who wouldn't hesitate to pull a quarterback if he threw an interception. Because of that we had a lot of quarterbacks looking over their shoulders. During his first season in '67, Lou made that terrible trade, sending two No. 1 picks to the Chargers for backup Steve Tensi. Because Steve was hurt so much, Max Choboian,

Jim LeClair, and Scotty Glacken played, too. The following season Lou brought in several quarterbacks to compete with Steve for the starting job—11 of them. Talk about lack of cohesion. Every time we ran a play in camp there was another quarterback behind center. We started four quarterbacks that '68 season. That's insane. Our offense was so out of sync it performed like a car with a shot carburetor.

Finally, Lou took a gamble and brought in Marlin Briscoe. As you know, Marlin played well, but after one season he wanted to be the highest-paid player on the team. Denver didn't have that kind of money, and he was gone.

The next two seasons, 1969–70, Lou hauled in seven quarterbacks at camp before settling on Tensi, Pete Liske, and Al Pastrana. Pete went to Canada and starred before coming to Denver. Al was a rookie who Lou had coached at Maryland. He was just green. In three starts he tossed eight interceptions. In one game Al was knocked woozy when we were in position for a game-winning field goal. Back then only quarterbacks could call timeout. The game ended with us trying to wake him up to call a timeout.

Pete, on the other hand, had potential. He was a good leader but forced a lot of bad throws. Once against Buffalo he was sacked five times and threw five interceptions. Lou went berserk. In 11 starts Pete tossed 14 interceptions.

In 1971, Steve Tensi retired, Lou cut Al, and shipped off Pete to Philadelphia. He decided he didn't need all those quarterbacks. He only invited four quarterbacks to camp and traded for Steve Ramsey and Don Horn. Lou was convinced Don was the answer, and he traded a great young defensive end, Alden Roche, and a first-round pick for him. Alden reminded me of a young Michael Strahan. He was tall, lean, and strong. He had no front teeth and looked like Dracula. We nicknamed him "the Count."

The first thing I noticed about Don and Steve was that neither was mobile. Steve didn't look like a quarterback. He seemed more like the Pillsbury Doughboy. I liked Steve. He was a gutsy quarterback; he just wasn't a great leader. He could never take command of a huddle like Charley did. Don was just too inexperienced. In his second game he faced his old team, the Packers, and threw six interceptions. I was standing behind Don near the end of the game, and I overheard a coach crack, "Don, you should have told me you were betting on this game so I could get in on the action."

Don separated his shoulder a few weeks later against the Bengals, and his short Broncos career was over. Lou resigned the next day, and offensive line coach Jerry Smith took over as interim coach.

When Ralston took over the next season, he brought in Charley but let Steve Ramsey start the first five games in '72. We went 1–4. Finally, 34-year-old Charley got a shot to start at Oakland and completed 20-of-28 passes for 361 yards and two touchdowns. We won 30–23. I caught my first touchdown from Charley, and I threw a 35-yard touchdown pass to Jerry Simmons on a halfback option. Jerry was such an instigator I had to kid him. I said, "Jerry that was a perfect pass. I can't believe you held on to it!"

Charley's performance was the best game by a Broncos quarterback since Marlin's huge game vs. Buffalo in '68. Charley became the Broncos starter during the next four seasons. Looking back at all the Broncos quarterbacks, one statistic sticks out to me. Of all the quarterbacks we had, only Marlin Briscoe threw more touchdowns than interceptions. Charley Johnson threw 52 touchdowns and 52 interceptions, not surprising for that era since he was a deep-ball passer.

Heir Apparent

When I joined the Broncos in 1967, the average career of an NFL running back was less than two years. As a 25-year-old rookie playing on a last-place team, I knew an injury could end my career at any moment. That's why I played every down as if it was my last.

The Broncos, of course, understood the precarious nature of an NFL running back and prepared each season accordingly. In my nine seasons they drafted 21 other running backs and traded for another six. Of those, one guy eventually became my heir apparent—Otis Armstrong. We drafted him No. 1 in 1973. He sat and watched me grind out 979 yards and 13 touchdowns that season while securing my third Pro Bowl. During training camp in '74, I injured my Achilles' tendon and tried to play too soon. It never healed properly and prevented me from playing with abandon. Otis got the opportunity to start and made one hell of a statement by leading the NFL in rushing, just as I had done three seasons earlier.

Although I was disappointed with my injury, I took my new reserve role as a professional. I always believed the best 11 guys should play regardless of who was on the bench. At 32, I had enjoyed a great career and was among the Top 10 rushers of all time. But more importantly, as captain and mentor, it was my duty to make sure Otis was prepared for each game. I told him that talent alone can only get you so far in the NFL. I made sure he stayed and worked with his linemen after practice. I coaxed linebackers to stay afterward, too, so Otis could improve his pass blocking.

During the best game of his career, Otis and I got into it a little bit. We were playing the Oilers, and Otis had already run for 165 yards and two touchdowns. We were winning 30–14 with two minutes left when Oilers quarterback Dan Pastorini was intercepted by John Rowser. Otis came over to me and said, "Hey, Floyd. Go ahead take it in. I'm exhausted." Now I hadn't carried the ball once that day, although I had returned punts and kickoffs. I said, "You want me to go in because you're tired— you mean you're not hurt?" He shook his head. "No, just dead tired. Go in." I said, "Otis, this is what being a starter and a professional means. You keep playing unless you're hurt or the coaches take you out." He again shook his head no. Well, I got mad. I grabbed him by the shoulder pads and pulled him close to me. "Listen," I said. "There's less than two minutes left. We're kicking their ass. This is the fun part. Now go in there and finish the goddamn job!"

Otis looked at me like, "Old Folks is nuts." Sure I wanted to play. During my career you had to break both of my legs and hide my helmet to get me out of a game. I loved Otis, but I wanted to teach him toughness. He went back in and, in a bit of irony, he cut me out of the record book. He gained three yards on his next carry topping my single-game record of 166 yards. Then on his final carry, he went 15 yards for his third touchdown—tying my team record of three touchdowns in a game—for a 37–14 victory.

That's actually one of my proudest memories. Knowing I made a young player better without any regard for one of my personal achievements.

TJ

Over the years there were a lot of players who came to me for advice. Because I was captain, some guys felt I had influence over who stayed and who went. That wasn't true. I just knew what the coaches wanted.

One guy who came to me for advice was Tommy Jackson. There's a whole generation of fans who know Tom as Chris Berman's sidekick on ESPN. But Tommy was a great player. At 5'11", 218 pounds, he was short and light for a linebacker. What he lacked in size he made up for with speed and a ton of heart.

Tommy used to ask me, "What can I do to make the team?" I told him, "You need to go all out on every play in every practice. They never cut you for going 100 percent or being aggressive." I told him that whenever we faced each other in a drill to really go at it. "Don't be afraid to lay me out and do a little shoving afterwards. Make a scene." So one day Tom gave me quite a shot in practice. The team gasped. John Ralston stopped everything and yelled, "Tom Jackson! Hitting our star running back like that is the quickest way outta here."

Tommy thought he had screwed up. "Did you hear the coach? They're going to cut me," he said afterward. "Really," I replied, "what did he call you?" He looked confused, "He, uh, called me Tom." "That's right," I laughed. "You're no longer 'Rookie' or 'Jackson.' You're Tom Jackson. They know you!"

When the coaches gathered for the next round of cuts, I'm sure they said, "Tommy may be a little out of control, but he goes all out. Let's keep him another week." And that's how you make a team. In fact, John started to keep Tommy out of certain drills along with me. He'd say, "We're going to do the Oklahoma drill. Floyd and Tom, you two sit this one out."

Tom All-Thumbs

Tom quickly became a great tackler and eventually started. But his hands needed work. One time he dropped two easy interceptions in a game. Billy Thompson went over to him and said, "Don't worry, TJ. Stay focused. You can do it." Then unbelievably, Tom dropped a third easy pick. Billy's mouth opened but nothing came out. Finally he said, "What the hell is wrong with you?"

This is one of my all-time favorite photos. That's me and my mom, Lula Little, on October 30, 1965, after we stomped Pitt 51–13 at Shea Stadium. I rushed for more than 100 yards and scored four touchdowns. My last score was a 95-yard punt return in which I must have zigzagged for 195 yards! Jets owner Sonny Werblin and head coach Weeb Ewbank were at the game and decided they were going to draft me. Of course, the Broncos beat them to it! (AP Photo)

Great picture, bad ending. Here I am charging down the field surrounded by a throng of Baylor players on September 16, 1966, in Waco, Texas. Baylor was a great team that year and they beat us bad, 35–12. Somehow I managed to gain 90 yards despite having nowhere to run. (AP Photo/FK)

In Week 2 of the 1969 season, the world champion Jets visited Mile High Stadium. We were pumped for the game and upset them 21–19. I rushed for 104 yards on 15 carries and a touchdown. Here I am returning a punt 52 yards as I bound over Jets punter Steve O'Neal (20) while John Dockery (43) is in hot pursuit. No. 62 is Broncos defensive tackle Jerry Inman. (AP Photo)

Here I am in the open field in a huge 16–10 win over the Los Angeles Rams at the LA Coliseum on November 12, 1972. There's no way I'm going to let linebacker Marlin McKeever (86) catch me; and although Clarence Williams (24) looks like he has a shot, you can see my man, Jerry Simmons (80), in the corner ready to lay on a lick. (AP Photo/NFL Photos)

I only played the Eagles twice in my career but have fond memories of both contests. My final game at Mile High was against the Eagles in which I accounted for more than 150 yards from scrimmage, scored two touchdowns, and was carried off the field by the fans. But this 1971 game at old Vet Stadium against Philly makes me smile now. It's not because I had 123 yards rushing and scored here on a 1-yard plunge. And it's certainly not because we lost this heartbreaker, 17-16, on Halloween. It's because sitting in the crowd that day was an 8-year-old boy cheering his heart out for his favorite player—me. Tom Mackie was at the game that day, thanks to his dad surprising him with tickets. It was the only time Tom saw me play in person. (AP Photo/Bill Ingraham)

I am blessed to have the greatest children any parent could ask for. From the left are my daughter, Kyra, son, Marc, and daughter, Christy. They are incredibly successful people who possess strong convictions and amazing spirits. Kyra, the youngest, is a triple-threat singer, dancer, and actor; she's appeared on Broadway many times. Marc is an attorney and author. And Christy, the mother of my grandchildren, also runs her own business. (Photo courtesy of the author)

Here I am in during Super Bowl XLV weekend in Dallas, Texas, on February 5, 2011, with my beautiful wife DeBorah. I am the luckiest man in the world to be married to this amazing woman. She is always there for me and every day we laugh about something. (Photo courtesy of the author)

It doesn't get any better than this! Hanging out at my Hall of Fame induction party with my fellow Broncos (from left to right): my teammate and best friend, Billy "BT" Thompson, Tommy Jackson, myself, and my son, Marc. I truly believe that BT and Tommy will join me one day in Canton. (Photo/Daryn Hollis)

Here I am posing with my bust after being inducted into the Pro Football Hall of Fame in Canton, Ohio, on Saturday, August 7, 2010. I was truly reveling in the moment, reflecting on all the family, friends, coaches, players, fans, and supporters who helped me along my journey. (AP Photo/Mark Duncan)

Later Billy and I teased Tom. "Tom, you trying to catch the ball is like putting perfume on a goat. It's not going to work." Tom, of course, cured his dropsies. During the 1977 Super Bowl run, he made some huge interceptions, including a 73-yarder for a touchdown against the Colts and two key fourth-quarter picks in the playoffs against the Steelers.

8

A NEW WINNING ALTITUDE

The First Winning Season

The closest we ever got to the playoffs during my Broncos career was that magical 1973 season. It was the beginning of the phrase, "Big Orange, How Sweet It Is!" Later it became "Orange Crush," until the soft drink company by the same name eventually took us to court to get us to stop using it. If anything, I'm sure we helped their sales.

Overall, Ralston's first season as coach in '72 season had been a disappointment. We finished 5–9. I had a productive yet injury-plagued season. I played the entire year with an injured knee that was further damaged against Kansas City. I needed surgery, but I decided to wait until the season was over. I still slugged out 859 yards rushing, 367 receiving, and 13 touchdowns.

I was 31 and endured off-season knee surgery. They didn't have the arthroscopic kind—this was the huge 8" slice down the side. Because the Broncos were unsure of how I would bounce back, John used the Broncos' first pick on Otis Armstrong. He also made a key trade for linebacker Ray May from Baltimore.

Holding Hands

Ray May was probably our biggest addition in 1973. He was a savvy veteran who had earned a championship ring with the Colts in Super Bowl V. He also brought with him a unique way of unifying the defense— holding hands. He started it in camp, and some guys felt stupid doing it. But Ray said it was a way to show guys unity that "I've got your back, and you've got mine."

I loved it and tried, doing it one time on offense, and one anonymous teammate said, "Folks, watch your hands. Only my wife and girlfriend can do that!"

We won the first game 28–10 against the Bengals, and I had another hat-trick touchdown performance. Then we lost three games to the 49ers, Bears, and Chiefs. The hand-holding experiment seemed to be losing its grip.

Monday Night Madness

Heading into Week 6, we were 2–3 and facing the biggest game in the history of the Denver Broncos. After four years of being ignored by the national media, we were appearing on our first *Monday Night Football* telecast. The whole city was elated. Announcers Howard Cosell, Frank Gifford, and Don Meredith were treated like royalty when they arrived days before the game. There were banquets and special appearances. The mayor proclaimed the day "Orange Monday." People donned orange outfits, wigs, and made huge signs. The fans wanted to show that Denver was a dynamic place to live with the greatest fans in the world.

The game was on October 22, and although Halloween was not for another week, the many orange outfits made for a spiritual event. That spirit went into the stratosphere during the first quarter when the Raiders were driving for what seemed like an easy touchdown and Clarence Davis lost a fumble. Billy Thompson scooped it up and raced 80 yards for a touchdown and a 7–0 lead. I think John Ralston ran the entire way along the sideline with him. BT was mobbed in the end zone.

The Raiders, as usual, came back and methodically scored 13 unanswered points to build a 13–7 halftime lead. When we got the ball back in the third quarter, we went to our basic offensive package of runs, traps, draws, and short passes. We got to Oakland's 10-yard line, and Charley gave me the ball four straight times before going over from the 1-yard line to make it 14–13. That carry put me over the mark of 5,000 career rushing yards. I was just happy we had taken the lead.

The whole game was a slugfest. I got clotheslined on a catch over the middle, and my neck and shoulders were stiffening up. Oakland had double the yardage we had on offense, and we were fighting our guts out just to stay with them.

Early in the fourth quarter, we tied the game at 20 on another Jim Turner field goal. Then Oakland did what they always seemed to do. They got the ball with 3:32 left and melted the clock down to 41 seconds before the ageless George Blanda booted a 49-yarder for a 23–20 lead. With the game almost over, a lot of the Raiders started joking. Some even took off their helmets.

Luckily, we got two breaks. Ray Guy, the Raiders' dependable kicking specialist, knocked two straight kickoffs out of bounds. Back then it was a 5-yard penalty and a re-kick. The third time Joe Dawkins returned it to our 38-yard line. There were only 30 seconds left. We needed to go at least 20 yards to give Jim Turner a chance at a field goal.

On first down Charley threw me a quick screen. I dodged two tacklers and ripped up the sideline for 13 yards. With the Raiders suspecting pass, Charley called a draw to Joe Dawkins for 12 more. Now with 17 seconds on the clock, the ball was at the 37 with one timeout left. We basically had one more play before we had to let Jim kick a field goal. Charley thought about tossing one in the end zone, but he needed time to throw. There was always a risk of a sack that would keep us out of field-goal range.

Charley decided to stay the course. He said, "Let's make it a bit closer for Jim. Folks, I'm giving it to you, 34 Power Trap. Just put your head down and get us a few more yards and I'll call timeout. Let's do it!"

I hit the hole, and there was a nice open spot for me to land. But I saw a crease open behind Mike Current's block and cut back to the right for nine yards. Charley called a timeout with seven seconds left, and Jim knocked a 35-yarder through the uprights for a 23–23 tie.

I know a tie isn't glamorous, but we were happy. We showed a lot of composure, coming back against a team known for its comebacks. We were now just 2–3–1, but we were brimming with confidence.

On a Roll

Following the comeback tie on *Monday Night Football* against the Raiders, the whole city rejoiced the next day. Neighbors cheered me as I drove to practice, newspapers captured every detail of the game, and I'm told the water coolers were getting extra attention in offices all over Colorado.

The good feelings flowed through every player, coach, equipment person, and staff member in the Broncos organization. We had finally been on national television and played an inspired game. Of course, the love fest quickly dissolved and it was back to business. We played the Jets the following week, and Leroy Mitchell scored on a 40-yard interception, propelling us to a 40–28 victory.

The next week we tied the Cardinals and sported a peculiar 3–3–2 record. Of course, having multiple ties was not out of the ordinary before overtime was instituted in 1974. I called a meeting and implored everyone to step up. "Let's get it done this year. I'm not getting any younger," I said. "That's because you're old as shit," a few of them joked. We won the next three games: 30–19 over San Diego; 23–13 at Pittsburgh; and a huge 14–10 upset at home against the Chiefs, a team we never seemed to beat.

Suddenly we were 6–3–2, but we had three tough games left: Dallas, at San Diego, and at Oakland.

Charged Up

After a tough loss to Dallas, we rebounded with a wild 42–28 win at San Diego the following week. Everyone played well. I scored my 13th touchdown of the season, which equaled the previous season's total. Best of all, the victory raised our record to 7–4–2 and, incredibly, ensured the franchise's first winning season ever.

I'll never forget the reception we got at the airport upon our return. Thousands of fans mobbed us at tiny Stapleton Airport as we stepped off the plane. There were no security people around, and the terminals were extremely narrow. I got hugged more times than a newborn baby. It was a circus atmosphere, and after seven seasons it felt great to finally be a winner. We had one game to go. It was a road game against—who else?—the hated Raiders. The winner would be AFC West champions and go to the playoffs. The loser would go home.

For All the Marbles

The Raiders game began with a bad omen. Prior to the kickoff, hundreds of pigeons were released, I guess, as a picturesque beginning to a championship game. Damn if those pigeons didn't shit all over us as they flew by. Luckily, we were wearing white so it wasn't that noticeable. It just stunk.

Without championship-playing experience, the team was jittery early on and the Raiders capitalized with a quick 14–0 lead. Down two touchdowns, our game plan to control the ball with runs and short passes went out the window. By giving up on the run, we played right into the Raiders' hands. Their pass rush was among the best in the league, and Charley started taking some shots. We managed a field goal, and by halftime it was 14–3.

Ralston gambled with an onside kick to start the second half, and it failed. The Raiders got the ball in good field position, but our defense forced a fumble and we took over near midfield. Now it was gut-check time, and we responded. We put together an 11-play drive that ended with a beautiful 13-yard touchdown strike from Charley to Haven Moses to make it 14–10. The score stayed the same going into the fourth quarter, and we felt good about everything.

That all changed on our first possession to start the fourth quarter. Charley completed three straight passes to Riley Odoms for 25 yards. Then with the ball at midfield, the Raiders blitzed and slammed Charley hard to the turf. He lay motionless for a few seconds. Ralston threw down his clipboard and galloped out to see his quarterback. Charley was helped to the sideline with a concussion and never returned.

Our hearts sank. It was fourth-and-10, but we still had a whole quarter left. No need to panic. Ralston felt otherwise and called another fake punt. Joe Dawkins was to take a direct snap and hand it off to Otis Armstrong on a counter. Otis wasn't normally in on the punt team and as soon as he jogged on the field the Raiders started pointing at him and yelling, "Hey, he's a new guy!"

We should have called it off. Joe had trouble with the snap and couldn't get it to Otis in time, so he kept the ball and was tackled immediately. Three plays later Stabler found Mike Siani alone for a 31-yard touchdown and a 21–10 lead. In less than two minutes, we had lost our quarterback and given away the game.

When Steve Ramsey came into the huddle, you could feel the confidence disappear. He just stared at the ground when he called a play, unlike Charley who always looked you in the eyes. A few plays later, Steve was picked off by Willie Brown.

The game appeared done. Luckily, with only a few minutes left, Raiders running back Marv Hubbard fumbled on his own 10-yard line and Pete Duranko recovered. After I got nine yards on a draw play, Ramsey found Riley Odoms in the end zone for a touchdown and suddenly it was 21–17 with three minutes left. The Broncos sideline exploded.

At that point we had nothing to lose and should have tried another onside kick. Ralston elected to kick it deep, and the Raiders offense ran all but 18 seconds off the clock. We lost 21–17 as the Raiders held on to win. We had played valiantly overall but couldn't overcome those costly mistakes. We played catch-up most of the game, throwing 38 times to Oakland's 20. Joe Dawkins and I only ran the ball 10–15 times.

Later in the locker room, a reporter came up to me and told me I had just missed out on 1,000 yards rushing. "You finished 21 yards short with 979 yards," he told me. I just stared at him and shrugged my shoulders. Frankly, I couldn't think of anything less important than another milestone. We had lost the game.

On the plane ride back, all you could hear was the engine's low hum. Lyle Alzado, as usual, was next to me and even he was as quiet as a stone. The requiem atmosphere all changed when our plane taxied at Stapleton. We looked out our windows and again saw the fans—5,000 of them—welcoming us home. I think it was even more than the previous week after we beat the Chargers. My eyes welled up. Those fans deserved a playoff team. They were so loyal. As we walked through the terminal, they kept chanting, "Wait until next year!" and, "We love you!" It was incredible.

9

THE AFC WEST AND OTHER HAZARDOUS TEAMS

Say Hello to Your Wife for Me!

As one of the smallest backs in the league, I learned pretty early that there was more to surviving in the NFL than merely hard work and taking care of yourself. Running backs were regularly gang-tackled and absorbed a lot of cheap shots. Personal fouls were rarely called because back then, they weren't personal fouls. Getting clotheslined, speared, spit on, kicked in the nuts, and slammed out of bounds were part of the game in the early 1970s. There were no quick whistles, and fumbles weren't analyzed. Any loose ball was a free-for-all that lasted until the refs felt like interfering. Because of all these hazards of the game, it paid to be sneaky smart.

One of the things I did was try to diffuse my opponents by getting to know them. The week before each game I would go to our PR director, Val Pinchbeck, and later, Bob Peck, to request a copy of the opponent's media guide. No wonder writers loved them. They contained all kinds of juicy information about a player, such as how long they'd been in the league, where they went to college, what their hobbies were, and even the names of their wives, kids, and pets. Along with studying game film, I used to study the media guide.

The idea came to me the first time I played the Chiefs in 1967. We were getting torched like a paper kite in a brush fire. They were humiliating us 52–9, and their horse, Warpaint, had run up and down the field so many times after touchdowns that he was exhausted. After the final touchdown, he just stood in the end zone and shit. On one of my final carries of the game, Buck Buchanan, all 6'7" of him, jumped on my back and rode me for five yards downfield before he crushed me into the ground. He made some whooping sound and pushed me into the dirt as he got up. At that point I was already too mad about the game. So I just took it like an old man in prison.

I decided it wouldn't hurt to get to know Buck and other bone-crushing defenders. Before the next Chiefs game I went over to him and said, "Hey, Buck. You know you guys played the Packers pretty tough last year in the Super Bowl. I'm sure you'll make it back soon. Say hello to your wife, Elizabeth, and your three kids for me. Stay healthy!" I'm sure Buck didn't know what to think. He didn't go half speed during the game, but after the whistle, instead of pushing me into the ground, he'd help me up. We became friends over the years, and it all started with that media guide. I didn't bother with the Raiders because I figured they'd just hit me harder. One guy on the Chargers I got to know beyond the media guide was receiver Gary Garrison. Gary and I became friends while volunteering for the USO Handshake Tour in Vietnam. We spent a few weeks touring several combat bases in 1970. That really changed my perspective, and I appreciated the sacrifices of all those young men and women, especially my courageous brother, Jitty, who did not one but two tours of duty in Vietnam.

Kiss My Butkus

Of course, there were some players who didn't go for my media-guide routine. One of the all-time greats, Dick Butkus, didn't fall for the banana in the tailpipe.

The first time I played the Bears was an exhibition game in 1970. I had met Dick years earlier in '64 with Gale Sayers at the All-America banquets. He was a load of fun off the field. But when the game was on he wasn't just intense, he was incensed. You would never know that during warm-ups. I went out and patted him on the back and said,

"Dick, great to see you. We're finally going to play against each other."

He said, "Yeah, it's about time. I'm looking forward to it."

"Me, too. Say, how's Helen and the kids?" I asked.

"Oh, they're great. And Joyce?"

"She's doing fine," I said. "Well, good luck. Stay healthy."

"You do the same, Floyd."

I thought, *This is great, nothing wrong with diffusing Dick Butkus a little.* But the game started, and he was the same old Dick. He'd curse me after each play. And it just got worse. I was gaining chunks of yards off tackle right past Butkus. When he tackled me, he'd twist my body to the ground like he did everyone else. Early in the game I stuck my hand out for him to help me up. "You gotta be fucking kidding me," he said. "Kiss my ass!" and he stomped back to the huddle. By the third quarter, I had rushed for 137 yards—the last was a 77-yarder in which I whisked right by him. I could hear him shouting my name all the way down the field, "You're dead, Floyd!" The coaches sat me in the fourth quarter, but Butkus kept looking over at me. At one point he waved for me to come back in. I just laughed and said, "No way."

After the game Dick walked over to me and said, "Good game, Floyd. Have a great season." It was like that cartoon with Wile E. Coyote and the Sheepdog. They'd beat the shit out of each other the whole day and when the whistle blew they walked home together arm-in-arm with their lunch pails.

Are You Alright, Floyd?

Despite being an AFC team, we played the Bears practically every year after the merger. We faced Chicago again near the end of the 1971 season after Lou had quit. Jerry Smith was the interim coach, and a lot had changed on the Bears side, as well.

Gale Sayers had already played his last game, and Dick was suffering from a slew of knee problems. The media speculated that Butkus wasn't the same player. I didn't believe it. Even at 50 percent, Dick was the best. And this time I got more carries than ever to prove it. For some reason the Broncos made me the workhorse that game. Usually I averaged about 14 carries a game, sharing the load with Bobby Anderson or another fullback like Willis Crenshaw. This time I got the brunt of the carries, 29. In the second quarter I went up the middle, and Butkus got a head of steam and tattooed me harder than I've ever been hit. He hit me under the chin and bent me backwards like a soft pretzel.

Now the first rule I taught myself in football was never let the defender know you're hurt. I was in another world. But I just popped up and hit Butkus on the butt.

"Good play, Dick," I said and started walking back.

Dick just watched me. "Are you alright, Floyd?"

"Sure, nice pop."

He continued to stare. "No really, Floyd. Are you sure you're alright?"

"Yeah, I'm fine. Why do you keep asking?"

"Well," he replied, "for one thing, you're in *our* huddle!"

I looked around the huddle and saw Dick, Ed O'Bradovich, and Doug Buffone looking back at me. "You're not my teammates," I huffed and put my head down as I returned to the Broncos' huddle.

Despite being completely dazed, I still rushed for 125 yards and we won a 6–3 thriller. I also extended my league-leading rushing effort going into the final two games. Dick, of course, didn't help with that shot.

Me and My Shadow

One of the more interesting albeit peculiar set-ups of some older stadiums during my time was the lack of advanced technology.

Some stadiums only had electricity on one side of the field, such as Minnesota's Metropolitan or Kansas City's Memorial. So both teams shared the same sideline. The only things separating us were tables of Gatorade in the middle.

The Chiefs were one of those teams that assigned a spy to limit my production. It was linebacker Willie Lanier. If I was out on a wing, Willie focused on me. If I stayed in to block, Willie kept me in his sights. This even happened off the field. One time after a series I went over to the table to get some Gatorade, and there was Willie filling his cup, too. A few series later, I went back and Willie was there again. Finally, I said, "Do you have to follow me everywhere?" He smiled, "Wherever you go, I go." After that I was afraid to duck into the bathroom.

Incentives

No one was making a lot of money during my era. Some coaches created incentives for players to help motivate them. Of course, depending on what team you played for, the "incentives" were called different things. For example, I was told that the Chiefs defensive players were paid cash "incentives" to keep my totals less than 100 yards.

As my spy, Willie also had the chance to make the most. So one time when his shoulder pad strap broke and he had to come off the field, I shouted for the coach to call my number. He did, and I went right up the middle for 40 yards before Jim Lynch tackled me. "No, no," Willie yelled from the sideline. Before his pads could get fixed, we called the same play and this time I went for 13 yards. "You son-of-a-bitch" I heard him blare as he finally ran back on.

After the game, Lanier actually came into our locker room. "How many yards did Floyd get?" he asked. "How many? Tell me!" The stats guy looked at the official sheet. "Let's see, yards from scrimmage, 131; yards rushing, 96." "Yippee!" Willie yelled, jumping up and down. "96 we just made it. Thanks, Floyd." And he ran out a few hundred bucks richer.

Incentives, Raiders-Style

One of my best friends during my career was Raiders defensive back Nemiah Wilson. He was with the Broncos before joining Oakland, and we became good friends. He still lived in Denver in the off-season, and we went into a tailoring business together. We also trained together by running the steps of Mile High Stadium in combat boots.

Nemiah shared with me one of the secrets to the Raiders' success. Each game they had bounties placed on certain guys, and I was the top one. He told me they had a guy, called the Spiff Coach who paid them in cash after every game. A "spiff" is a term for a cash payment based on an incentive. The players would line up and say, "I knocked Floyd Little out for two series," or "I gave Charley Johnson a concussion," and the Spiff Coach would hand over an envelope with hundreds of dollars.

One time against the Raiders, I was running a trail pattern behind tight end Riley Odoms. Riley ran a crossing pattern behind the linebackers, and I trailed five yards behind. It was Charley's job to hit the open guy. I made my cut and started to get open when I looked over and saw Riley a step ahead of the linebacker. Charley threw a perfect pass, and Riley made a fingertip grab. Raiders safety Jack Tatum came up and knocked the snot out of him with a helmet-to-helmet lick. Riley landed on his back and was out cold, but somehow he held on to the ball. Jack, as usual, stood over him to enjoy the moment. I looked at him and thought, *Shit, that could have been me.* Tatum, no doubt, got a nice payday.

Ruthless

The Raiders definitely earned their reputation as a bunch of ruthless renegades. We rarely beat them because we always sank to their level. They'd start delivering cheap shots and punch, bite, kick and scratch and we'd do the same in retaliation. They didn't try to tackle you as much as try to maim and hurt you. After what Nemiah told me, I tried to protect myself as best I could against Oakland. But as a running back there wasn't much I could do. Instead of tackling me, guys would try to hold me up— so their buddy could take a shot at me. They'd even pull your arm out and expose it so someone could ram his helmet into it.

I'd see John Madden at the Pro Bowls, and he was the nicest guy. The first time I met him he told me what a great player I was and how much he respected me. "Every time we play Denver I tell my guys, 'We got to get Floyd. We got to stop that guy,'" he said. That made me feel good. Of course, I didn't let on that I knew there were bounties to knock me out of the game.

Not Today, Fat Man!

Coach John Madden was an amusing guy to watch. He waved his arms like a maniac during games and always wore a short-sleeve shirt, even when it was minus-20. I don't know how he never caught pneumonia. He also kept his field credentials dangling from his belt loop so security knew he was allowed on the field. As if they didn't know who this 6'5", 260-pound coach was. But what was so funny was his every-guy persona. Guys treated him like another player and loved to trash talk him. You never saw opponents teasing Saban. Madden, however, was fair game.

Surprisingly, the top trash talker on our team was Tom Jackson. You see him now and he's the most courteous, professional guy on TV. But as a player, Tommy was one of the biggest loudmouths. No one talked more trash to Madden than Tommy. The Raiders would try some double reverse, and Tommy would stop it for a loss. Instead of jawing at some of the Raiders, Tommy would turn to Madden and say, "Not today, Fat Man. You're going to sweat some weight today." John hated listening to Tom, too. "That Tom Jackson never shuts up," he used to say.

Who Took My Clothes?

Another tough linebacker I played against was Mike Curtis of the Baltimore Colts. Mike went all out on every play until the whistle blew. One time I was running around the left end and passed the first down marker. I looked up and had no lane to cut back, so I was forced to go out of bounds. Well, Curtis came out of nowhere and just leveled me. He hit me between my shoulders and helmet, and I went flying out of bounds. I was out cold. When I finally woke up, I was naked on the shower floor. I don't know how I got there, and worse, I don't know who took off my clothes. I was just thankful I wasn't naked in the Colts' shower! I learned a lesson never to assume you're not going to get hit.

Tails, You Lose

For two teams that hated each other, I became friends with a number of the Steelers. I played in Pro Bowls with Joe Greene, Jack Ham, Andy Russell, and I even knew the voice of the Steelers, Myron Cope, from his reporting days. This friendship continued for years when we all participated in Andy Russell's annual golf tournament.

Of those players, I probably became closest friends with Andy. Yet, there's one thing that I did to Andy that still makes him mad to this day. As team captains we were out calling the coin toss before a Broncos-Steelers game. The referee, I believe, was Tommy Bell. He said, "Captain Little, this is Captain Russell. This side of the coin is heads, this side tails. Captain Little, you make the call."

I thought for a second and as Bell flipped the coin I joked, "Heads we win, tails you lose." As the coin hit the ground, Bell looked at Andy and said, "Tails you lose, Captain Russell. Okay, Captain Little, you want to receive?"

Andy was furious. He said, "Wait a minute. What's going on here?" He tried telling Bell what I had done, but the longtime referee was either embarrassed or didn't believe him. Bell just shook him off and told him to return to his side.

That whole game Andy was trying to get back at me. Because of our friendship we never wanted to embarrass each other. He used to give me a heads up if he was blitzing. His function was not to get to the quarterback but to keep me from going out in a pass pattern. This time, though, he started giving me false signs, pretending he was going to blitz and instead he'd break out into coverage. After a few plays I went over and said, "Why are you so mad?" He was still upset. "Kiss my ass," he said, "You fucked me, now I'm going to fuck you."

Even today, we can joke about most things—but he still gets mad about that coin flip.

Son of Stram

I played in an era when there were a lot of great coaches. One of the best was Hank Stram. We rarely beat his Kansas City teams, and many times they flat-out killed us. The fans sure as heck hated the Raiders, but the Chiefs were our real rival. We really respected them, and the few times we beat them were huge victories.

One time at Mile High against the Chiefs I was in the locker room putting on my uniform. As I went to grab for my No. 44 jersey I realized it wasn't there. The equipment guys swore they put out my jersey. We quickly determined that someone had stolen it. While an assistant drove back to the practice facility to get another one, I went out to warm up wearing No. 46. Despite my size, I stuck out because of my bowed legs. My knees were so far apart that my college teammates called me Mr. Parentheses. There weren't too many guys who had my physique.

As I went through calisthenics and began fielding punts I looked over and Stram was staring at me. His eyes were fixated on me like I had knocked over his mailbox. Suddenly, I felt this presence behind me. I turned and Stram was 2' away.

"Who are you?" he said, trying to see past my facemask.

"Huh? It's Floyd, Coach."

He said, "Floyd Little? You're wearing No. 46. You've got the wrong jersey on."

"I know. Someone stole my jersey."

He looked at me, and a smile broke out. "Whew, for a second I thought you guys had a secret weapon."

The irony is I found out years later that Stram's son was the one who stole my jersey. I was in Kansas City doing a motivational speech, and he came up to me and confessed. "I was a big fan of yours as a kid and wanted your jersey," he said. He apologized and also admitted to stealing Joe Namath's helmet once. I started laughing. Maybe Hank got his kid to steal memorabilia from opponents so they'd lose focus before games.

This Little Pinky's Named Floyd!

Over the years I've played in a lot of charity golf tournaments. One time I was playing in Arizona and ran into Earl Edwards, a former Pro Bowl defensive end with the 49ers. He looked at me and blurted, "Goddamn, it's Floyd Little. You son of a bitch!" I was taken back. I only played against San Fran a few times, so I had no idea why he was giving me a hard time. "Look at my finger, Floyd. You see what you did?" Turns out the first time we played them he got his pinky caught in my shoulder pads while trying to tackle me on a long touchdown jaunt. He bent his finger like one of Chuck Bednarik's mangled digits. It looked like a protractor. He said, "You know what I call this finger?" I shook my head. "I call it my Fucking Floyd Little finger!" he said. "Every day I look at that twisted pinky I think of you, dirty bastard."

I was touched!

Keep Your Chin Up, Sweetness

It's hard to believe, but there was a time when the great Walter Payton was a young running back trying to make a name for himself. It was the last game of the 1976 season, and I was calling a Bears game with my colleague Ross Porter. After the game, Jim Finks, the Bears GM, came up to me and asked me to talk to their young running back because he had just lost the rushing crown to O.J. Simpson.

"Floyd, this kid is really dejected about losing the rushing title," Finks said. "You've led the league. Could you please talk to him and let him know he'll be okay?"

"Absolutely," I said and followed Jim into the Bears' locker room. There sitting by himself near his locker was Walter, head down, slowly getting dressed. I said, "Hi Walter. I'm Floyd Little." Walter looked up, and his eyes brightened, "It's great to meet you, Mr. Little." I replied, "I just want you to know I think you're a great young player. Don't get discouraged about the rushing title. Remember, this is just one season. I've heard you're a hard worker, a dedicated guy. That's going to take you a long way. When your career is over, I wouldn't be surprised if you hold all the records."

He smiled. "Thank you, Mr. Little. That' means a lot." Knowing that Walter went on to accomplish so much, I'm honored I got the chance to give him encouragement.

Porter the Pro

As mentioned, after my playing days, I worked as an NBC analyst for a few seasons. I broadcast games with some of the all-time greats, such as Jack Buck, Jay Randolph, Jim Simpson, and former Syracuse alumni Dick Stockton. But the guy I was most impressed with was Ross Porter.

One of my first games was covering a Buccaneers-Dolphins game during the Bucs' inaugural 1976 season. It was a blistering day in Tampa, and I was on the field before the game interviewing the two opposing quarterbacks from my '67 rookie class—Bob Griese of the Dolphins and Steve Spurrier of the Bucs. After the interview I raced up to the press box and when I got there Ross, who suffered from Bell's Palsy, was having an episode. Bell's Palsy is a condition where a temporary paralysis causes facial features to distort. It resembles someone having a stroke, but it's not as serious.

Well, Ross's face was half paralyzed and he could barely speak. Meanwhile, the director was counting down 30, 20, 15 seconds to airtime. I was trying to help Ross through it, but the whole time I'm thinking, *Shit, I'm going to have to do both the play-by-play and the commentary!* Sweat was pouring down my face. But as soon as we went on air, Ross miraculously recovered. His voice became as smooth as ever, and his face somehow returned to normal.

The Biggest Cheap Shot of Them All

I've retold a lot of my favorite stories in this book that originally appeared in *Tales from the Broncos Sideline*. I did this because only 5,000 copies of my first book were printed before the publisher went out of business, and I've received countless letters and emails from people asking if the publisher will be printing more copies. The answer is no, that's why I decided to retell some of my favorites here. Copies of my first book are in such demand, I typically see sellers asking $50 or more for it—of course, I get zero royalty from it.

But there is one story that wasn't told in the first book that I'd like to tell now. It's about the biggest cheap shot I ever experienced playing in the NFL.

In 1972, we were playing the Falcons in Atlanta. Our quarterback, Charley Johnson, called a rollout pass to the right. To make sure the play was successful, I faked a handoff going left. After my fake, the defense froze. When they saw I didn't have the ball, they dashed to the right to pursue Charley, who tossed a long gainer to Jerry Simmons down the right sideline. At that point I was a good 40 yards from the play, watching from afar down the left sideline.

Then BAM! Out of nowhere one of their linebackers, Greg Brezina No. 50, tattooed me with the biggest cheap shot of my life. He hit me in my head from my blindside with the force of a jet propeller. Completely unnecessary. I did a cartwheel and a somersault at the same time and landed with such a thud it was like watching a piano fall 200' off a building. Wham! I was completely dazed. But I saw it was Brezina and all my hurt evaporated. I stayed in the game and went after him on two consecutive plays, drawing two flags for unnecessary roughness.

Coach Ralston pulled me aside and said, "What the heck are you doing?" I said, "Did you see what Brezina did to me? I'm going to kill that sonofabitch!" I was so furious I spent the rest of the game chasing that guy. He knew it, too, because he avoided me on every play.

I was doubly angry by the end of the game because we had lost. So I got dressed quickly and shot back over to the Falcons locker room to wait for Brezina to come out. After a half-hour, I saw Claude Humphrey. He knew who I was waiting for. "He ain't coming out, Floyd," Claude said. "He knows he screwed up."

Still, I waited. Finally, Ralston came up to me and said, "The bus is leaving. Either you get on the bus, or we're leaving Atlanta without you." Guys on my team finally had to get off the bus to haul my ass back on it. I was like a mule, kicking and screaming the whole time. I did not want to leave.

So I waited two years to pay back Brezina. Wouldn't you know, a few days before we played Atlanta I twisted my ankle and was ruled out. But I played anyway. I lasted just the first quarter before I was literally hobbling on one leg. I was even angrier two years later that I didn't get the chance to get him back.

Even Randy Gradishar came up to me and said, "Floyd, Brezina told me he's sorry. So let it go. It was two years ago!" I said, "You can let it go because it didn't happen to you." Randy told me that Brezina had found God and had become a Christian. "Well," I snarled, "I wished he had found God before he tried to take my head off!"

I believed in an eye for an eye, a tooth for a tooth. Hitting a guy like that is horseshit. The really good players never did that. Brezina's teammate Tommy Nobis never played like that. Neither did Claude Humphrey. It's been 40 years, and I'm still angry about it!

The Chief with the Biggest Hurt

I probably never got hit harder than when I played the Chiefs. That whole defense was filled with Hall of Famers—Willie Lanier, Bobby Bell, and Buck Buchanan. You felt like you were in a car crash every time you carried the ball against them. But they didn't cheap shot you. They would hit you hard then pick you up and say, "Are you alright? Don't come back here again, or the same shit will happen to you." I'd say, "Thanks for the warning. Now go get a Gatorade, you look exhausted." If you want to know what guys say between plays, that's how we talked.

One game I was running down the sideline and was tackled near the goal line. After the whistle, their defensive end, Marvin Upshaw, was frustrated and speared me in the back. Well, Buck picked up Upshaw from the jersey and said, "Don't do that shit to him. Not Floyd, he's one of us." That just shows you the mutual respect great players had for one another back then.

I loved Buck Buchanan. He was this massive guy at 6'7" and played the game with a ferocity that I admired. He played in six AFL All-Star Games and two Pro Bowls and was one of the truly dominating players. He was a great guy off the field. He passed away in 1992 when he was only 51. He died of lung cancer not long after his induction in Canton. He was gone much too soon from this life. But fans, teammates, and guys who played against him will never forget Buck.

Coach Stram to the Rescue

In my nine seasons I played the Chiefs 18 times and got to know guys like Buck Buchanan, Willie Lanier, and Bobby Bell well. We bonded at the Pro Bowl, before and after games, and during off-season charity events.

That's why a particular play against the Chiefs in a 1972 game at Arrowhead Stadium stands out so much. It was a brutal, cold day and I had rushed for about 90 yards by the end of the third quarter. Snow was swirling around, and the wind chill made it feel like minus-25.

I got the ball on an off-tackle play near the goal line and after a few yards linebacker Jim Lynch came up and grabbed my thighs. Meanwhile Curley Culp, a former teammate, had his shoulders wedged between my legs. I continued to try to lunge forward when once again defensive end Marvin Upshaw stuck his helmet under my chinstrap, hitting me backward. The impact forced my legs apart like a wishbone. I could feel my cartilage tearing, and I reacted with a blood-curdling holler. Buck and Jim saw what was happening and grabbed Marvin and Curley and yelled at them to stop. "Don't you dare hurt him," they hollered. Unbelievably, the players stopped.

As I began to fall to the ground, a couple Chiefs grabbed me and kept me from landing. I looked over and the coach was running to my aid. Not Ralston, but Hank Stram. He got there first. The game was held up for five minutes to make sure I was okay. In fact, instead of my teammates, it was Stram and a couple of the Chiefs who helped me to the sideline where I sat the final quarter.

John Ralston told me he had never seen a player garner so much compassion and respect from the opposition. "We've faced the Chiefs a lot," I said. "We respect the hell out of each other."

After the game a number of Chiefs stopped by the locker to see if I was okay. Of course, Willie also wanted to check to make sure I hadn't gained 100 yards, too.

A "Little" Snack

One of the great thrills about watching today's NFL is seeing all the sons whose fathers I played with in my era. One of them is tight end Daniel Graham, who played for the Broncos. His father, Tom, also played for the Broncos from 1972–74. Tom was a strong, tough linebacker with a lot of talent. Midway through the '74 season he had a falling out with John Ralston and was shipped to the Kansas City Chiefs. He lasted just eight games there before being traded to the Chargers the next season.

In my last game against the Chargers, I was tackled by half the San Diego defense on one play. In the middle of the pile I heard this cursing and—worse—I felt someone biting my leg. It was Tom gnawing on me like a coyote. Now why he was taking out his frustration about the Broncos on me—a year after the fact—I don't know. But more curious was how he was able to bite my leg with his helmet on!

10

MORE MEMORABLE
GAMES AND PLAYS

Insult to Injury

Even though I finished with 729 yards rushing during the 1969 season, it could have been an even bigger year than the year I led the league in 1971. It was the third season playing together with my young offensive line, and we were starting to build a cohesive rhythm. They understood the way I ran, and I was learning to be more patient. The previous season in '68 we showed glimpses of greatness. I gained 147 yards against the Patriots and 126 yards versus the Dolphins and my buddy Larry Csonka.

I started the '69 season with back-to-back 100-yard games and followed that up with more than 130 yards from scrimmage against the Chiefs and another big day against the Raiders. After five games I was the AFL's rushing leader, averaging more than 100 yards rushing per game despite missing a game due to injury.

Then we played Cincinnati in Week 6 at tiny Nippert Stadium, and I had my biggest day as a pro. It was located in the worst section of the city, but we weren't intimidated. Our offense moved the ball at will that day. I'd gain 5, 10, or 20 yards on the same play in a row. I always felt the secret to breaking a long run was to run the same play over and over. Even if you don't make many yards the first two times, you see how the defense reacts, then swoosh! You're gone. I had that kind of day against the Bengals and punctuated it with a 48-yard touchdown run after setting up the defense with the exact same play before. I rushed for 166 yards that game and suddenly was more than 300 yards ahead of every back in the AFL. I was on pace for a 1,400-yard season.

Unfortunately, after putting up 110 yards from scrimmage the next week against the Oilers, I injured my knee in Week 8 against the Chargers. I was in a cast and missed all but the last two games. It took that long for San Diego's Dickie Post to overtake my rushing total. Gale Sayers was the only player to gain 1,000 yards that season with 1,032.

Sometimes I think *What if?* about that '69 season. But injuries are part of the game. You play every play like it's your last because it just might be.

Running Smarts

Throughout my career I always played hurt. I always felt it was important to play as long as you weren't hurting your team. I believe you only get so many plays in a career, and I didn't want to leave the game thinking, *I wish I had* or *I should have*. Not me. The thing is, running backs get hit so much that you have to be able to distinguish the difference between pain and injury or you'll never suit up.

A few times I crossed the line and played when I should have been getting operated on. Looking back, I probably shouldn't have played at all during the 1970 season. I broke a bone in my vertebra the first week called the transverse process bone—it was the most painful injury I ever had. Somehow I played all 14 games and managed to lead the AFC in rushing with 901 yards. I averaged 4.3 yards a carry and would have reached 1,000 but Lou called my number just 209 times.

My best game that year was against the 49ers at old Kezar Stadium. They had a phenomenal team and just missed the Super Bowl, losing in the NFC title game. Once again we finished last. Playing a great team was motivation enough. I scored from 80 yards in the first quarter, punching through a hole on the left side. I cut across the field to the right, and no one could catch me. By halftime I had more than 100 yards rushing and finished with 140 even though we passed most of the fourth quarter as we fell short 19–14.

Looking back, it was pretty stupid to play. I was probably one shot away from living the rest of my life in a wheelchair. But I always say, if you don't want me to play, then don't put my uniform in my locker. Otherwise I'm going to do everything I can to go out on that field. To be honest, if I could live it all over, I still would have played.

Victory Snatched

It may seem strange to have a game you lost remain so vivid in your mind. But the 1972 game against the Minnesota Vikings is one of those games that affected me like few others. It was a game in which we had no business winning. When we grabbed the lead near the end it appeared there was no way we could lose.

The game had special motivation for me. Clint Jones, the first running back taken in the 1967 NFL Draft, was starting for the Vikings. I had nothing personal against Clint. I met him at Bob Hope's All-America TV special and liked him. But I constantly wanted to prove to people who doubted me that I was the better pro. Every time I strapped on a helmet, I set out to prove all the critics and naysayers who said I was too small and too old to make it in the pros wrong. It's just the way I played the game.

The other motivation was going against the relentless Vikings defense. I always believed you tested yourself against the best. That's how you know if you're any good. The Vikings were the Purple People Eaters. They supposedly devoured offenses. We were a last-place team, but I knew our fans would be behind us, so I was excited to play them.

By the second quarter the Vikings were winning 6–0. We had done little offensively, so in the next series John Ralston made a switch and Charley Johnson took over. Charley marched us down the field. With a critical third-and-3 at the 36-yard-line, Charley changed the play from a run to a quick screen to me. I caught the short pass and weaved through a handful of tacklers and turned on the afterburners for a 36-yard touchdown. We went into the half confidently ahead 7–6.

Then in the third the Vikings took control and scored 10 points to pull away 16–7. It looked like a typical Broncos game for us. Close for half the game, then we watched it slip away. When all seemed lost, we got the ball on a turnover and I turned in one of the better runs of my career.

I took a handoff deep in the backfield and cut up the middle, eluding Alan Page. I was met by linebacker Roy Winston who grabbed my jersey and held on for a couple of yards. I did a 360-degree spin and cut back to the outside. Then I traversed across the field for the final yards. I think all 11 Vikings had a chance to tackle me at one point. I must have zigzagged for twice the yards during this 27-yard touchdown. That play cut the lead to 16–14.

We got the ball back with 7:27 left in the game and put together an incredible 12-play drive. It was perfectly executed, and I could see the Vikings players were getting frustrated. I finished off the drive with my third touchdown of the game to take a 20–16 lead with just 58 seconds left. The Mile High crowd went nuts. The Vikings needed a miracle.

They had one by the name of Francis Asbury Tarkenton. He quickly moved the Vikings 63 yards in 45 seconds, completing 3-of-4 passes. The last was for 31 yards to Gene Washington who beat a hobbling Randy Montgomery for a dramatic 23–20 win with seconds left.

I was speechless after the game. It was the first time where I felt like I couldn't have done more. I scored three touchdowns, gained 100 yards on 18 carries, and had another 39 yards receiving. Usually with a loss I'd walk off the field thinking, *I could have gained one more yard or made one more block.* This time was different. I sat with my head in my hands in the locker room for almost 20 minutes. I was upset because my best wasn't good enough. I remember yelling to no one in particular, "What do we have to do to win around here?" It was perhaps the most bitterly frustrating loss of my career. I was told afterward that Vikings coach Bud Grant kept repeating, "That Little is some back!" My one small consolation was I outgained Clint Jones 100 yards to 7. But he left Mile High Stadium with a win, and I didn't.

One-Yard Wonder

It seems crazy, but one of the best touchdowns of my career was a 1-yard run against the 49ers. It was 1973, and we were in one of those shootouts at Mile High. Late in the game I got the ball on a straight dive play. I was supposed to go inside Marv Montgomery's block. But his opponent got past him, and Marv inadvertently pushed him into me. I quickly bounced to the outside and was hit at the 3-yard line by the 49ers Pro Bowl corner-back Bruce Taylor. He tagged me hard underneath the shoulder pads and began to push me back. I sank my legs down low and started pumping my feet. It was a test of wills—two No. 44s out on an island, fighting for the end zone. No one was within five yards. Slowly I started to gain an advantage, but Taylor continued to fight. I pushed him back to the 2, the 1, and finally lowered my shoulder and drove him into the end zone. Teammates say it was the darnedest thing they ever saw. I went from losing three yards to scoring a clutch touchdown. They engulfed me in the end zone. It gave us a short-lived 34–33 advantage. Predictably, the 49ers kicked the winning field goal minutes later.

Brownouts

Except for that Vikings game which still stings, I try to focus on the wins. In my nine seasons, the Broncos went a paltry 47–73–6. But every once in a while there were games that we not only won, we dominated. One of those was at the Cleveland Browns in 1971. The game had all the signs of a classic upset. They were a perennial playoff team, and a couple of years earlier during the merger talks, Browns owner Art Modell made the comment that his Browns would never play in a losing AFL city like Denver and that he certainly wouldn't allow "those Denver Donkeys" to come to his grand Municipal Stadium. Lou had saved all those comments and tacked them onto our bulletin board. He was a former Browns star and took great offense.

Our passing game was non-existent at that point, so Lou's philosophy was simple. "We're going to ram the ball down their goddamn throats," he roared before the game. And that's what we did. It was a perfect day for smash-mouth football—overcast, rain, and plenty of mud. We ran the ball 30 times in the first half and built a 24–0 lead. The Browns couldn't stop us. And our defense was superb. They intercepted three passes and held the Browns entire running game to 24 yards.

I gained 113 yards, and by the fourth quarter we were up by more than three touchdowns, so Lou sat me down in the fourth quarter and I cursed him for it. Despite being mad, it was great to see the other backs on the team get some reps. Fullback Bobby Anderson, a Colorado legend in his own right, gained 71 yards. But I was happiest for my roommate and backup halfback, Fran Lynch, who got to pound the rock for 53 yards. By game's end we had rammed the ball down their throats to the tune of 280 rushing yards.

I even got in a wrestling match with Browns defensive tackle Walter Johnson. He wouldn't let me up after a run, and we started going at it. Fred Swearingen was the umpire, and I think he took special delight in seeing a little guy get the best of a defensive tackle. He didn't even throw a flag.

By the fourth quarter it was 27–0, and it started pouring. They had no recourse but to try to pass, and we knocked the snot out of them. The 27–0 victory was the first time the Browns had been shut out since the early 1950s. That's 274 games—an NFL record. We were yelling, "Hee-Haw!" at them. This great playoff team was getting embarrassed at home by the Denver "Donkeys." It was like a championship game for us.

I don't know how we got home safely. We were jumping up and down on the plane ride home, racing up and down the aisle. The pilot was no doubt nervous. It was the first victory in a long line of huge wins over the Browns. Fittingly, it also was Lou Saban's last win as Broncos coach.

11

MILE HIGH SENDOFF

My Final Season

Looking back on my final season as a Bronco, I'm still amazed that it ended on such a high note. At 33, I was ancient for a running back. My painful Achilles injury had forced me to surrender the starting job to Otis Armstrong the previous season, and I told John Ralston that I would come back for one more year and do whatever the team needed me to do. I was happy to play special teams, return kicks—I didn't care.

I trained just as hard in the off-season, but when you're no longer mentally focused on starting, your whole mindset changes. That's why when I hear athletes teetering on whether to play another season, I know that mentally they're already shutting down. I figured I'd carry the ball maybe 15–20 times the whole season. I was already among the Top 10 all-time rushers, so I didn't care about adding to my total.

I went through the first few games in 1975 returning kickoffs. In the third game we felt we could run the screen well against the Bills, so I came in and scored on a 35-yard play from Charley Johnson. I jogged off the field satisfied that it was going to be my last NFL touchdown. Then Otis tore his hamstring the next week against the Steelers and was done for the year. Suddenly, I was back in the lineup. It took me a few games to get back to the mentality of being a starter.

We played the Chiefs, and I rushed for 58 yards, had 13 receiving yards, and another 14 yards on kickoff returns. Then we played the Bengals, and I had 86 yards from scrimmage and a touchdown. A couple weeks later against the Falcons I combined for 119 yards from scrimmage, including 5.3 yards a carry. Mentally and physically I was playing as well as a 33-year-old running back could perform, considering most backs hang it up before age 30. Unfortunately, our injury report was mounting. We were losing more and more guys and games.

Pregame Emotions

By the time I suited up for my final home game at Mile High Stadium against the Philadelphia Eagles, we were a disappointing 5–7 and had lost a dozen players, including six starters, the biggest was Charley Johnson.

The week before the Eagles game I started getting a slew of cards and telegrams from former players and coaches. Local and national sportswriters wrote articles. Dolphins linebacker Nick Buoniconti sent me a great article about me by *Miami-Herald* writer Edwin Pope. I think Dick Connor of the *Denver Post* and Chet Nelson of the *Rocky Mountain News* wrote a column a day about me. But the majority of the well-wishes were from fans. Many of them thanked me for representing the Denver Broncos so well for nine seasons. Some thanked me for saving the franchise. Some simply told me that I was their hero and a true role model for kids. It was an emotional week for an emotional guy. I'm a Cancer in the Zodiac world. My birthday is July 4. Cancers cry watching cell phone commercials. *Brian's Song?* Forget it. I need 12 dozen tissues.

The Final Good-Bye at Mile High

As I was introduced for the final time I remember marveling at the stands being filled despite the frigid 18-degree weather. It was the week before Christmas, and we weren't playing for anything. But the fans were bundled up and cheering like it was Opening Day.

There were all kinds of signs. One of them had my face on the body of Superman. Another read, "No one can ever replace our 'Little' gap." My eyes were already welling up. When I got to the sideline before the game, I was hugged by Billy Thompson, Charley, Fran Lynch, Lyle Alzado,

Rick Upchurch, and the rest of the team. A couple of Eagles, Harold Carmichael and Bill Bergey, ran over to wish me good luck. "The NFL will miss you," Bergey said. Harold added, "You've been a great pro and have the respect and admiration of everyone in the league." I almost started bawling right there.

The game had a magical atmosphere. Snow had fallen, and flurries continued throughout the game. By halftime we were up 10–7 thanks to a Jim Turner field goal and a touchdown by my roommate, Fran Lynch. I had gained only 12 yards, and any butterflies I had before the game were gone.

John Ralston decided that we were going to start the third quarter by running the ball. Jon Keyworth and I ran the ball seven times in a row before Billy Van Heusen had to punt. I finally started to feel comfortable. Near the end of the third quarter, the game was tied 10–10 and we had the ball on our own 34.

At this point we were having fun in the huddle. Since Charley was ruled out of the game, the guys were yelling for backup quarterback Steve Ramsey to run plays behind them. "Give me Folks," they'd say. "Let Folks run behind me. I'll carry his geriatric ass." A screen pass play came in and I immediately got excited. I said half-joking, "Hey, this is a great play. Make your blocks because I'm taking it all the way." The funny thing was that deep down I believed it. Throughout my career I always excelled at screen plays. Most of my receiving touchdowns came on screen passes that I turned into big runs. Over my career I averaged 42 yards per touchdown reception! Screen passes gave me the space I needed for my cutbacks.

I always thought my success in turning screen passes into big gainers was something that only I noticed. That's until a couple years back when Tom interviewed Coach Mike McCormack, a Hall of Fame lineman, and the Eagles coach that day. Mike said this about me:

"In my opinion, Floyd was as good as I've ever seen at perfecting the screen pass. He helped establish it as a dangerous play—with his ability to encase the pass and turn it into a game-breaking play. He was just phenomenal at executing that play—and he did it against us [the Eagles] at Denver in the snow."

The thing I remember about catching Steve Ramsey's perfect floater was my linemen were still behind me. I teased them about it later. Right away I was like a scuba diver in shark-infested waters. I had Eagles coming after me from all directions. I made a couple guys miss, then Billy Van Heusen threw a great block and Haven Moses moved out in front to lead me down the right sideline. When I got to the 30, several Eagles had an angle on me so I cut back to the inside and headed for the goalposts. The last Eagle dove at my legs around the 10 and missed as I galloped into the end zone. The touchdown went for 66 yards, and I was mobbed by my teammates. The noise at Mile High climbed an extra 10 decibels as we took the lead.

Later in the fourth quarter I scored again from two yards out on a sweep to make it 25–10. Bill Bergey helped me to my feet and said, "Great game, my friend." After a rather pedestrian beginning, I finished with 150 yards from scrimmage and two touchdowns. As the final minutes of the game ticked down, I lost it.

When you're drowning they say your whole life passes in front of you. As the two-minute warning sounded, I realized my career was finally coming to an end. I just stared at the clock and my teammates. You start playing when you're a kid and now you're 33 and you realize it's over. Mentally I was ready to leave. I could have stuck around and padded my stats like some running backs have done, but I was never about the yards or the records. I cared most about the game, about winning, and doing everything I could for the good of the team. In those final few moments, Ralston put his arm around me and tears streamed down my face. There's a great picture of that moment that hung in the Pro Football Hall of Fame. It was on a large plaque with another photo of me being carried off the field moments later. Two burly fans hoisted me on their shoulders and led me off the field for the final time at Mile High.

That was surreal. I've seen coaches and players carried off a field by teammates but never by fans. That was the single greatest moment of my career, and it came at the end. Being carried off by the greatest fans in the world on my last game at Mile High Stadium is something I'll cherish until the day I die.

In the locker room every player and person in the Broncos organization congratulated me. Players and coaches were asking for my chinstrap, shoes, elbow pads, you name it. I happily obliged. I was the last to leave, and as I walked out a limousine pulled up and out popped Charley Johnson dressed as a chauffeur. "Your car, sir," he said. Inside sat my wife. They had planned a farewell party for me at a nearby hotel. It was an extravagant affair with coaches, players, and wives. There was great food and even an ice sculpture with the No. 44 jersey. We all stayed late, laughing and talking about the game and funny things that happened through the years.

The players gave me a special gift that I still carry with me almost everywhere I go. A Bible signed by every member of the team. When I'm not reading it or studying verses, every so often I spend time just looking at the names. Remembering all those teammates of mine who gave everything they had. Teammates who were instrumental in helping me get to Canton. Teammates, some of them no longer with us, that I won't ever forget.

The Selfless Hero

The person who really stood out for me in my last game at Mile High was Charley Johnson. Here was a guy who was one of the best and still the most overlooked quarterback of my generation. People didn't realize that this, too, was his final game at Mile High Stadium. He played 15 great seasons. He led the league in passing a few times, and he made the Cardinals competitive during the 1960s. And a year after he came to Denver in 1972, Charley led the Broncos to their first winning season in franchise history.

While Charley played professional football, he also got his doctorate in chemical engineering and was an active-duty officer in the United States Army. He would drive to his army post on Saturdays and play on Sundays. If he played today, Charley would be talked about like Tim Tebow regarding his too-good-to-be-true character.

Needless to say, Charley was the epitome of professionalism. He should have been sharing the limelight with me. Instead he humbly and unselfishly took a backseat. Charley was just an amazing person for doing that. Today he continues to be one of my best friends. We touch base a few times a year, and I'm not happy until I see his smiling face at our Alumni weekend.

Miami, Not So Nice

Although that memorable game at Mile High Stadium was my last home game, people forget there was still another game to play the following Saturday at Miami. As it turned out, I wish the game had never been played. We lost to the Dolphins 14–13 when, in typical Broncos fashion, Jim Turner's game-winning field-goal attempt was blocked. Charley Johnson was the holder, and I felt horrible that his last play was spent running after a loose ball. Meanwhile, I had stood on the sideline for most of the game after severely twisting my ankle early in the second quarter. Charley, sore shoulder and all, was told he could go in for one play at quarterback to hand off. "Nah," he said, "I'd probably try to throw long."

Miles away in Wilmington, Delaware, a 12-year-old boy cried on his living-room floor after that game. He was upset that his hero's career was over and that it ended with a loss. That boy was Tom Mackie. Little did anyone know that someday this kid would become my hero.

Vrrrooom, the Car Business

After I hung up my cleats for the final time, I focused on what I was going to do for the rest of my life. A reporter for *Sports Illustrated* asked me what I was going to do next, and I told him, "I'm 33 years old; I'm not going to wait around for the NFL to take care of me."

Actually, I thought the Broncos would just hire me as an assistant coach or to work in the front office, but that never happened. I had gone to night school during the past few seasons to get a law degree from the University of Denver's College of Law. The intent was to become a Juvenile Court Judge. But after graduating and seeing all the kids who faced trouble, I didn't want to be the guy who might have to send someone to jail. So I became a distributor at Coors for a couple years, but that didn't excite me.

Then I found a Ford Motor Executive Management Training Program and decided that's what I wanted to do. I had always loved cars, and the thought of owning a dealership really appealed to me. So I learned everything: sales, marketing, accounting, financing, and purchasing. I brought a Lincoln-Mercury dealership in Englewood, Colorado, then I moved to Los Angeles and had a dealership in Santa Barbara and then West Covina. In 1990, I had the opportunity to buy my first Ford dealership in

Seattle and moved there. I owned Pacific Coast Ford for the next 20 years. Finally, the economy bottomed out a few years back after 32 successful years in the business, and I had no choice but to sell it back to Ford in 2009. I retired as the longest-tenured minority owner in Ford's portfolio.

12

POSITIVELY OLD SCHOOL

The Obvious Question

There are a lot of great things about today's game. Obviously, dozens of rule changes over the years give offenses a big advantage over defenses. Naturally, fans and people in the media ask me, "Do you think so-and-so could have played in today's era?" I just laugh. I'm sorry, but I've got the old-school mindset. I reply, "Shit, the better question is could he have played in our era!" Don't get me wrong, today's players are bigger, faster, and stronger. But are they tougher? I think if you go back and look at some of the incredible guys who played in my era, it would be difficult to say today's players are tougher.

I could probably write a whole book on the differences between today's game and my era. Instead, I'd just like to point out some of the more interesting things I've noticed.

Shoes Glorious Shoes

Years ago, I took a tour of the Broncos facility at Dove Valley. Boy, oh, boy was that impressive. The players have everything you can imagine. They have three outdoor practice fields: one with grass, one heated, and the third the latest carpeted turf. There's also an indoor field covered with that new plush Field Turf. A fully catered cafeteria, brand new weight room, a training room with three large whirlpool baths, players lounges, and game rooms with Web hookups, a sweet locker room, and separate meeting rooms for every position, including larger rooms for team meetings. There was even an old photo of me in the training room. I just want to go on record saying I wasn't in the training room that much!

I'm sure every team in the NFL has a similar setup. But I can't imagine any of them nicer than the Broncos. I'm proud to see how much the organization has grown over the years. I know some of the things seem unnecessary, like game rooms, but I think that's to keep the players around one another as much as possible to increase their opportunities to bond. Obviously our training facility was nothing like that. It was more like a series of huts—like where'd you go if you had detention.

But the thing about Dove Valley that stood out most to me was the shoes. Every player seemed to have a dozen or so different pairs. We had only one! We wore the same cleats in practice as we did for games. We just washed the dirt off 'em. If the field was soggy, we didn't change into longer cleats. We unscrewed the shorter cleats and screwed in the longer ones. It reminded me of an episode of *The Simpsons* where Marge is in New York City and she's mesmerized by a line of new shoes in a store window. "Wow, look at all the shoes," she sighs. "Too bad I've already got a pair!"

Third-and-Five Guy?

As I was winding up my career, the NFL was already changing. There were some running backs in the league who were becoming specialists. The Colts had a guy, Don McCauley, who was like that. He'd come into the game on third downs and was usually the main target on a swing pass or some draw. I was asked if I'd consider coming back as a specialist. Since I never considered myself a part-time player, I declined. I'm sure if I had I could have extended my career a few years. I may have even played in the Broncos' first Super Bowl in 1977, or I could have gone to another team, like Calvin Hill did with the Browns. But once I was a Bronco, I wanted to remain a Bronco. I didn't want to play for anyone else, and I definitely didn't want to pad my totals as a role player. I take great pride in that I was an every-down back and I was still returning kicks in my final game.

John Madden said he admired me because I could run, catch, block, and return kicks. And Jack Ham called me "the most complete back" he ever played against.

Now you've got third-and-five guys and short-yardage guys. Everyone's a role player it seems. Case in point, until Peyton Hillis finally did it in 2008, I was the last Broncos running back to have a 100-yard receiving day when I had 127 yards receiving 34 years earlier in 1974 vs. the Chargers. That's significant.

It's the same with guys playing defense. I was listening to ESPN's *Mike and Mike in the Morning* last fall, and Mike Golic was trying to downplay the Broncos 18-point comeback win over the Dolphins in Tim Tebow's dramatic first start. It was evident he was a Tebow hater. Couldn't give the guy credit for anything. He tried to explain that when Tim ran in the two-point conversion to send it to overtime, which, by the way, the whole world knew he was going to run, the reason he scored wasn't because the kid made a great play but because, as Golic said, "The Dolphins didn't have their tacklers in the game." Really?

A Runner's Game

I would love to carry the ball in today's NFL, especially when the Broncos implemented the zone-blocking scheme. I remember Clinton Portis had rushed for more than 1,500 yards and averaged 5.5 yards per carry in each of his first two seasons with the Broncos behind the zone scheme. Then the next year he got traded to the Redskins, who were still running the old counter trey, and Portis' average plummeted to 3.8. Don't get me wrong, Portis had a terrific career, and I'm a fan, but he was never able to duplicate the numbers he put up while playing in the Broncos zone scheme.

In my day, very rarely did you see a clear lane to run and, even better, a backside lane to cut back. Today's game is more finesse. Our linemen couldn't use their hands. You fired off and went helmet to helmet. You blocked with your shoulders and arms, not with your hands. You couldn't extend your arms. Today it's all about positioning and technique. You can basically hold; it's just the interpretation of holding. You see guys hook their hands and arms around players' outside shoulders and move them to an area. Linemen in our era had to keep their hands and forearms close to their chests like priests.

It's tougher for defenders to stop offenses these days. When I was tackled it was usually up around the neck or helmet. That shortened your career. Fortunately, they changed it and now you can't tackle that high. But you can't really play bump and run against receivers, and you can't even lay a lick on the quarterback anymore.

Moving the hash marks to midfield changed the game a lot, too. That happened in 1972, after I turned 30. It gave offenses more room to either side. Willie Lanier said it made his job as a middle linebacker tougher because you had to cover more space. It also was the first rule change to increase the number of 1,000-yard rushers. When I led the NFL in '71, I was only the 13th back in history to gain 1,000 yards. We had a banquet and everything. Then in '72, they moved the hash marks closer to midfield, and 10 rushers got 1,000 yards that year.

More records went out the window in 1978 when the regular season was extended from 14 to 16 games. And in the early 1980s, Redskins coach Joe Gibbs went to a one-back offense so he could have an extra blocker to combat the likes of Lawrence Taylor. Teams followed, and suddenly fullbacks were no longer splitting carries, they were just blocking. Tailbacks went from carrying the ball 200 times a season to more than 300 and sometimes 400.

That's why it's so hard to compare eras. We played under a completely different set of rules, and every year it seems the NFL gives offenses more advantages because people like to see touchdowns, not great defensive struggles. I'd love to see the NFL reinstitute some rules to help the defense. Can you imagine an announcement like, "In order to halt the excessive holding by offensive linemen, we're bringing back the head slap!" I think Tombstone Rich Jackson would scramble to go find his helmet in the attic.

The NFL's Black Eye Finally Getting Attention

Baseball is no longer our national pastime. Football has replaced it and continues to be the nation's greatest sport. The NFL is the only league that does it the right way with revenue sharing and a salary cap. The only guaranteed money is your signing bonus—the rest you have to earn. I think fans like that approach because they can relate to it. That's how the real world works.

Still, guys are able to earn incredible incomes as NFL players. They don't have to work in the off-season like we did. And I don't have to go into detail to know how many billions of dollars the NFL makes. In my first book I talked about how, as former players, we helped pave the way for this amazing level of prosperity. We sacrificed our bodies and our well-being by playing in the most violent sport of them all. Yet our health benefits and pensions were dramatically less than those in any of the major sports. It had become the NFL's black eye.

I've been lucky. I got out of the game when I was relatively healthy. I didn't wait around for the NFL to take care of me; I worked hard for 30 years to achieve financial security. But many guys have not been so fortunate. They have serious financial problems and do not have the money to pay mounting health-care costs from their playing days. Many have crippling diseases. Remember Johnny Unitas a few years back before he passed away? He was the NFL's greatest quarterback who helped grow the sport in the 1950s. He had to have both knees replaced, and he couldn't even pick up a fork with his throwing hand because the middle three fingers didn't work. But when he needed money to cover these expenses, the NFL turned its back on him, citing some stipulation that he didn't file until after he was 55. It made me sick.

Finally, in the new collective bargaining agreement (CBA), some of the money was put in a Legacy Fund to help players from previous generations (those who retired before 1993) deal with mounting medical bills and health-care issues. The new CBA contributed $620 million to the Legacy Fund. Over the next 10 years it promises additional funding for retiree benefits between $900 million and $1 billion. CBA also promised to make improvements to post-career medical options, the disability plan, the 88 Plan (known as the John Mackey Plan), career transition, and degree completion programs, as well as the Player Care Plan.

I'm not going to shout a big hallelujah because it's been long overdue. I do think it's a good start. But there's more to be done.

Good friends like Dave Duerson and guys like Andre Waters have taken their own lives, due in large part to chronic traumatic encephalopathy—known as CTE. It's a degenerative and incurable disease that compromises neural activity and is linked to memory loss, depression, and dementia. It's the same trauma-induced disease found in many deceased players, including my friend, the great Cookie Gilchrist. And I can tell you there are probably hundreds more. I know Dave had complained about headaches, blurred vision, and he couldn't remember things like what he had for breakfast the day before. In his suicide note he even wrote: "Please see that my brain is given to the NFL's brain bank."

I know the NFL gave $1 million to financing research after it acknowledged long-term effects of football brain trauma, but I hope they do more. Our life expectancy is only 58, a good 15 years below the national average. Many of us are divorced. Some have battled alcohol and drugs. Still, we're directly responsible for the success of the league.

The sad truth is that a lot of people became rich from the NFL. Our generation hasn't benefited like the later ones.

The NFL Code

There is a code in the NFL about being a professional. I believe it still exists today despite all the talk by some current player about being "entertainers." Regardless of our record, my teammates were dedicated to working hard each week to get better. We took our status as professional athletes seriously. We worked hard to be prepared for each opponent and gave it our all. Players who dogged it in practice, who forgot plays, or didn't go all out did not last in the NFL. When I saw guys quitting in practice or in the fourth quarter, I didn't want to play with them anymore.

No matter the score I always looked at how we played in the final quarter. Who went all out until the final whistle? It's an attitude that you looked for in players on other teams, too. Players simply collecting a paycheck were not respected and held little value.

I was proud that my teammates upheld that code. They played with character and pride. They were incredible team players who cared about you. If there was one thing players in the league knew about me was that I went all out. I played every play as if it was my last—even in preseason.

One time against the Colts in an exhibition game, a rookie punt returner on our team got hurt. No one would go in. So I grabbed my helmet and returned a punt 89 yards for a touchdown. I was in my thirties, and people made a big deal that a "star" would volunteer to return a punt during a nothing game. I looked at it like, "That's what I got paid to do." Guys around the league respected me. They'd tell me, "You never quit." That meant more to me than anything.

13

SUPER BOWLS AND THE FINAL, FINAL GAME AT MILE HIGH

Super Fan

In the 35-plus years since I retired, I've continued to be a diehard Broncos fan. I became a season-ticket holder after I retired, and I was there with other Broncos fans when we won those two spectacular playoff games at Mile High in 1977 to reach the Super Bowl. I was even in line the day after to get Super Bowl tickets. I waited in line for four hours in frigid 10-degree weather and came up empty. The Broncos didn't give me any tickets, and the team only allocated so many to season-ticket holders, so I waited in line like everyone else. Fans couldn't believe it. One guy said, "If Floyd Little can't get Super Bowl tickets, how the hell can I?" and he left. The Phipps owned the team then, and even though they were good owners, they didn't always treat former players well.

Since Pat Bowlen became the owner in 1984, things improved. He developed the Ring of Fame to honor former players and has enthusiastically embraced the alumni network. I thank him for that. But as you will read later in the book, the Broncos organization has made some questionable decisions recently on the way they have treated me and, I'm sure, other former players who deserve better.

Shut Up and Eat Your Hot Dog

After missing out on the Broncos first Super Bowl, I went to Super Bowl XXI in Pasadena and sat with Sam Brunelli, my Broncos teammate and Jack Kemp, the former Bills quarterback and senator.

We were sitting in the end zone when the Broncos had that first-and-goal at the 1-yard line before halftime. They tried three runs and lost yardage each time, then missed an extra point–length field goal. Before the last play, a sweep to the left side, I knew we weren't going to make it. I could see it in the linemen's eyes as they walked up to the line of scrimmage. They had no confidence in the play. I remember thinking, *Why are we trying a sweep? We just need a yard.* I was getting ticked. My competitive juices were flowing. I started shouting, "Give me the damn ball. I'll get that yard. I don't even need linemen." Jack started laughing, knowing all too well about my intense playing days. Sam shook his head. He told me to shut up and eat my hot dog. "Folks, you can't play anymore. You're 44, and I'm not talking about your old jersey number."

We Won?

I went to see the Broncos face the Washington Redskins in San Diego for Super Bowl XXII, and I was in New Orleans for the brutal loss to the 49ers in XXIV. That's what made Super Bowl XXXII the greatest sporting experience of my life as a fan. Even if you're not a Broncos fan, if you saw the reaction on the Broncos bench when linebacker John Mobley knocked away that last Brett Favre pass to secure Denver's first World Championship, you had to get goosebumps. Personally, I wept like a baby. I think the Broncos were 12-point underdogs and were up against the Green Bay Packers, the epitome of NFL supremacy during my era.

You couldn't have written a better script for John. The 15-year veteran, 0–3 in previous Super Bowls during the 1980s, earned perhaps his one last shot at glory against the reigning Super Bowl Champions in the city that crushed his team 10 years earlier.

Once again I attended the game. But this time the only reason I needed someone to hold me down was to keep me from floating away. Like a lot of fans and former Broncos players, I felt like I had also finally won a Super Bowl. Terrell Davis had a game for the ages, as did the offense, defense, and special teams. All the loyalty and frustration we experienced and endured through the years came pouring out of us in an eruption of utter joy, especially since we won so dramatically at the end.

I think fans and everyone who had ever played for the Broncos had to pinch themselves—simultaneously. To see John carried off the field amidst streams of confetti and fireworks was amazing. I didn't sleep a second that night. I remember catching ESPN later after the game, and there was Tom Jackson, sitting with Chris Berman, misty-eyed and prouder than the NBC peacock. Chris gave a champagne toast to Tom and Broncos fans. The Super Bowl victory the following year was great, too. It further validated the Broncos as one of the true marquee teams in the NFL. But that first championship was a reawakening of the thrill and camaraderie from years of pure devotion to a team.

Blown Away

I have known John Elway since his rookie season with the Broncos in 1983. The team sponsored a Broncos cruise for fans. I spent time getting to know that generation's Broncos like John, Keith Bishop, Dave Studdard, and Steve Watson. We had a good time and visited different ports during the trip. One day we saw an advertisement for parasailing. This was 1984 when it was popular. I wanted to try it but I'm afraid of heights, so I declined. A few of the younger Broncos were ready to do it, too—until the parasailing instructor casually announced that the waters were pretty shark-infested. I was thinking, *If John decides to do it—we owe it to the organization to pick him up and throw him back in the boat before he puts the parachute on.*

The thing I liked right away about John was that he treated everyone the same. John made a point to get to know not just me but a lot of the former Broncos. He was hounded by the media to the point where they were reporting on what kind of candy he gave out on Halloween. But it never affected his performance on the field. He had the best arm I'd ever seen, and he made plays that a robo-quarterback couldn't make. John got into the car business after me, and we used to give each other a hard time about who was the better salesman.

Whenever I hosted a charity event, John would graciously sign a few items for me. And I'd participate in his golf tournament each year. I know he respected me as a former player, but I never knew how much until after the Broncos beat the Packers.

During his golf tournament that spring, I was told to stop by his hotel room for an impromptu party. I came into his room and there was a crowd of people. Somehow John saw me and pushed through the crowd. He gave me a hug and thanked me for laying the foundation in the Broncos organization. I looked around like, "Is he talking to me?" He said that without my signing and the impact I had on the team that the Broncos would never have stayed in Denver. I was shocked and speechless, which is unbelievable because by now you know I can talk! My glasses looked like they just went through a car wash. I was so overcome with joy that all I remember was uttering some words of thanks and running out, so I didn't flood the room with my tears. Boy, oh boy. I'll never forget it. In my mind John's the greatest quarterback of his era, including Dan Marino and Joe Montana.

The Final, Final Farewell

I had mixed emotions when it was announced they wanted to tear down Mile High Stadium. I understood that the stadium was more than 50 years old. But it was still the shrine where all that Rocky Mountain magic happened—usually as the sun began to set and the sky was a blazing orange.

Everyone remembers all those incredible last-second, John Elway–orchestrated comebacks there, but I held similar memories from my playing days. I had arguably the greatest—and the worst—game of my life at Mile High against Buffalo. I set a Broncos record with 295 combined yards and still got fired. It was also the scene of the infamous Half-Loaf game, the Broncos first *Monday Night Football* game, the NFL's first regular season overtime game, and my final home game when I was carried off the field. After I hung up my cleats, the Red Miller "Orange Crush" Broncos continued the magic at Mile High. In 1977, the Broncos beat the AFC's two dominating teams, the Steelers and the Raiders, to go to the franchise's first Super Bowl.

I've been to Sports Authority Field at Mile High a number of times. It's a magnificent facility. I'm sure all the corporate suits enjoy the view and the delicious cuisine from their luxury suites. Heck, I even came back to campaign for the new stadium to help get the deal passed as a favor to the Broncos. But when I look out the window on the outside of Sports Authority Field and see where Mile High used to stand—that hallowed ground now a 120-yard plus parking lot—it saddens me a bit.

Field of Dreams

As big a treat as it was for the fans to watch some of their legendary Broncos play one final game—albeit a flag football game—at Mile High against NFL legends Joe Montana, Roger Craig, Dave Krieg, and William "The Refrigerator" Perry, I think it was an even bigger thrill for us players.

It was surreal to be reunited with teammates like BT, Rick Upchurch, Randy Gradishar, Riley Odoms, Haven Moses, Louis Wright, Barney Chavous, Bobby Anderson, and Steve Foley. And it was like an out-of-body experience to line up with younger guys Mark Jackson, Vance Johnson, Craig Morton, Karl Mecklenburg, Dave Studdard, Keith Kartz, and, of course, John Elway.

The thing I'll always remember about that week of practice was catching footballs from John. I couldn't believe how hard that guy could throw. And he was retired! Steve Watson used to joke about the Elway Cross. How John would throw the ball so hard that the point of the ball would leave a cross impression on receivers' chests. When I heard that I thought, *Well, you're not supposed to catch the ball with your chest, you're supposed to catch it with your hands.* I quickly learned that was impossible with John. I thought perhaps the best way to catch passes from him was to let the defensive back try to catch it first and then grab the pop-up.

The finale was fun because it was sandlot football. We diagrammed plays in the huddle and teased each other unmercifully. There also was a lot of gamesmanship, wisecracking, and even talking a little smack. Imagine an older guy like me talking smack with a young guy like Everson Walls! He must have been like, "Old man, drink your Ovaltine."

Despite being the oldest guy there, I may have surprised a few people. I could still play. I had participated in charity flag football games in recent years, playing in the Margarita Bowl in Phoenix with guys such as Tony Dorsett, Billy "White Shoes" Johnson, and Jim Plunkett.

With two minutes left in the finale, I experienced John's last two-minute drill ever. Down 27–26, John threaded a nice 15-yard touchdown pass to me to pull us ahead 32–27. I remember it was the same end zone where I had scored my final touchdown. We went for two and, just like in Cleveland during The Drive, John completed the pass to Mark Jackson. Then with about a minute left, the NFL legends scored on a long pass and went for two to win. Even with the game on the line, we were laughing on the sideline as they lined up in the wishbone. "Where's Barry Switzer?" I joked. They fumbled the ball, and we ran out the clock.

I'm honored to say that I got the final carry at Mile High Stadium, taking a handoff from John's 12-year-old son, Jack. The final score: Broncos legends 34, NFL legends 33. We all stayed on the field as fireworks ensued. It was the perfect sendoff for a grand, grand stadium.

14

BRONCOS FANS,
THE WORLD'S GREATEST

Standing Up for the Broncos

After leading the NFL in rushing in 1971, the Pro Bowl rosters were announced. I figured several Broncos deserved recognition: Rich Jackson, Dave Costa, and Billy Thompson on defense; and offensive linemen Larron Jackson and Mike Current. After all, I didn't lead the NFL without my line's help.

To my shock, I was the only Bronco selected. And, incredibly, I was an alternate. How was that possible? I was disgusted. I checked the AFC roster and the Chiefs had nine players, the Dolphins and Colts had seven, and the Raiders had six. No team had fewer Pro Bowlers than the Broncos.

At the Pro Bowl luncheon before the game, Bob Lilly and I were there to represent the two conferences. The national press only asked Bob questions and ignored me for the entire luncheon. Finally, the host said, "Thanks everyone for coming," then looked over and saw me. "Oh, wait a minute," he said. "We've got Floyd Little here from the AFC. Floyd, do you have anything to say?"

Some media had already left. I got up and said, "Well, that's about right. Once again the AFC has gotten no respect, especially the Denver Broncos. I can't believe I'm the only Bronco chosen by the media. This is supposed to be the Pro Bowl—the best players from each team and conference. There are nine Chiefs here and one of them—my friend Buck Buchanan—has been hurt most of the year. The Broncos are so disrespected we've never even been on *Monday Night Football*."

One reporter said we weren't on because Mile High Stadium didn't have any lights, which was a lie. "Did you ever hear of an away game?" I replied. My tirade went on for another five minutes as I passionately defended my team.

The next day the headlines read, "Little wants to be traded." A reporter had taken everything I said out of context. The Broncos front office got some calls, and even some teammates believed the story.

But some guys like Larron Jackson defended me. "C'mon," he said, "this is Folks. He loves us. He would never say those things."

That night I was supposed to accept the award for Pro Athlete of the Year from the Colorado Sports Hall of Fame. I was afraid to go and get booed. Bob Peck, the Broncos PR director, told me that people who knew me realized it wasn't true and, if anything, this was the perfect forum to set the record straight. I was afraid of what I might say to defend myself. I had a colorful speech all prepared just in case. But when I walked out to accept the award, not only did no one boo me, I got a standing ovation for five minutes. People were chanting, "We love you, Floyd!" I was about to cry. I had never been so surprised in my life.

Bob looked at me and said, "See, I told you."

A Day in My Honor

I always knew the Broncos fans and the city of Denver appreciated the way I stuck with the team my entire career and how they could always count on me to play my heart out whatever the score. They also admired my community work, which was something that came natural to me. I had to overcome many obstacles as a child, so I have a special attachment to kids. I still make speeches all over the country. Of course, first I show them a clip of who I was so they know a little bit about this short, stocky, bowlegged older gent standing in front of them.

When the city of Denver honored me with Floyd Little Day on October 29, 1972, for my impact on and off the field, I was so taken back that I felt like royalty. It was held at Mile High Stadium before a game with the Cleveland Browns. I remember the announcement was made at the Broncos Quarterback Club luncheon the week after that wretched last-second loss to the Vikings. It was one of the best pick-me-ups of my life.

I was given all kinds of incredible gifts from friends and teammates, including a set of golf clubs. I made a speech, thanking the fans, and I looked over at my wife and baby girl, Christy, and my eyes welled up like an over-watered fern. I was grateful for the ceremony and the opportunity to thank the great Denver fans. The game was emotional, too, because Rich Jackson had just been traded to Cleveland and I knew he wanted to give me a special "hello" smack. On one play Rich had a chance to grab me on a quick screen from Charley, but I cut past him and scored on a 19-yard catch and run. On the way back I smacked him on his ass, "You missed me!" He laughed and said, "You dirty dog."

In the following years I was recognized nationally for humanitarian service, winning the YMCA's Brian Piccolo award in 1973 and the prestigious Byron "Whizzer" White award in 1974. I also was the first Bronco to have a ceremony to officially retire my number and was among the first inducted in the Ring of Fame. In 2010, I was finally inducted into Canton. These honors all meant a great deal to me. But none meant as much as Floyd Little Day because that came from the fans.

The Fans

The thing I hope Broncos players never forget is that the reason they're able to put on a uniform and play in this great city is because of the Broncos fans. Pat Bowlen doesn't really pay their salaries. The fans do by buying tickets and purchasing Broncos jerseys, hats, shirts, and other memorabilia. Broncos fans are the most passionate, loyal group in the NFL. Many of them have been season-ticket holders since 1960. Some have passed away and handed down tickets to new generations. Watching the Broncos on Sundays is a heartfelt ritual the entire city and the state of Colorado embraces.

In my era it was even more special. We weren't rich athletes but well-paid working-class people. It was a neighborhood atmosphere. We were seen all over town. We didn't live in mansions or drive around in expensive Cadillacs. We worked here in the off-season. Guys sold cars, life insurance, worked construction, and ran small businesses. The fans loved us. Even if we lost by 30 points, they'd cheer, "You'll get 'em next time!" There was always a crowd waiting after games. Fans wanted to get your autograph or give you a hug or just pat you on the back. This was their team. There was no greater honor than to play for a city where every time you pulled on your jersey, laced up your cleats, grabbed your helmet, and ran onto that field you felt like you were at the center of the universe with people who loved and respected you.

Selling the Sizzle

As an owner of a car dealership, I learned a long time ago that you don't sell the steak, you sell the sizzle. During my years with the Broncos, I did a lot of advertising for different businesses. I did TV commercials, radio, print, and my face was plastered on billboards all over Denver. One billboard my teammates teased me about was for Sigman's Hotdogs. The ad was a close up of me wearing a helmet without a facemask and holding a hotdog. The billboard read, "Floyd Little Chooses Sigman's Top Dog. It's Dog-Gone Good." Of course teammates chided me saying, "Folks is so old he don't even wear a facemask."

Another ad was for Day Chevrolet in which I actually sang, "Any day you can beat a Day Deal, that'll be the day!" For some reason I never won a Grammy.

I still do ads in Denver. For the past 30 years I've been doing ads with my friend, Darrell Elliott, a personal injury attorney. Friends like BT give me a hard time because in every ad I look at the camera and blurt out, "It's an All-Pro move!" Cracks him up every time. The past couple of years we changed it to "It's a Hall of Fame move!"

Wrong Little, Part I

As a sports hero in a sports-crazy town, I experienced my share of imposters. One guy used to frequent this singles club downtown and tell women he was me. My wife even got a call from another woman at 2:00 AM attempting to rat me out. "I just want to tell you that Floyd is here at this bar talking to three women, and it doesn't look like he's leaving anytime soon." My wife looked over at me in bed and said, "Floyd is right here. Good night."

Apparently, the resemblance was uncanny. He could have been a twin. My brother, Ranger, visiting one time, went to the club and confronted the guy. "Hi. I'm Floyd Little," the guy said. "No you're not," Ranger said.

"How do you know I'm not?" "Because he's my brother, and he's a lot better looking than you. He takes after me." We never heard from that guy again.

Today's NFL

With free agency, it's tough to get attached to a favorite player these days. And it requires a small loan for families to go to games. The fault's not all on the players or all on the owners, either. As you saw in the tough labor negotiations in 2011, there's a fair amount of greed on both sides. Veteran players are getting cut right before bonuses are due because teams can't afford to pay them. The joy of the game has become secondary. It's a business. I'm sure players think, *The owners don't care about me, why should I care about them.* There are some players who probably don't even like playing. They forget that beyond the bonus they still get paid millions a year to play a game. That's a pretty damn good living. Maybe they don't make the money that players in other sports make, but the other major sports stink compared to the NFL.

Of course, there are players out there who still put the game first. A few I met who fit that old-school mold were guys like Rod Smith, Al Wilson, and John Lynch. I believe Tim Tebow is cut from the same mold.

I'm a huge Rod Smith fan. Rod could have played in any era. My record of 12,157 combined yards lasted for more than 30 years. It was finally broken in 2006 by Rod Smith. There's no player I would want to have that record than Rod. I would have loved to have him as a teammate. He was a consistent hard worker and took being captain seriously. Al Wilson was like that, and so was John Lynch. Back in 2005 when the Broncos played the Redskins, it was Alumni Weekend, so a few of us former players participated in the coin flip. Before we walked onto the field, John Lynch came over to me and said, "It's nice to meet you. I'm glad to make your acquaintance." That was five years before I was inducted into the Hall of Fame. It blew me away. So many players don't seem to care about players from our era who helped pave the way. But we alumni are very appreciative of the ones who do.

If I were a coach I would get a team of guys who truly played for the love of the game. Guys who were at their fifth training camp in three years. Guys who had played in the Arena Football League, NFL Europe,

Canada, and toiled on practice squads and semi-pro teams playing on rocky fields—guys who proved a lot of people wrong. Of course, I also would ask management to buck up a few ducats so I could have Rod Smith and Al Wilson leading them.

A World of Influence

The thing I am continually humbled by as the years pass is the influence that NFL players have on kids. There are some who say athletes shouldn't be role models; parents should. I agree. But there's something innate about a child looking up to sports heroes. I mean, how many kids put up huge pictures of their parents in their rooms?

I continually meet people who tell me, "You were my hero." One such person is broadcaster Jim Gray, a Denver native. In 2010, Jim was honored with a star on the Hollywood Walk of Fame. You probably know Jim as a tenacious reporter who got into it a bit with Pete Rose during an All-Star Game. Well, Jim is one of the most respected broadcasters in the industry. More people came to Jim's ceremony than anyone in the last 20 years. Guys like Mike Ditka, Al Davis, Jim Otto, Bill Walton, Jeffrey Osborne, and Larry King. He invited me, too. But I didn't really know why until I was at the banquet and he told the crowd that I was his idol growing up. Out of all those people, he told the crowd that I was his hero, his motivation to succeed. He wanted a special picture with me. He said he used to wear my jersey and go to the games and cheer me. Once again, I was speechless and overwhelmed with pride.

It reminded me of all the times I've signed autographs. Sometimes there were lines of people waiting for my autograph after games. It was especially tough after a loss when I was in a lot of pain and emotionally spent. But I always signed. I felt if they took the time to stand there, asking me for my signature, then obliging them was the least I could do, especially when they are kids. I never understand when players snub a child for an autograph. Whether you think you're a role model or not, that child believes you are one. You never know what a snub will do to a child. But by signing you never know what that will do to lift the kid's spirits. You never know who you might influence. When I played, I know of two kids who looked up to me and went to great lengths to get my autograph: Jim Gray and Tom Mackie. Think about the impact they've had on my life simply because I conducted myself the way a role model should.

Wrong Little, Part II

Ever get a lottery ticket and think for a minute that all your numbers have lined up and you're suddenly the big winner? That same feeling happened to me about 20 years ago. I was at a charity event in Los Angeles and some supporter recognized me and yelled, "Floyd Little, Floyd Little. Congratulations, I just heard the great news!" I said, "What are you talking about?" "You've been elected to the Pro Football Hall of Fame. It was on the radio." I was flabbergasted. "Really?" "Yeah, they just announced it. Congratulations!"

I was smiling so much I was almost panting. Then I thought, "Wait a minute, is this really true? No one even told me I was nominated." So I called BT to check it out. He said, "No, man. You didn't make it. They said, Larry Little, not Floyd."

It was as if someone had jammed his fist down my throat and ripped out my heart. I try to laugh about it now. But damn that was upsetting.

15

FINALLY, CANTON!

Why Did It Take So Long?

When I retired in 1975, I was considered one of the top running backs of my era. The Pro Football Hall of Fame Selection Committee voted me to the All-Pro Squad of the 1970s. They hung a large plaque in Canton commemorating my career. For years after my retirement, writers mentioned me in articles as, "Future Hall-of-Famer Floyd Little." But for 35 years after playing my last down, I was overlooked.

In 2005, 30 years after retiring and sick of constantly fielding questions from fans and former players, I decided to look for some answers. I asked the powers that be—the nine Seniors Committee members who vote for the old timers—why I've been overlooked. I sent personal letters to each of them. Plus I sent a note to Paul Zimmerman of *Sports Illustrated* because he was one of the 39 voters (there are now 44) and I loved his insights on SI.com. Of those 10, three replied: Paul Z, David Goldberg, and Edwin Pope.

Through my correspondence, the writers told me only two criteria go into evaluating a running back's candidacy: yards rushing and Super Bowls." That's it. Pro Bowls, receiving yards, combined yards returning punts and kickoffs, impact to your team and the league, years captain, and overall reputation are not given much weight. So I checked out the criteria for the Baseball Hall of Fame in Cooperstown, and it was totally different: "Voting shall be based upon the player's record, playing ability, integrity, sportsmanship, character, and contributions to the team(s) on which the player played."

Why the criterion for induction of these two major sports is so different still intrigues me. Has football's criteria always been this shortsighted or has it changed since the Hall opened in 1963? And what kind of message does it send to kids who dream about someday being inducted in the Pro Football Hall of Fame—that character, sportsmanship, leadership, integrity, reputation, and community work don't matter as long as you've got great stats and played in Super Bowls? As a Hall of Famer, I think it's something our Hall of Fame committee should re-evaluate because I know the NFL prides itself on positively influencing children.

After being informed of the basis for candidacy, my lack of Super Bowls continued to be a strike against me. But really, is there a running back who could have willed the 1967–75 Broncos to a Super Bowl? Like a lot of positions, I think running backs play a role but there's a lot that goes into a championship team. You have to have a great owner, a superior coaching staff, a winning system, a smart GM, talented players on both sides of the ball, and a good deal of luck. I think when it comes to Hall of Fame selection, too much emphasis is put on Super Bowls. It's one game. What about a player's entire career?

During my prime, 1968–73, I led the league in both rushing and yards from scrimmage. Heck, in my nine seasons only O.J. Simpson rushed for more yards. When you consider I came into the league as a 25-year-old rookie, played for a perennial losing team, was the Broncos' only real offensive threat for most of my career, played special teams, and still placed seventh on the list of all-time rushers. I think my numbers speak for themselves.

In 2000, Marcus Allen was a first-ballot selection to the Hall after he retired seventh all-time. Tom Mackie researched to find out that all running backs ranked seventh in 1980, '85, '90, '95, and 2000 all got into Canton. And the six guys ahead of me when I retired: Jim Brown, O.J. Simpson, Jim Taylor, Joe Perry, Leroy Kelly, and John Henry Johnson— were selected years ago. So why did it take me so long?

Although my numbers may not compare with today's backs, the selectors finally realized that it's an unfair comparison. Ball carriers today tote the rock almost twice as much as backs in my era. In 1970, I led the AFC in rushing with 901 yards on 209 carries. In 2000, Edgerrin James led the NFL with 1,709 yards on 387 carries. You can't compare the eras. Just imagine how the stats of today's runners will measure up with NFL stars 30 years from now in the year 2042? It's all relative.

I realize the writers who vote for the Hall of Fame have an incredibly tough job. I appreciate their task and realize they vote based on the criteria the Hall has established. I'm grateful to the ones who have passionately spoken on my behalf. I know nothing is promised in life. There are a lot of deserving players out there. But I'm glad the Hall of Fame committee finally took a look at my 12,157 yards of production and overall impact on the Broncos and decided I was as worthy as any. I was a trailblazer who, along with Denver's great fans, helped keep this organization going when the club could have easily folded. Plus I had the numbers to boot.

I think being immortalized in the Hall of Fame is the greatest honor. It's a tribute that the fans and the whole Broncos organization can share. Right now there are only four Broncos in the Hall of Fame: John Elway, Gary Zimmerman, Shannon Sharpe, and me. We're too good of an organization and that's not enough.

Who's Tom Landry?

Another reason it may have taken so long is something that happened years before that I only found out about a half-dozen years ago. From time to time sportswriters call me to talk about the old days or about the current Broncos. Back around 2005, Larry Felser, a great sportswriter for the *Buffalo News*, called me about a project he was working on that became the book, *The Birth of the New NFL*. Larry worked for the *Buffalo News* during my playing days. He also was on the Hall of Fame committee for years. Now he's retired from both. We talked about some great Broncos-Bills games. He was there, of course, for that infamous Buffalo game in 1968, so we laughed about that. After a few minutes on the phone, my curiosity got to me. So I asked him point blank why, at that time, I had never been nominated for the Hall.

He told me the last time my name seriously came up for consideration was back in the early 1990s. The Dallas Cowboys legendary coach Tom Landry was one of the people asked to give his opinion on candidates that year. The Hall of Fame committee discussed my credentials with him, and Felser said Landry had this blank stare on his face. Felser asked him what was wrong, and Landry turned to him and said, "Sorry. I don't remember Floyd Little." Years before I read the book *North Dallas Forty*, by former Cowboys tight end Peter Gent, and I saw the movie. It was based on Landry and the Cowboys. Obviously, the way Landry was portrayed as being out of touch was Gent's version. But after that conversation with Larry, I don't know what to think about the man. Because the Broncos were in the AFL and the Cowboys were in the NFL, we never played during the 1960s and only played once after the merger in 1973. The game was played at Mile High.

The funny thing is we scrimmaged the Cowboys each year during training camp. They were in Thousand Oaks, and we were nearby at Cal Poly Pomona. Hell, I led the NFL in rushing the year Landry won his first Super Bowl. And after I retired I even played in a foursome with him at a celebrity golf tournament. Maybe he wasn't impressed with my golfing.

His Hall of Fame players definitely remembered me, though. Bob Lilly told Tom, "Floyd was one of the top running backs of his era…. He was the Broncos playmaker for years and years. In my opinion, Floyd is one of those great players who has been overlooked for the Hall of Fame." Roger Staubach also chimed in that I was "long overdue" for Canton.

At any rate, I wish Landry was still alive so I could knock on his door and introduce myself.

Nominated, Finally

A lot has been written about the day I finally got the call—the one that I had waited 35 years for—the call from the Pro Football Hall of Fame telling me I had finally been nominated as a finalist. Gary Smith penned an awe-inspiring narrative about it in *Sports Illustrated*. I have so many vivid memories about that day. The funny thing is, the Hall of Fame was not on my mind. I thought they had already voted the week before, and I didn't make it. The Broncos were announcing the 50th Anniversary Team around that time, and I was hoping to get a call that I had made that team (which I did!).

After I heard the news from Joe Horrigan of the Hall of Fame and thanked the voters, I got off the phone and embraced my wife, DeBorah. We marveled at the incredible news as our eyes became flushed with tears. Then I picked up the phone. Tom Mackie was the first person I called, even before I dialed my kids. I just had to phone him first. Tom was the one who had done seven years of heavy lifting to get my name on the minds of voters.

In 2003, just a few months after I met him for the first time, Tom put together an incredible presentation called "44 Reasons to Elect Floyd Little to the Pro Football Hall of Fame." He compared my career to Hall of Fame running backs and showed my numbers were better than many of the backs already enshrined. He compared my rushing, receiving, kickoff and punt returns stats to theirs. He also showed that my numbers made me one of the greatest running backs of my generation. Tom discovered that during my career, only O.J. Simpson rushed for more yards. He also researched all the running backs of my generation and discovered that during a six-year period, 1968–1973, no one rushed for more yards or had more yards from scrimmage than I did.

Tom really dug down deep to find information about my career that no one had uncovered before. He noticed that when the NFL moved the hash marks closer to midfield in 1972, it doubled the number of 1,000-yard rushers from when I led the league in 1971. By '72, I was already 30 years old, ancient for running backs. That meant I had played the majority of my career on what many referred to as a short field. And I still retired seventh all time. Willie Lanier used to tell me that when they moved the hash marks closer to midfield in '72 that it made it a lot more difficult for defenses to stop the run. Tom put together this eye-popping presentation and mailed it off to all the Hall of Fame writers. He also sent the presentation to Broncos PR guru Jim Saccomano. Impressed by the stats, Jim promptly distributed Tom's presentation to the local media and sent it to all of the Hall of Fame voters, too.

Tom did this again the following year and the year after that. One year he put together a packet that included more stats, his published stories about me, letters of recommendation from Hall of Famers, and a DVD highlight reel of my playing days. He also started emailing and sending letters to Seniors Committee voters about my career.

On top of that, Tom noticed that my bio in the Broncos Media Guide did not mention any of my major achievements. It omitted the fact that I led the NFL in rushing in 1971 and led the AFC in rushing two years in a row. It also failed to mention that I had retired as the seventh-leading rusher in NFL history. There was also a huge error about my number of Pro Bowls. The media guide said I played in two AFL All-Star Games and only one Pro Bowl. The truth is I played in three Pro Bowls and two AFL All-Star Games. I believe these omissions and errors sold me short in the eyes of Hall of Fame voters for years. Whenever a player is mentioned in an article, sportswriters typically pull up that guy's bio from the team's media guide. I remember reading stories about me that were inaccurate, saying, "A Pro Bowl participant in 1971, Floyd twice played in the AFL All-Star Game in 1968 and 69...." Instead, it should have mentioned my major achievements, such as, "A five-time Pro Bowl player, Floyd led the NFL in rushing in 1971 and retired as the seventh-leading rusher in NFL history." Tom contacted the Broncos about the errors in the media guide, and the PR department happily revised my bio to include my top achievements.

In 2006, Tom co-authored my autobiography, *Tales from the Broncos Sideline*. Along with my life story, the book stated my case for the Hall of Fame. Tom's stats had already appeared in stories by Hall of Fame voters. One of them was my career won-lost mark of 47–73–6, which Tom used to illustrate my Pro Bowl achievements despite always playing on dismal teams. Ron Borges mentioned this won-lost stat in a 2003 column. Borges said that although John Elway was up for election, the world should not forget about me just because my teams sported a dismal 47–73–6 career record. Rick Gosselin mentioned Tom's stat that during my career only O.J. Simpson rushed for more—in a 2006 article. Even *Sports Illustrated*'s Peter King, who went out of his way to bash my Hall of Fame credentials, used one of Tom's stats in a "Monday Morning Quarterback" column:

during a six-year period, 1968–73, I rushed for more yards (and more yards from scrimmage) than anyone.

But the thing that Tom did that had perhaps the biggest impact was the book of quotes he put together "44 Hall of Famers on 44 Floyd Little" that I believe finally helped push me over the top and get nominated. Tom spent several months tirelessly interviewing Hall of Famers about me and asking them point blank whether I deserved to be in Canton. He talked to Hall of Famers that I played against, including Bobby Bell, Willie Lanier, Joe Greene, Mel Blount, and Nick Buoniconti. Some of the quotes he found were letters from Hall of Famers like John Mackey who wrote that if there wasn't room for me in Canton, then the Hall of Fame should take him out and put me in because I deserved it that much. To be honest, I've only read those quotes a couple of times. I can't get through all 44 quotes without getting really emotional. The things these Hall of Famers said about me are so humbling.

So Tom was the first person I called because, more than anyone else, he was responsible for me getting nominated. And you know what? I got his voicemail! But Tom called me right back. He was on the road and had to pull over. We were both so emotional. Tom cried, "Floyd, I'm so happy for you. You finally did it!" I told Tom it was all because of him. He had pulled me out of the depths of hell in the eyes of the Hall of Fame voters. Writers who had forgotten about me finally started to recognize my impact and achievements. Tom had worked tirelessly for seven years to make sure the voters realized that I should no longer be penalized for being a great player on some bad teams.

Understand that I had only been nominated. I still needed to receive 80 percent of the votes on the day before the Super Bowl to be inducted. That was six months away. But for me, being nominated was the greatest feeling. I had been passed over for more than three decades. I had never been nominated once during that time. That's what hurt. To know that I had the deck stacked against me from the beginning. Being drafted by a struggling AFL team that never had a winning record. To be one of 26 rookies on the team that first season but somehow lead the league in combined yards my first two seasons. Then to lead the league in yards per game and yards per carry and go on to win back-to-back rushing titles, play in five Pro Bowls, and retire as the seventh-leading rusher in NFL history. To accomplish all this while playing with 27 quarterbacks and 50 offensive linemen in my career. And still to never be recognized with a single nomination.

So when I got the call, I celebrated with DeBorah, thanked Tom, and called my children and other family members and friends. After all that I sat on the edge of my bed and just gazed out the window. I thought about all those years of being snubbed. My emotions began to overwhelm me and I got choked up, feeling a lump in my throat. When I first got the call, my heart stopped beating for a moment. Then it started up again, beating faster and faster to the point of racing. Now I was sitting quietly by myself. DeBorah didn't know quite what to think, but she left me to reflect on everything. It had been so long, I had been denied for what felt like an eternity. I took a deep breath and started reveling in the moment—finally feeling the joy of being nominated.

As I sat there on my bed, I began to own it. I had told my kids many years before that if I ever got nominated to the Pro Football Hall of Fame, I would take them to the Super Bowl to be there for the announcement and the game. They immediately reminded me of my promise. I said, "Yeah, but that was back when Super Bowl tickets were $35. Now they're $1,000!" They didn't flinch, "Dad, you gave us your word. You can't go back on your word!" Those dirty dogs. I laughed. "Of course we're going!" It wasn't a question that I would not be elected. I had come too far to be denied. My positive attitude came pouring out of me. "This is going to happen. I will not be denied my place in Canton."

I started thanking people for their love and support over the years. I called Jim Gray, BT, and many other teammates. I also knew I had to thank Tom Mackie in a big way. I decided to send him a thank-you note every day for 44 straight days. In the *Sports Illustrated* article, it says that I sent those thank-you notes to Tom after I was elected to the Hall of Fame. The truth is, I sent them to Tom after I was nominated because I knew getting nominated was the biggest hurdle. I wanted him to know how much his efforts had changed my life. I wanted him to know that he was my hero now. When I talk about the importance of being a role model because you never know who you're going to influence, Tom was one of those kids. He was just seven years old when he picked me as his favorite player, his hero. Now Tom was family. Who could have come up with such a story? He needed to know how blessed I felt to have him in my life. I wasn't going to wait to be elected to tell him. I was convinced that I would receive the votes necessary to get in. I was already celebrating.

Waiting Is the Hardest Part

It's not just a popular tune by Tom Petty and The Heartbreakers, it's the damn truth. Waiting is definitely the hardest part. For someone like me who never puts off anything for tomorrow, waiting to find out if I would be elected to the Pro Football Hall of Fame was really tough. I'm the guy who files his income taxes in January and can't let a bill sit for more than five minutes before cracking open the checkbook. Now I had to wait six months to find out if I would receive the ultimate honor or be denied and thrown back in the abyss of candidates forever.

Modern players don't have to wait long. They find out if they are Hall of Fame finalists just a month before the voting. Not only did I have to wait 35 years to finally be nominated, I had to live through that excruciating realm of suspended animation—August 2009 to February 2010—to finally hear the verdict. Dr. Seuss said, "Waiting is the most useless place." You got that right. No wonder so many of the senior nominees are already pushing up daisies when they finally get the call.

Even though I probably thought about it every day, I did my best to enjoy those six months. I traveled and spoke to youth groups across the country. I became a spokesperson for some great causes. One was Youth Lifeline America, a life-changing organization headed up by Roland Williams, who played tight end at Syracuse and won a Super Bowl with the St. Louis Rams. I also participated in many golf tournaments and went back to Syracuse a number of times to help with fundraising. I received a lot of congratulatory phone calls and emails from former teammates from college and the pros, coaches, friends, family, and fans. They were all excited for me, and some were nervous. They wanted me to make it to Canton so bad.

I decided I wasn't going to sweat it out. I had been passed over so many times, that to finally be nominated was a blessing, one that I had given up on the year before when Bob Hayes was nominated for the second time in five years. Marshall Goldberg, a running back from the 1940s, was nominated a second time the year before that. I thought, *Not only do I keep getting passed over, other guys are getting second chances!*

Now that I was finally nominated, Tom, Jim Gray, and others kept telling me I was going to get elected. It was going to happen. That being nominated was the toughest hurdle. They told me to enjoy the ride. So that's what I did.

I was determined not to think about whether or not I would make it. Like I always preach to others, I wasn't going to allow negativity to creep into my thoughts. There are so many people, the Denver fans who waited for this day, and the Broncos organization that has seen its stars passed over so many times for this honor. I looked at it as fate. This was the time for me, my family, and Broncos fans. I told family and friends who were worried, "We all have to revel in this experience and try to enjoy the moment." I believed that when the final vote was cast that I would be one of the 2010 inductees. I felt Dick LeBeau and I should both get in. Both of us wore No. 44, both of us played in the same era. It was the 44th Super Bowl, there are 44 writers, Obama was the 44th president, my son, Marc, was 44 years old. I believed it was in the stars.

The Manifesto

Although Tom Mackie believed I would be elected to Canton on the day before the Super Bowl, he was leaving nothing to chance. As I said to Tom, "We are owning this." After seven years of pit-bull persistence, Tom spent those months putting together one final document, one final presentation. This one was a 47-page manifesto that he sent to the guy who was going to present me to the Hall of Fame voters—Jeff Legwold of the *Denver Post*. Jeff was the guy chosen by the Seniors Committee to present me. Usually, it's one of the nine Seniors Committee voters who presents a seniors nominee. But they felt Jeff could do a better job. Tom had been in contact with Jeff for a few years and had emailed Jeff regularly after I was nominated. He sent Jeff stats and nuggets of information about my career that would help address any objections the voters might have. Tom became even more dogged in his preparation. He also mailed copies of our book to all 44 voters to give them more insight and perspective about my career. We had come this far. We weren't going to let this final opportunity slip through our fingertips.

Tom told me what the possible objections could be to my getting in. I had one 1,000-yard season. I played on a losing team. My career average was 3.9 yards per carry. Tom came up with multiple responses to these and other objections that could be aired. For my one 1,000-yard season (in which I led the NFL in rushing in 1971 with 1,133 yards), I was only the 13th player in NFL history to gain 1,000 yards. Tom noted that I played the majority of my career in an era before the hash marks were moved closer to midfield in 1972. The first year this new rule was put in place, 10 running backs rushed for 1,000 yards—twice the number when I led the year before in '71. Moving the hash marks gave running backs the ability to equally use both sides of the field. During my playing days, the ball was placed closer to the sideline, cutting off nearly half of the field. I was already 30 years old when they moved the hash marks. I played the '72 season with torn knee cartilage that required surgery after the season. I still slugged out nearly 900 yards and scored 13 touchdowns.

I was told Peter King of *Sports Illustrated* had an issue with my one 1,000-yard season and my 3.9-yard average. He also questioned the legitimacy of my candidacy because he thought my career average 54 yards rushing per game was poor. Regarding 1,000 yards, he tried to justify his point by saying that 33 running backs rushed for 1,000 yards from 1971–75, so why couldn't I have rushed for more? But his assertion was grossly misleading. It didn't take into account that moving the hash marks in '72 was a major rule change that benefited running backs from those in previous eras. If you take the number of 1,000-yard rushers over a four-year period before the rule change, 1968–71, only 10 players went over the 1,000-yard mark. That's just a tad over two running backs per season. Then if you look at the number of 1,000-yard rushers over a four-year period, 1972–75, after the rule change, 28 players achieved it—that's nearly three times as many!

I had come close to multiple 1,000-yard seasons a number of times. In 1969, only one player—Gale Sayers—gained 1,000 yards (1,032). I averaged more than 100 yards rushing per game during the first half of the 1969 season until I injured my knee and missed six games. I was on pace for a 1,400-yard season before my injury. In 1970, I led the AFC in rushing with more than 900 yards while playing the season with a broken bone in my back—something our team physician told me was impossible. In 1973 at the ripe old age of 31, I rushed for 979 yards, just 21 yards shy of 1,000. That was after undergoing knee surgery in the off-season. I also led the NFL in rushing touchdowns that year.

Tom also pointed out in his presentation that Hall of Famers Paul Hornung and Lenny Moore never rushed for 1,000 yards after each had played in seven 14-game seasons. Actually, Hornung and Moore never came close. Neither of them rushed for more than 600 yards in a 14-game season. And if you want to compare 1,000-yard Hall of Fame rushers to 1,000-yard Hall of Fame receivers, Charley Taylor only had one 1,000-yard receiving season. The fact that I was 30 years old before the NFL moved the hash marks to essentially quadruple the number of 1,000-yard rushers gave Tom's argument a lot of credence. I was told by one Hall of Fame voter that this was a pivotal point that changed a lot of opinions when it came to voting me in. The funny thing is this isn't something that Tom spent a lot of time on in his presentation. He had addressed the hash mark argument back in 2003 in his first "44 Reasons" presentation.

Regarding playing on losing teams, Tom noted that I had played with 27 quarterbacks in nine seasons—quarterbacks who as a group completed just 43 percent of their passes and threw 65 more interceptions than touchdowns. The year I led the NFL in rushing, our two quarterbacks combined for eight touchdowns and 27 interceptions. Coach Lou Saban resigned after just nine games. We became the league's top rushing team with interim coach Jerry Smith.

As for the argument about my 3.9 career rushing average, Tom noted that Hall of Fame running back John Riggins also averaged 3.9 yards per carry during his career. Well, Riggins was 6'2", 240 pounds, running behind The Hogs, probably the most celebrated offensive line in NFL history. I played with 50 linemen over the course of nine seasons, none of whom played in the NFC-AFC Pro Bowl. He also noted the difference in 3.9 yards a carry and 4.0 yards is just 3.6", less than the width of a 4x6" card. His argument was: You're going to deny Floyd a place in Canton because he averaged 3.6" less than another Hall of Famer who played behind a slew of Pro Bowl linemen and even some Hall of Fame linemen?

Finally, King's argument that my 54 yards rushing per game was not Hall of Fame worthy was ludicrous. Tom's presentation pointed out that you also must consider how many rushing yards per game the other Hall of Fame running backs from my era put up. John Henry Johnson averaged 48 yards rushing per game; Leroy Kelly, averaged 53; Larry Csonka, 55; and Paul Hornung averaged only 36 yards. Tom also pointed out that rushing was just part of my game. I was a multi-dimensional back who averaged more than 20 yards receiving a game—few Hall of Fame running backs were even close to that.

The question I have is why would a Hall of Fame voter like King take so much time trying to disparage my career before the final vote was ever cast? I know he was a huge supporter of getting Dick LeBeau nominated. Since only one of the two seniors candidates were voted in the two years before Dick and I were nominated, King probably felt like he needed to rip my career in hopes of swaying voters. Just like politicians who opt to rip their opponents by staging negative campaigns before an election.

I felt King tried to take advantage of his national platform in his "Monday Morning Quarterback" column to make sure that Dick, not me, got into Canton. If he wanted Dick to get into the Hall of Fame so much, why not just extol Dick's achievements? I love Dick LeBeau. I was so happy when he got elected. We both deserved it. You don't have to tear down one person just to build someone else up. King must have felt otherwise. He went so far with his case for LeBeau that two weeks before Dick and I were even nominated, he predicted in his column that only six players would be elected to the 2010 Hall of Fame class—he selected LeBeau and five modern players. He already assumed the other seniors nominee, whoever that was, wouldn't get the votes.

When people question whether any of the 44 Hall of Fame voters ever have a personal agenda, I have to agree that some do, considering the unprofessional way King acted during those months.

Frankly, I didn't care what King thought. I never got the sense he knew football like more established NFL writers, including Paul Zimmerman. Zim was an old AFL writer who actually watched me play. He had incredible insight into the game. I used to read his columns in *Sports Illustrated* religiously until he tragically suffered a stroke four years ago. I was so saddened that I immediately sent him a get-well card.

To me, it didn't matter what one subjective Hall of Fame voter thought. It just bothered me that King was trying so hard to ruin my chances. I've always lived by the credo, "Someone's label or opinion of you should never become your reality." He was just one guy, one opinion. I had faith in Tom's manifesto and Jeff Legwold's presentation. I had faith that the other 43 voters would see that I was deserving. I needed 38 votes (80 percent) to be elected to the Pro Football Hall of Fame. I got 42 of the 44 votes. King and a voter who represented the Tennessee Titans didn't vote for me. Despite King's attempt to poison my candidacy, I was overwhelmingly elected to the Hall of Fame.

The Celebration

I can't tell you how difficult it was waiting for the final envelope to announce the Hall of Fame Class of 2010 the day before the Super Bowl. It was held at a convention center in Ft. Lauderdale. Charles Haley and I were both sharing a green room with our families next to where the Hall of Fame announcement show was being broadcast. We were watching the whole thing unfold on television. We were glued to the tube like we were witnessing the Apollo 11 moon landing. I have to admit at that point, I started to have some negative feelings. What if they only elected one of the seniors nominees like they had the past two years? The year before me the great Claude Humphrey was denied. The year before that it was Marshall Goldberg.

When Charles got cut from the finalists, it just raised my doubts. He was so deserving, I felt awful for him. To see him get up with his family and wish me well before leaving was heartbreaking.

So there we were, waiting in a room for an announcement that still felt a lifetime away. Tom was too nervous to sit. He got up and kept walking in and out of the green room. He was talking with Jeff Legwold, Jim Saccomano, and Broncos executive Joe Ellis to find out if I had made it. No one knew anything, not even Legwold who was there for the vote.

Finally, Hall of Fame executive director Steve Perry got up to make the announcement. My mind was spinning. As he opened the envelope, I leaned forward in my chair. I was teetering on the edge. So was my family. Tom finally sat down and told me to breathe. My hands were fists resting on my forehead. Then all of sudden the TV froze. I was like, "What the #*$?" Then the show came back as Perry started reading the names. When he said, "Dick LeBeau," I thought, *Oh my lord, I didn't make it.* Then my name rang out like a chorus—"Floyd Little." I was so overcome with emotion I toppled over onto floor. My daughters, Christy and Kyra, and my son, Marc, engulfed me. Tom slapped my leg and screamed, "You the man!" My beautiful wife, DeBorah, kissed me. Then we all embraced for a prayer before Jim Saccomano came bursting through the room and hugged me. Jim congratulated me and sighed, "Well, Floyd, I think maybe the voters decided they were tired of hearing from Tom Mackie."

Minutes later I was escorted onto NFL Network's live broadcast with Rich Eisen and Jerry Rice. Emmitt Smith came on later. It was surreal. Thinking about it still gives me goosebumps. I was still overwhelmed with joy, and it gave me a chance to publicly thank my Lord and Savior Jesus Christ for blessing me. Jeff Legwold, who presented me to the voters, was the first person I thanked. I knew Jeff had done an incredible job. I also thanked my family and friends for years of love and support, as well as the great Broncos fans and my teammates for all their hard work and sacrifice. I also thanked Tom for all those years of persistence that helped make this all possible. Jim Gray was another person who went above and beyond. The day before the vote, Jim personally called all the voters to convince them I was worthy of their vote.

After I appeared on NFL Network, I was on my way to do a radio show with Gil Brandt, the longtime Cowboys vice president of player personnel who had followed me since I was at Bordentown. A gentleman about my age stopped me and asked if we could talk. He said he had met me more than 45 years ago at the Pensacola Naval Base right before the 1965 Sugar Bowl. I was shocked that I was so old and that this gentleman remembered meeting me so many years ago. He looked at me and said, "I told my son that you were the greatest running back I had ever seen." I wasn't sure what he meant by that, so I asked him who his son was. "Emmitt Smith," he replied. "I'm Emmitt Smith Sr." I was shocked and gave him a huge bear hug. For the father of Emmitt Smith to say something like that was just incredible—a fitting end to an emotionally draining six months.

The Celebration Dinner

That night we all went out to a fantastic dinner in South Beach. I was just elated. We dined, gave toasts, and celebrated like it was spring break. I don't drink, but I had a glass of champagne. I got a stream of calls from people congratulating me. Eddie Murray, the Hall of Fame baseball player and a good friend of mine, showed up to surprise me. He told me he was so proud and happy to have me as his friend and now I was a fellow Hall of Famer.

I got so many goodwill calls that soon my voicemail was full. Many of the calls were from the Hall of Fame voters themselves, extending their congratulations. John Clayton of EPSN was one of those callers. He asked me to be on his show sometime. It was shaping up to be the ultimate perfect day.

During dinner, my cell phone rang again. I was going to let it go but decided to answer. It was Peter King. I thought, *Well, he's finally going to give me my due.* I excused myself from the table so I could hear what he had to say. Much to my disbelief, Peter told me he was calling to tell me that the only reason I got elected to the Hall of Fame was because Jeff Legwold had given the greatest presentation he had ever heard. King also wanted me to know that despite Jeff's convincing presentation, he didn't vote for me and he still didn't think I deserved to be in the Hall of Fame.

I was shocked. What was King trying to do—rain on my parade? He knew I was out celebrating. What could he possibly think he was going to accomplish by telling me he didn't vote for me and that he didn't think I deserved to be in Canton? Seriously, what kind of person calls someone up to say such a thing? What the hell was wrong with this guy? Obviously 42 of the 44 voters didn't agree with him. It was just his sullied opinion. But it got me angry. I could have responded a million ways. I could have told him to go f— himself. But I wasn't going to allow this horrible person to ruin one of the greatest nights of my life. So I told him he was welcome to his opinion. Then before I hung up I said, "See you in Canton!"

King didn't need to tell me what a great job Jeff Legwold did. I had just thanked Jeff in person and live on NFL Network. For months Tom told me how dedicated Jeff was to putting together a great presentation. I had met Jeff after I was nominated, and I could tell he was a serious NFL writer who did a lot of research. Frankly, I think every Hall of Fame candidate deserves the ultimate presentation. They deserve to have someone who is committed to doing an incredible job. For seniors nominees like me, this is our only chance. It better be great. I don't know who presented Claude Humphrey. But I bet his presenter didn't do his very best. Otherwise, Claude would be in the Hall of Fame where he belongs.

After that call from King, I had to laugh. I shook my head and thought, "That's a new low even for that guy!" I went back to dinner and immersed myself into the frivolity of my loved ones. I raised a glass and thanked everyone for their love and support. We celebrated late into the night.

In the end I didn't need King's vote. And now I belong to the most exclusive fraternity in pro football—and they can't trade me, cut me, or fire me.

Super Bowl XLIV

The next day was even more magnificent. The Hall of Fame moved us out of our hotel and into the Ritz Carlton. We now had a driver to take us around. I felt like the queen of England—football royalty. The first stop was going to be an outdoor reception to welcome all the new Hall of Famers.

On the way I received two calls. The first was from Joe Greene, the legendary Steelers Hall of Famer I battled many times. He congratulated me and said, "Floyd, I just want you to know that you are the greatest player I ever went up against." My mouth dropped to the floor. He called me the greatest player. Not the greatest running back—the greatest player. My young driver heard me repeat that and asked, "Did you just talk to Mean Joe Greene?" I told Joe how much I appreciated those kind words, and we laughed about a couple of games.

Then the phone rang again. The caller said, "Floyd, this is Joe." I was shocked. "Joe Biden?" I said, recognizing my college friend's voice. The driver heard this and almost caromed off the road while looking back at me. He must have thought, "Who is this guy I'm driving? He knows the Vice President of the United States!"

Later that day we made our way to the Super Bowl where the Saints and Colts were going to battle it out. As new Hall of Famers we were now part of the coin-flip ceremony. While I stood there waiting to walk out on the field with my fellow Hall of Famers, Peyton Manning tapped me on the shoulder. "My father wanted me to congratulate you. He told me you were a tremendous player. He sends his best wishes. We're really happy for you." Again, I was speechless. Here's a future Hall of Famer warming up right before the biggest game of his life, and he takes a moment to come over and congratulate me? I just smiled and told him thank you.

It was just one emotional moment after another. At that point I didn't walk out onto the field, I floated. Now I was a Hall of Famer, flipping the coin at the Super Bowl. I beamed like a lighthouse. I didn't think it could get any more emotional after that. But it did.

All the new Hall of Famers shared a suite during the game. At halftime there was a knock at the door. It was Jim Gray. He was working the game with Westwood One and came to interview me. He hugged me and told me how much I deserved this honor. I thanked him for everything he did. Then Jim quickly set up to do the interview. Right before he asked me his first question, he looked at me and broke down crying. I saw that and I became a human fountain myself. After a few minutes we regained our composure and tried it again. Jim started to ask his first question, and then he had to stop. The tears started flowing again.

It's no wonder. Jim grew up in Denver, and I was his hero. His dad had season tickets, and they went to all my games. When he got a plaque on the Hollywood Walk of Fame years back, Jim told hundreds of guests that I was his hero. When he broke down at the Super Bowl, I just hugged him and told him I loved him. We never did finish the interview.

2010 Hall of Fame Class

Before I was elected to the 2010 Hall of Fame Class, I had made the choice to be there in Ft. Lauderdale to hear the announcement. The truth is, that when I told the Hall of Fame committee I was bringing my entire family, they gave me the choice of waiting in the green room to hear the final verdict or sitting out in the parking lot. The idea being if I didn't make it, as they suggested, we could drive away without feeling humiliated. I said, "No, my family and I have come too far. We are going to sit in the green room and await our fate. Besides," I joked, "if I don't make it, my son and I are burning the place down!"

Luckily for everyone's safety, we got the votes! Part of the joy of being there was being able to thank everyone on NFL Network's live telecast. Rich Eisen commented that the great thing about each Hall of Fame class is there's always a mixed-bag of NFL greats. He was right. I was sitting there on stage with Jerry Rice, a first-ballot Hall of Famer, and I had waited more than 30 years to get the call. Dick LeBeau had waited even longer than me. Emmitt Smith was another first-ballot guy. John Randle, Rickey Jackson, and Russ Grimm had to wait a number of years, too. But now we're all Hall of Famers. There's no degree of Hall of Fame; we're all the same.

I'm so proud to be in my class. We were all able to connect, and we've all become pretty solid friends.

It's been an incredible pleasure to know Jerry Rice. He is probably one of the nicest people—not nicest football players—but nicest people I've ever met. I can't recall ever meeting someone kinder, gentler, and more approachable than Jerry. One time I was with him and he accidentally walked in front of some fans taking a picture. Not only did Jerry say he was sorry, he apologized profusely. He signed autographs and let them take numerous pictures with him. Here's a guy who is considered by many to be the greatest football player in NFL history, and he's a regular guy. Drew Brees is the same way. I got a chance to meet Drew a few times; once was at the 2010 NFL Draft when we each got to announce a pick for our respective teams. Both of those guys are nice folks.

John Randle is the cat's meow. He and I are like two peas in a pod. We laugh at the same jokes and carry on like two incorrigible rascals. But he is always there to represent our class and he, Randall McDaniel (2009 class), and I are inseparable whenever we get together.

It's also been great to get to know Dick LeBeau and Russ Grimm. Both of them are still coaching, so I don't get the chance to visit or talk to them as much. But we had a grand time at our Hall of Fame ceremony. Dick has a great dry sense of humor, and I'm so glad he and I both finally made it to Canton. Russ has been nothing but a gentleman. I really respect him a lot.

Emmitt Smith and I have had some great conversations. He's learned a lot about my career from his father, Emmitt Smith Sr., who followed me from the time I was a sophomore at Syracuse. Emmitt also loved the movie *The Express* and told me he was thrilled to have someone like me in our class who helped lay the foundation for smaller backs like him. I've made it a point to play in his golf tournament every year.

That leaves Rickey Jackson. To be honest, Rickey didn't start off well with our class or with the other members of the Hall of Fame. In the beginning he seemed standoffish and disrespectful. So much so that Deacon Jones even called him out. I think everyone reacts differently when they are first elected. It might have taken Rickey awhile to loosen up. But he's definitely turned around. The past few times I've seen him, he's been very appreciative. Now Rickey embraces his fellow Hall of Famers when he sees us. He's finally allowing us to get to know him, and he's a really good guy.

Gary Smith

When I was told that *Sports Illustrated* was going to do an article on me, I was ecstatic. I knew as long as it wasn't written by Peter King, the story would be positive. Shortly thereafter I received a call from writer Gary Smith. He told me he was coming up from his home in the south to interview Tom Mackie in New Jersey. Then he would fly out to Seattle and spend a few days with me. *Days?* I thought. Well, okay.

When Gary showed up at my door, he didn't look like a typical sportswriter. He was dressed casual in jeans, sneakers, and a lumberjack shirt. His hair was kind of a mess, and he was sporting a moustache from the 1970s. If he had been holding a cup, I would have put a dollar in it.

I can joke like that about Gary because we had such a great time hanging out. We laughed a lot, and I really admired his unassuming, down-to-earth personality. He was very nice and personable. You never would have known that he was a big-shot writer from the most recognizable sports magazine in the country. Gary had this big yellow legal pad, and he sat there and asked me question after question. He asked me about growing up in Connecticut and scribbled something in a corner of the page. Then he asked me about Lou Saban and flipped a few pages and wrote something on the back. Frankly, I don't know how he was able to keep track of everything. He also talked to DeBorah, my kids, my nephew, teammates, associates of mine at my old Ford dealer, the neighbor's cat—everyone.

Never had a writer asked me so many questions and interviewed so many people. There was also a lot of chitchatting when he didn't ask any questions. We went out to breakfast a few times, and DeBorah cooked dinner for him one night. There was also a photographer who snapped a lot of shots. It was such a pleasure to have Gary around that after a while I didn't feel like I was talking to a sportswriter. We formed a nice friendship and talked about a lot of things, like playing guitar. Gary plays, and I have three acoustic guitars. I'm still taking lessons, but when I get some downtime I want to learn Bill Withers' song, "Ain't No Sunshine." I figure since Bill's a friend of mine, I should learn his songs.

Before I knew it, Gary had been visiting for five days. It wasn't until a week after Gary left that I heard anything about him. I was doing an interview with someone from a Colorado newspaper, and I mentioned that a guy from *Sports Illustrated* had just been here.

"Oh really, who was it?" the writer asked.

"Gary Smith," I said.

"What? Are you kidding me? You had Gary Smith at your house? He's the best writer in the country. He only does three or four articles a year."

I was shocked. "Are you serious?"

"Yes. Gary Smith has won every major award in the business. He's like no other writer you've ever read. And he's doing a story on you?"

I didn't know what to think until I asked a few more sportswriters, and they confirmed that Gary was the best hands-down. I remember Tom mentioned that Gary was his favorite writer before he flew out here. But I've always told Tom that he's my favorite writer, and he just laughs.

So you can imagine how much I was blown away when the article came out. I mean, it wasn't an article. I can't even call it a feature story. It was like a full-length screenplay! Gary's incredible narrative stretched over nine pages. I had friends tell me they couldn't read it without bawling. One friend said he was reading it while sitting next to his son and had to get up and leave the house. He didn't want his son to see him crying.

I've always thought the way Tom and I got together—a boyhood fan finally meeting his idol, and the friendship that came out of all that—was special. I knew it would be a great story someday. But Gary wrote it like he was there watching the whole seven-year friendship and journey unfold in front of him. I can't begin to tell you the hundreds of emails I got from friends and fans about the impact of that story.

I'm so appreciative of Gary's talent and his skill in weaving together such a remarkable story. That's why I was so happy when he agreed to do the Preface for this book.

The fact that Gary's *Sports Illustrated* story came out the week before the Hall of Fame induction just made the entire experience even more unforgettable. Since then I've been told by countless people that it would make a great movie. I agree. I hope it happens someday. Of course, Denzel Washington would have to play me. Tom's holding out for Brad Pitt.

Hall of Fame Weekend

People have asked me what Hall of Fame induction weekend was like when I officially became a member of pro football's most exclusive club. I have to admit, it was much like your wedding day—a blur.

We were on such a tight schedule with something going on every minute, it really was overwhelming. I didn't get the chance to spend time with family, much less friends. I felt bad. So many people had come a great distance to share in the moment, and I didn't really have a chance to thank them.

I also thought I would have time to rehearse my speech. I already had spent a great deal of time crafting it before I left for Canton, thanks to DeBorah. She was able to help me with some rough spots where I had difficulty making transitions to the next part. When the induction ceremony was a few weeks away, she could tell I was nervous about it because I would get up and pace the room, sit down, stand up, talk to myself. Finally, she said, "You're being a pain in the ass. Why don't you recite your speech, and then you can decide whether you want me to help you."

So DeBorah had me stand in the kitchen in my pajamas and practice my speech. She helped me make a smooth transition to different parts then said, "It's a great speech, but don't talk like you're reading it. Talk from your heart. Don't think of it as a speech. Think of it as you telling a story." No wonder she's a professional speaker and presenter. My lady is great.

That's when it clicked. That's when I started to feel really good about my so-called speech because I wasn't going to give a speech. I was going to tell a story.

Weeks later when I was busy rushing around in Canton, my son-in-law, Adrian, stopped over at my room to see if I needed any help. I told him the one thing I wanted to do was practice my speech. I said, "Well, it's not really a speech; it's not about football. It's a story about my journey." He smiled and said, "That's cool. Hey, I'm a good person to practice on because I don't get emotional when it comes to things like that."

So I began to recite the speech, and after a few minutes I could see him starting to get emotional. Then when I got to the part, "No one travels this road alone. I can never have imagined the impact of a phone call I got from Tom Mackie's wife…" and I could see tears welling up in Adrian's eyes. He looked away quickly. He just started repeating, "Oh dad, oh dad…" I started thinking, *Oh boy, oh boy*… I knew that if I could get Christy's husband to get emotional, I had a pretty good speech. At that point, I didn't even need to finish. "I'm ready," I said.

My Presenter

Nearly 20 years ago, my son, Marc, and I were having lunch at the Varsity—a great eatery on the Syracuse campus. The Varsity has been a landmark since my college days, and I took Marc there to soak in the atmosphere and let him experience a slice of my college life. We weren't there five minutes before two students approached our table.

One of them said, "Mr. Little, my friend and I have a bet that we want you to settle. We were discussing what year you were inducted into the Pro Football Hall of Fame. I say it was 1982. My friend says 1984. Who's right?"

I swallowed my drink and looked up at their hopeful faces. "Sorry," I said, "But I've never even been nominated," as my voice trailed off. Marc saw the sadness in my eyes that day, having to tell yet another fan that I wasn't in the Hall of Fame. When we got home, Marc sat down and wrote a letter to the sports editor of the *Denver Post* extolling why I should be a Hall of Famer. I was blown away by the passion of his letter. So I made a promise to Marc that if I ever did make it to Canton, he would be my presenter.

True to my word, 20 years after my promise, Marc was there to present me. Although it had to be taped, Marc's words resonated with me and my whole family. He did a magnificent job. He told everyone that either of his two sisters, Christy or Kyra, could have done an excellent job in presenting me, but he was asked to represent our family. I thought that was marvelous.

You can probably tell how much Marc means to me. We are very close. When he was in college at USC he was shot in the leg after being held up at gunpoint. He was rushed to the emergency room and flatlined a few times. He survived but lost his leg. Because he came so close to dying, he and I go on a father-son trip somewhere fantastic each year on his birthday to celebrate his life.

A song that we play a lot on those trips is "Wind Beneath My Wings." Not the Bette Midler version, but the Eddie and Gerald Levert version. It's this beautiful rendition with this incredible sax performance. For those who don't know the story, Eddie and Gerald were an incredible father-son musical group. Eddie was the lead singer of the O'Jays back in the 1970s. Gerald performed in some great groups before teaming up with his father. They had many hits, including "Wind Beneath My Wings." The song always meant so much to us. But several years ago it meant even more after Gerald tragically passed away in 2006 at age 40. He was Marc's age.

I always told Marc that he and his sisters are the wind beneath my wings. So as I'm watching Marc present me at the Hall of Fame, I'm thinking about our incredible relationship. He's telling everyone how much I deserve this honor and how much I mean to him and our family. Then right at the end of his presentation he slips in, "Dad, you are the wind beneath *our* wings!" When I heard that, I lost it. I got up with tears in my eyes as I hugged Marc and said, "You dirty dog. You rolled me under the bus." Marc just looked at me with his eyes flushed and said, "Straighten your tie, Dad. Go knock him dead."

Right then, I knew God had saved Marc for me just for that moment.

A Man of Few Words

Since my induction into Canton, I have heard from hundreds of people who told me how much they loved my speech and how it inspired them. Many people have told me it's the best Hall of Fame speech they ever heard.

I have to admit, even though I'm a humble guy, I'm proud of it. I really put a great deal of effort into it. I was asked by the Hall of Fame not to exceed nine minutes. As you know, I'm a man of my word. So it was a challenge to thank everyone I needed to thank and to say everything I needed to say without going over the limit. There was a lot I had to cut out. But in the end, I think my message was pretty powerful.

Looking back, I'm glad I had to cut some of my speech. The few times I've seen the re-broadcast, it flows pretty well. There's no fluff. It's like watching a commercial. Sometimes the 30-second commercials are much better than the 60-second or the infomercials. That's how I view my Hall of Fame speech—short, to the point, with fireworks at the end.

My Hall of Fame Speech

Thank you. Thank you. I am still standing. And I give all the glory to my Lord and Savior Jesus Christ. I am truly blessed to be standing here on this day to celebrate my journey as a person and as an athlete.

I only wish my mom and dad were here to celebrate with me. I know my mom is looking down on me today and she's saying, 'Floyd, I'm proud of you, you done good.' I also miss my two brothers. Fred, known as Ranger, and Charles, known as Jitty. Jitty was the real hero. He served two terms in Vietnam and was a war hero. I miss my two brothers.

But God continues to bless me with three living sisters—Betty Jackson, Rosalie Johnson, and Priscilla Goodson. These three ladies have been my biggest fans since I first put on a football helmet at Troop Junior High School. You have been my rock and strength on this journey. I could not have made it without your prayer and your support. Thank you for always being there for me.

I also have three very special and talented kids. You've already met my son, Marc. He was my presenter. Marc is not like a regular son. He's also my lawyer, my advisor, and my best friend. Life would be real different for me if Marc wasn't around. I love you, man.

My daughter, Christy, who has blessed me with four grandkids, A.J., Skye, Blaze, and Hayes. Christy is a proud mommy in training and has created a career teaching other mommies to be better mommies, and I'm so proud of her for that. Christy, I am so proud of all the things you do because when I look at you I see all the things you do for our family. We are a close family because of you. I have been truly blessed to have you as my daughter. I love you, Christy.

My daughter, Kyra. I have watched you perform on Broadway and on stages across this country. I have not seen anyone with more talent than you. You truly are a triple threat with abilities that make me proud to stick my chest out and say, 'That is my daughter.' I love you, Kyra.

To Joyce Davis, the mother of my two daughters. Joyce, you did a great job as a mother. Thank you for your support during those early and challenging years as a Denver Bronco. Thank you for your support.

To my beautiful wife DeBorah, my friend, my partner, and everything a husband can want. You stand shoulder to shoulder with me. You never wavered in your steadfast resolve, always willing to go to battle on my behalf, always ready to help me finish the fight. Thank you for always being by my side. You are my Hall of Famer, and I love you.

No one travels this road alone. I can never have imagined the impact of a phone call I got from Tom Mackie's wife, Emily. She called asking if I would consider meeting Tom for his 40th birthday because I was Tom's hero. Not only did Tom and I meet, but he became the co-author of my first book, Tales from the Bronco Sideline. My biggest advocate for my Pro Football Hall of Fame consideration. Now Tom is my hero. Thank you, Tom Mackie, for all you've done. I truly appreciate it.

Lastly I want to thank my biggest friend and supporter, Jim Gray. Thank you, Jim Gray, for all you've done that contributed to my moment of being here today. I'm truly grateful, Jim, for all you've done.

The list of those that's had an impact on my life and career is long, but I must give thanks to Ernie Davis, to Jim Brown, to John Mackey, to Hal Williams, to Ernie Barnes, to Billy Thompson, and my coaches Dan Casey, Al Verdel, Jay Lou, Ben Swartzwalder, Lou Saban, John Ralston. A special thanks to the Hall of Fame committee, Jeff Legwold, Jim Saccomano, and my Syracuse family, Dr. Nancy Cantor, and Dr.

Daryl Gross, and the Vice President of the United States, Joe Biden. To all my classmates, all my teammates from Hillhouse High School, Bordentown Military, Syracuse University, and the Denver Broncos. To Pat Bowlen and the entire Bronco organization, and to all the Bronco fans around the world. To all my friends and family who are here, and those who could not be here, thank you for your loyalty and your support over all these years. I am truly, truly grateful.

There's no words to describe the joy of experiencing this final sports chapter in my life. This is obviously the highest honor any football player can garner. I stand here today celebrating my athletic life journey, and I understand its significance. Everything else pales in comparison. Every player wakes up wishing to have this honor. I encourage you all to continue to dream for this moment. I have been favored by God and by those who have had a say in what happens to me.

But the road was not always so easy and clear. I remember being a strong but angry young man in school. I used my strength in ways that became my weakness. After being kicked out of school, I had reached an impasse in my life. Everything was done. My hopes were shattered and done. And then I had a vision from my late father that came to me and said, 'Floyd, I've chosen you to take my place, to do what I could not do, and to finish what I could not finish.'

I came to myself. With the help of those who saw the good in me, I was re-enrolled back in school with determination. Not only did I become the president of my class, but I started my journey as a leader in everything that I did, and I never looked back.

Because of those [who] encouraged me in those early years, I am here today. So I want to encourage you, every student, every athlete, every person who will hear my voice, don't listen to the naysayer. I had plenty of those. Don't listen to those that will judge you for your rough edges. Don't focus on your weakness so you won't become a victim. Find the goodness in you that says, Yes, I can be a good student. Yes, I can be a good son and daughter. Yes, I can be a positive role model. Yes, I can, because the good in you is better than the worst in most. The choice is yours. Be the best that you can be.

I truly believe that none of us is anything until the least of us is something. The great writer James Baldwin said, 'Naked I came into this world

*and naked I shall leave.' We are bound to leave everything we accomplished
in this lifetime behind, passing it on. So leave a legacy that you and your
family can be proud.*

*I've given you the best that I've got. And I'm a better person for it.
Thank you for being here with me and for me. I thank God for His favor
today, and may God bless us all. Thank you so much.*

The People in My Speech

I was told my Hall of Fame speech could only be nine minutes. As a
man of my word I did all that I could to stay within the limit. That means
I only had time to mention some people by name, even though I would
have loved to espouse on how much they've meant to me. You know, the
Jim Browns, John Mackeys, Lou Sabans and many of the other people I
mentioned in my speech. But here are some who you might have said,
"Who's that?"

Ernie Barnes

Ernie Barnes played guard and tackle from 1960–64 in the early years
of the AFL. Drafted by the Colts in the 10th round in 1960, he instead
chose to play for the New York Titans of the AFL. He also played for
the Chargers and the Broncos. When I got to Denver in 1967, Ernie was
already retired. I got to know Ernie through Charlie Mitchell, a great running back who also played for the Broncos. So Ernie became my adopted
teammate. But to say that Ernie was just a former football player was to say
that Dr. Martin Luther King was just a preacher.

Ernie's real gift was art. In my mind he was the greatest African
American artist of my generation. His work was powerful, showing grit
and fierce emotion. His paintings appeared in some of the finest muse-
ums in the country. His work also appeared on album covers, like Marvin
Gaye's 1976 album, *I Want You*. Ernie became the official artist of the
1984 Olympic Games in Los Angeles. I own four of his pieces, including
one called *The Fullback*, which I was told was inspired by me.

Ernie was just an incredible guy. His best friend was Bill Withers, the
great singer/songwriter. DeBorah and I became great friends with Ernie
and his wife Bernie (yes, they rhymed!). After 9/11, Ernie did a painting

commemorating the Twin Towers that he donated to the Natural History Museum of Seattle.

The year before I was inducted into Canton, Ernie went in for surgery. I called to wish him luck, and he came out fine. Then there were complications, and he was rushed back into surgery. Shortly thereafter, I got a call from Bernie telling me Ernie had died. I was devastated. I had just talked to him. We had discussed them coming to Canton if I got elected. After he passed, I wanted people to know he was there in spirit.

Ernie's legacy will live on in his paintings that will inspire generations to come.

Hal Williams

Hal Williams, or the guy my family calls "Uncle Hal," is a movie and television star. He appeared in movies like *Private Benjamin* and also starred on *Sanford and Son* and *227*. I got to know him through my first wife, Joyce, who did a lot of acting. She and Hal both had roles on the television version of *Private Benjamin*.

I used to come down to watch tapings. We'd hang in the trailers and talk. That's how I got to know Hal. He was so personable and sincere. We shared a lot of laughs. He was a heck of a football player in college, so we had plenty of gridiron stories to tell. Even after Joyce and I divorced, Hal remained a close family friend. He's been to all our family's events, kids' graduations, daughters' weddings. Whenever we have cookouts, we make sure to invite Hal. He's probably the best barbecue man in the country. He and Marc are really good friends. He's Uncle Hal, he's family! Of course, he was there at my Hall of Fame induction. He said he wouldn't miss it for the world.

Dr. Nancy Cantor

As the chancellor of Syracuse University, you would think Dr. Nancy Cantor would be a rather formal, very buttoned-up leader. Ah, no. Don't get me wrong, Nancy is very professional, and one of the smartest people I've ever met. But what I love about her is how dynamic, outgoing, and supportive she is of everything that goes on at Syracuse. You won't see her sitting high up in some executive suite at athletic events. Hell, no. She's down by the players, cheering her heart out with her husband, Steven. She's fully committed to her job. She knows the players, and you'll see her high-fiving them quite a bit.

Nancy has also done a lot to integrate the faculty and students at Syracuse with people of color. She's appointed African Americans to head up the Management School and the Newhouse School. This past year, our freshman class at Syracuse comprised of 32 percent minorities. She doesn't just talk the talk, she walks the walk. We are so fortunate to have her at Syracuse.

My first impression of Nancy has not faded in the least. When I first accepted the position here at Syracuse, I received an email from her that said, "Yay, yay, yay, yay, yay, yay, yay, yay!!!!!"

Dr. Daryl Gross

My boss, Daryl Gross, is the athletic director at Syracuse. He is an outstanding athletic director who learned from the best—Mike Garrett, who beat me out for the 1965 Heisman Trophy!

After being at USC for more than a decade, Daryl came to Syracuse in 2005. One of the first things he did as AD was retire the No. 44 worn by Jim Brown, Ernie Davis, myself, and some other great backs. Daryl knows about football. He was a pretty good player at California–Davis where he played receiver and caught passes from former Jets quarterback Ken O'Brien. Daryl also did a lot to make sure the movie *The Express* was told the right way. He made sure the 2008 premiere was held right here in Syracuse, not Hollywood.

What can I say, this man changed my life! I was resigned to retiring after I gave up my Ford Dealership in 2009 and had spent a year enjoying life as a newly minted Hall of Famer. I sold my house in Seattle and my stuff was on its way to my new home in Las Vegas when he called me to ask if I would become his special assistant at Syracuse—to help with fundraising, recruiting, and most important, restoring the Orange's proud athletic tradition. Coming back to Syracuse has changed my life, and I am so grateful to Daryl and all the people at this university.

He's been so appreciative of my efforts, too. He told me recently, "I'm glad you're here, Floyd. Because of you, I sleep better."

Jim Saccomano

Jim Saccomano is one of the finest men I've ever known. He's been the Broncos public relations guru since 1978. And although I retired in 1975, Jim has gone out of his way to make sure fans have never forgotten me. He's a Colorado native, and though we were never part of the organization at the same time, he probably saw all my games.

This is the kind of guy Jim is. He doesn't call me Floyd, he calls me the Franchise. Even after all these years. That was my nickname back in my playing days because my signing in 1967 as the first-ever No. 1 pick helped lead to the expansion and yearly sell-out of Mile High Stadium. Jim never forgot that, and I appreciate all he's done for me.

When I was working on my first book back in 2005, Jim invited Tom Mackie and me to spend the day at Broncos headquarters, allowing us to look through old files to find photos we could use for the book. Jim has also always made sure the writers who vote on the Hall of Fame never forgot my name. When I was finally nominated for the Hall of Fame, Jim told me, "This is a great day for Broncos fans and, on a personal note, a great day for me." What a guy!

The Ray Nitschke Luncheon

For years outsiders have asked about the famed Hall of Fame Luncheon during induction weekend. It's officially called the Ray Nitschke Luncheon after the late, great Hall of Fame linebacker. The purpose of this ultra-private luncheon is to welcome the new class of Hall of Famers.

In the year our 2010 class arrived, there were almost 100 Hall of Famers in attendance. I was glad because quite a few of these legends passed away the following year, including John Mackey, Joe Perry, John Henry Johnson, Andy Robustelli, Pete Pihos, and Ollie Matson.

As new Hall of Famers you are sworn to silence. Literally. You are not allowed to speak during the luncheon. My friend Willie Lanier presides over the event and does a sort of roll call.

He will go around the room and randomly pick different Hall of Famers to get up and talk. Sometimes he asks them about a certain subject. Sometimes he asks the person to tell about his journey to Canton. It's a fascinating and humbling experience. You witness how some of these all-time greats have difficulty talking about themselves. Sometimes you see a lot of emotion, a lot of tears. You sit there in awe and pinch yourself that you are now part of this exclusive brotherhood. You are now family.

My Celebration Party

After the Hall of Fame luncheon, the parades, the induction ceremony, and all the speeches, each player was given their own private celebration party in tents not far from the stadium. The tents were the kind you see at outdoor weddings. My tent was filled to the brim with family, friends, former teammates, coaches, and fans.

I had two emotions as I walked over to the celebration: pure elation and pure exhaustion. The speech that I was so nervous about had gone extremely well. Jerry Jones and Eddie DeBartolo told me how great my speech was and said that Marc had the best presentation they had seen.

Yet along with feeling happy and relieved, I was barely running on fumes at that point.

Every moment of my time was taken up during the weekend. It was like a rollercoaster of non-stop events—luncheons and dinners, parades, press conferences, media events, autograph signings, then the induction itself. I barely had time to catch my breath. That feeling went away when I stepped into the tent and was literally engulfed by well-wishers. So many people I hadn't seen in years were there, as well as so many friends and relatives that I was so glad had made the effort. Unfortunately, I barely had time to say hello before I was pulled in another direction. Still, it was important for me to stop and shake everyone's hand. Stop and sign a helmet or a ball. Stop and pose with people in front of my bust. But it quickly took its toll.

I maintained a second wind for a while. There were people from my high school days, from my days at Bordentown, from Syracuse, the Broncos, my Ford dealership associates, and relatives that I hadn't seen before. Even some of my ex-wife's relatives came to be part of the celebration, which was touching. I mean John Mackey's wife, Sylvia, was there. It was unbelievable to see so many people who had bridged the span of my life—all in one place! It was beyond surreal. It was magical. Seriously, when does that happen? Maybe at your wedding, if you invite 400 people.

I'm especially glad my Syracuse friends were there. And my closest Broncos teammates, BT, Rich Jackson, Tommy Jackson, and Jerry Simmons. Three great Broncos who deserve to be in Canton someday and one, Jerry, who caught my only NFL touchdown pass!

After a couple of hours, though, I didn't think I could stand anymore. I finally saw Tom and gave him a hug. He looked concerned and asked me if I was okay. I said, "Tom, I haven't slept in two days." He said he was sorry, then he still made me smile and pose with him in front of my bust. That dirty dog!

The one great thing our family did was hire our own photographer, Daryn Hollis, to take photos of everyone at the event so we will always have them. He did an unbelievable job.

Around midnight, my son-in-law, Adrian, saw that I had had enough. He and my nephew basically kidnapped me and tossed me in a car to take me back to the hotel. I had to get up early the next morning for an autograph session, and they knew I was long overdue for Z-town. Needless to say, I was out before I hit the pillow.

There is one sour note from my celebration party that is unforgiveable. As is customary with Hall of Fame tradition, the player's team is asked to pick up the tab. Well, much to my dismay, I was told by the Broncos that they would only pay for the tent. No food, tables, or anything else. So I had to pay $12,000 out of my own pocket so my guests could eat, drink, and have a place to sit down. Someone told me I also had the smallest tent. A few of the Hall of Famers were teasing me, "Did you see Emmitt Smith's tent? They've got chandeliers in there. Did you see Rickey Jackson's? He's got a jazz orchestra in his." I can bet you that Emmitt Smith and Jerry Rice didn't have to pay for the food at their private parties. I was shocked and hurt that the team I had helped laid the foundation for, the team that signed me to bolster fan support and keep the Broncos in Denver, the team for which my performances helped to begin a string of sellout games that's lasted more than 40 years, would be so damn cheap. I just don't understand. It was incredibly disappointing, and it's something that still upsets me.

A Special Ovation

Tom Coughlin and I remain good friends. We trade emails and phone calls during the year, and I always make a point to play in his Jay Fund charity golf tournament in Jacksonville, Florida, every year. Tom puts together a nice banquet the first night of the tournament and introduces many of the attendees.

A couple of years ago, I was sitting there as he went around and introduced just about everyone. I thought, *Well, I guess Tom forgot about me.* A moment later, Tom stood up and said, "I've got one more introduction. This is someone I truly admire. He's someone I've known for many years. Someone I've always aspired to be like. Someone who when he was in college could climb two 20' ropes, one hand at a time, without using his legs. Someone who was such a great leader and such a great player that anytime he was in the huddle, I knew we had a chance to win. Someone, who after an incredible Pro Bowl career with the Denver Broncos, was finally inducted into the Pro Football Hall of Fame this year. Ladies and gentleman, a great friend and my teammate from Syracuse, Hall of Famer Floyd Little!"

The place erupted with a standing ovation. I was so surprised and so humbled by Tom's gesture, I could have kissed him.

That's the kind of guy Tom Coughlin is, the kind that few people see. The kind the media and the fans are finally starting to appreciate.

Receiving My Hall of Fame Ring

A month after I was elected to the Pro Football Hall of Fame, I received my Hall of Fame ring at halftime of the Colts game in front of the great Broncos fans. The Friday before the game the Broncos Alumni put together a tribute for me, and Saturday was our annual Alumni golf outing. It was a great three days culminating with me receiving my Hall of Fame ring in front of my family and the great Broncos fans. I say it all the time but it's true—Broncos fans are the greatest in the NFL. They have never forgotten me, and every time I come back to Denver I always get the second-biggest cheer—next to John Elway, of course!

The coach at the time, Josh McDaniels, had asked me to speak to the team before the Colts game. I was planning on doing so until the tragic death of Broncos receiver Kenny McKinley just six days earlier. I politely postponed speaking to the team until another time because the team was still reeling emotionally about his passing.

Kenny's death really impacted me. I couldn't fully celebrate receiving the Hall of Fame ring because of it. My heart went out to his family and especially the young son he left behind. I had never met Kenny, but speaking to young people is what I do. It reaffirmed my belief that NFL players need someone on each team in a support role. I'm not sure the Broncos have that, maybe they do. But I remember when the Dallas Cowboys had players with some off-field issues, they hired the great Calvin Hill and his wife, Janet, to develop some internal programs, including assisting players with how to deal with celebrity as well as personal issues.

When you're young and you grow up without money, then all of a sudden you have money and responsibilities, like Kenny had with his son, then you get injured, the world can seem too much. I just wish to God that Kenny had someone he trusted that he could have spoken to who could have helped him avoid this tragedy.

A Special Athletic Center

I've achieved a lot in my life through hard work and sacrifice. But I never thought that I would have anything named after me. That's what happened last fall in 2011 when the newly built New Haven Athletic Center next to my high school, Hillhouse High, was named the Floyd Little Athletic Center.

There were hundreds of people at the dedication. I used my opportunity to address the crowd to encourage students about the importance of getting an education. I told them how I struggled in school so badly that I had to take the SAT five times. I went from a 200, which is what you get just for writing your name, to a 1280.

A lot of my high school classmates were there, including my favorite teacher, Robert Schreck. He was the teacher who worked so hard to give me another chance after I was thrown out of school in the eighth grade. He helped give me one more chance when no one else would. I asked teachers there to keep believing in students who may be struggling, like Mr. Schreck did for me.

Walter Camp Distinguished American Award

One of the greatest honors I've ever received occurred in January 2012 when I received the Walter Camp Distinguished American Award. It's given annually to an individual who has used his or her talents to attain great success in business, private life, or public service. The person also has to exemplify teamwork, integrity, dedication, and be a leader, innovator, and pioneer.

Needless to say I was blown away and completely humbled by the honor. Past recipients have included Pro Football Hall of Famers like Chuck Bednarik, Red Grange, and Len Dawson, as well as coaches like George Halas, Tom Landry, and Dick Vermeil.

The event was doubly special because it was held in my hometown of New Haven, Connecticut. It was a great weekend where some of the greatest players and coaches came together, including Stanford quarterback Andrew Luck, Hall of Famer Harry Carson, Lions great Chris Spielman, and LSU coach Les Miles—all of whom won awards.

The biggest thrill for me though was being asked to address 2,500 middle school students at the athletic center that bears my name. I talked to the students about how I was at a crossroads when I was their age and how I was frustrated because I wasn't a very good student. But I never gave up. I told them, "You have to choose to better yourself because life is a challenge." I also talked about focus, commitment, sacrifice, and dedication. And I told them never listen to the naysayers, because you can accomplish anything with a positive attitude.

I was just one of a handful of speakers who took part in the Walter Camp Foundation's "Stay in School" rally that weekend. After my speech one of the foundation's organizers pulled me to the side and asked me if I could give the closing speech at that night's award ceremony.

I said, "Absolutely, I would be honored." I always look at making a speech as a chance to inspire and motivate someone. It doesn't matter whether I'm talking to students or some of the most accomplished people in the country, I have something to say.

That night I addressed an audience that included Andrew Luck and his other Walter Camp All-American teammates, fellow Hall of Famers like Harry Carson, and coaches such as LSU's Les Miles. "You are all here because you are game-changers. Now I challenge you to be life-changers." I urged them to look beyond their success and become committed to using their talents and their platform to change young people's lives.

"The world needs role models. Not every child has parents who are there for them. We have all accomplished something great in our lives. But what purpose does that serve unless we can help someone else accomplish something in their lives? I know you have the power to make a difference in the community and in someone's life. But will you? That's the question."

I went on for several minutes and really challenged this audience of overachievers. After my speech, I got a rousing standing ovation and was literally mobbed by people. They were blown away by my speech. I have to admit it's been something I've wanted to say for a long time, but I never had the opportunity to speak to such an audience of accomplished people until then.

It is my hope that the young athletes like Andrew Luck take my urging and continue to be positive role models. Even Les Miles pulled me aside and said, "That was one hell of a speech. Next year please come and speak to my players." Then he leaned in and said, "Too bad I didn't have you address my kids before the BCS Championship because I believe the outcome would have been different!"

The Broncos Drop the Ball

It would be one thing if the Broncos frugalness that I mentioned earlier, having me pay for my Hall of Fame private tent party, had been an isolated incident. But I've experienced a series of inhospitable episodes with my old team that hurt so much I can't internalize them any longer. I'm one of those guys who have bitten his lip a number of times when I've been treated poorly. In my professional football career, in business, and in my life I've tried to go along to get along.

Part of the reason is I never wanted things I said in the heat of the moment to come back and bite me. It never made good business sense to do so. But I'm at an age now where I realize I must be true to myself. After all, this is what I preach.

The thing is, the Broncos somewhere along the way have gone from one of the marquee organizations in the NFL, like they were in the late

1990s, to becoming on par with notorious tide-wad teams like the Lions, Bengals, and Cardinals. I just don't understand why.

After I retired from the Broncos the one thing I wanted more than anything was to remain with the team in some capacity. Whether it was in player personnel, serving the community, it didn't matter. Hell, I retired from football with a degree from Denver Law School. So it's not like I didn't have the capacity to become an executive. Still, in the more than 35 years since my retirement, the Broncos never once offered me a position with the organization. In fact, after my retirement, the Jets offered me a position with their team. So did Hank Stram, who had just become the head coach of the Saints. So I told the Broncos about those two offers, hoping they would say, "There's no way we're going to let Floyd Little work for any NFL team except for this one." Nope. Instead they said, "Okay, we'll be happy to give you a recommendation if you need one."

I was heartbroken. Deep down, the Broncos were the only team I wanted to work for. After all, I had poured my heart into that organization for nine years and had been the face of the franchise during all those tough years. So I decided to move on with my life. I went into the beer distribution business for a couple years. Then there was an opportunity to get into an executive management class through Ford. A while later, I purchased my first Lincoln-Mercury dealership in Englewood, Colorado, before moving to Los Angeles to own dealerships in Santa Barbara and West Covina, so my then-wife, Joyce, could pursue an acting career.

Still, whenever the Broncos needed me I was there. Like when the Broncos were experiencing backlash when it was announced they were tearing down beloved Mile High Stadium to build the more corporate-focused Invesco Field at Mile High, they asked me to help generate enthusiasm for the new structure. So I did, even though deep down, I hated watching Mile High being torn to shreds.

Then finally the day came when I got nominated to the Pro Football Hall of Fame. Since I promised my family 20 years earlier if I was ever nominated, I would take them to the Super Bowl, I asked the Broncos for eight Super Bowl tickets. Initially they said yes. But then some administrative confusion ensued that was their fault. Days before the Super Bowl they announced they could only give me four tickets. And, oh yeah, I had to pay for them—$1,000 each. I had promised my family, so I scrambled to get the tickets. I asked two of my best friends, BT and Darrell Elliott, if they could somehow get the other tickets. After a lot of effort on their part, they came through. Then at the Super Bowl, I ran into my good friend Fred Biletnikoff, the Hall of Fame receiver for the Raiders. I asked him how he got his Super Bowl tickets. He shrugged, "Oh, I asked the Raiders for 10 tickets and they just mailed them to me." Then I asked how much he had to pay for them. Fred looked at me like I was nuts. "What do you mean, how much did I pay?! They were free, of course!"

I already mentioned the $12,000 I had to pay for my Hall of Fame celebration party in Canton. I assure you the Broncos were the only organization that charged their Hall of Famer for his own party.

A month later, when I was to receive my Hall of Fame Ring at halftime of the Broncos-Colts game, the Broncos allowed me to invite 10 people to the ceremony. They paid for airfare and hotel, which is customary. But then, I discovered they didn't pay for incidentals, which I found out when I got a hotel bill for a bottle of water that I took out of the fridge in my room. Weeks before the ceremony, I asked the Broncos for an extra ticket so my one sister could come. The Broncos said absolutely not. So I had to tell my sister she couldn't come. At the ring ceremony they put us in a suite but made it clear they were not going to pay for any food. I told them that was outrageous. So they told us they could bring food to our suite but it would cost me more than $2,500. So my daughter made me a cake instead.

I thought I had seen everything, until the dedication of the Floyd Little Athletic Center last year. One of the organizers contacted the Broncos to ask if they wanted to place a $250 ad in the program to congratulate me. Coming from a franchise with a net worth of more than $1 billion, it was obviously a rhetorical question. The Broncos' response floored everyone. "No, we've already done enough for Floyd," they said. Somehow my alma mater, Hillhouse High, was able to fork over money for a full-page ad. So was Syracuse University. And so was a high school classmate.

A similar scenario happened a couple months later when I received the Walter Camp Distinguished American Award. Syracuse took out a full-page ad in the program and the organizers contacted the Broncos to ask them. After what happened before, I could only guess what their response was going to be. So the night of the event, I picked up a copy of the program and leafed through it—page by page of beautiful full-page ads. Then I saw it. The Broncos actually came through with an ad congratulating me—a half-page ad! I laughed because I couldn't believe how ridiculous it looked. Here is a $1 billion NFL franchise with one of their only four Hall of Famers in team history getting a prestigious award, and they only purchased a half-page ad. Unbelievable.

It's not that the Broncos never do anything nice for me. At the Broncos Alumni event the year I was inducted, they put together a nice tribute for me. They did the same in London when the Broncos played the 49ers. But it's the cheapness, the nickel and diming, which you might expect from a mom-and-pop shop—not an ultra-successful NFL franchise. DeBorah has been a saint through all of this. She knows I hate cheap people and she's been the one that communicates with the Broncos. For the last couple of years it's been constant negotiation. The Broncos will itemize what they will cover and go to the mat on other things saying, "No, we will not cover this or that."

Don't you think they should be embracing any opportunity they have to support one of their best players? My Hall of Fame induction should have been a huge celebration for them. Hell, anytime one of us Ring of Famers ask the Broncos for something they should bend over backwards to accommodate us No questions asked. We helped make this organization what it is today. We're just asking to be loved and respected.

I mean, are they hurting that bad? The team has sold out every game since the NFL-AFL merger. I'm sure having Tim Tebow for two years and this year with Peyton Manning that merchandising has been through the roof. C'mon, you're a $1 billion franchise and you can't pay $12,000 for food at a party for one of your newly minted Hall of Famers? Or even $250 for an ad in a program? I have to be honest, I don't know who is the pulling the trigger when it comes to these short-sighted decisions. Is it Pat Bowlen or somebody else? I do know that usually this kind of stuff trickles down from the top.

To be honest, the Broncos have given me such a bad taste in my mouth there are only three reasons I ever come back to Denver anymore. The fans who I love dearly, friends like BT and Darrell, and to see my old team-mates and guys like Jim Saccomano during the Broncos alumni weekend. That's it.

I feel slighted. Maybe it's because I'm the only HOFer who didn't play for the current ownership? I don't know. I just don't understand. I've bled orange for this organization ever since I became the Broncos' first No. 1 pick to sign 45 years ago.

All I know is the Broncos aren't the same organization they once were. It's puzzling, sad, and I'm extremely hurt by it.

16

COMING BACK HOME TO SYRACUSE

Home Again

After my Hall of Fame induction, my schedule became busier. I flew back to my alma mater, Syracuse, for many fundraising events and dedications, such as when they unveiled the Ernie Davis statue. I also was asked to speak to more youth groups than ever. I spent a year traveling all across the country. My joy has always been talking to young people—students of every age. I had been such a troubled kid that my heart goes out to youth looking for someone to care about them. There are few things that bring me more joy than to reach a kid who needs direction. It's nearly impossible for me to say no when I'm asked to address a group of young people. Sometimes I go weeks without a single day to myself. It can be exhausting, but it's so incredibly fulfilling.

I started looking at my life. I was 69 years old. I had been in the auto business for 32 years and had finally sold my last Ford dealership the year before. DeBorah and I talked about taking it easy and smelling the roses, so to speak. We decided to move south to a warmer climate and buy a home in Las Vegas. I know it's called Sin City, but it's always been a favorite place of mine to play golf, see a show, play a little poker, and enjoy the great weather.

We bought a house and started packing for Vegas. We were literally surrounded by moving boxes when the phone rang. It was Daryl Gross, the Syracuse athletic director. His assistant, Scott Sidwell, had just accepted the AD job at the University of San Francisco. "Floyd," he said, "I was asked who would be the best person to take Scott's job at Syracuse, and you were the first person who popped into my head. We want you to come back here and be my special assistant. To help with fundraising, recruiting, and help restore our football program to its glory days. Be a positive influence here on campus. What do you say?"

The first thing I thought was, "Wow, this is too bad. The timing is terrible. I'm on my way to Las Vegas!" I told him I would have to get back to him. Truth is I was stunned and a bit taken back by it all. Years before, my dream was to be part of the Broncos organization, but sadly I never got a single offer to come back. As I put down the phone, DeBorah and I sat down to discuss it. After wading through a few of the pros and cons, I realized something. What was I really doing moving to Las Vegas? To relax and piddle around, look through old scrapbooks, catch the early bird special so I could be in bed by 9:00 PM? I grinned and started salivating. Who else gets offered a new career at my age? Who gets the chance to influence young people every day—at the place that gave me an education and a roadmap to success. Holy crap, this is a dream job! I grabbed my phone and started punching numbers so fast that I misdialed Daryl four times. "Yes, absolutely, I will come home to Syracuse!" I said when I finally got through.

Home Is Where the Heart Is

The year I've been back here at Syracuse as the special assistant to the athletic director has been the greatest of my life. It's been even more amazing than the year before when I was inducted into Canton. After my induction, the rest of the year became a victory tour of sorts. I was invited across the country as the guest of honor at multiple events celebrating my career.

My new position at Syracuse as the special assistant to the athletic director has afforded me the opportunity to influence so many kids—not just football players. I instituted an open-door policy from Day 1. Every morning when I get to my office, there's a group of student athletes waiting to talk to me—young men and women. Whether they're on the men's basketball team or the lady's lacrosse teams, soccer, field hockey recruits, you name it. I am here to engage with them, offer encouragement, and inspire them.

The student athletes come into my office and they see my accomplishments hanging on the wall. I adorn my office with posters, plaques from the Hall of Fame, my retired jersey, and various honors, such as my Walter Camp Distinguished American Award that I received last year. This is done on purpose to inspire these kids to accomplish their own goals. I want them to look around my office and see how bright their future can be. The first thing I do is listen to them. Find out their goals, their dreams, ask them what they want to accomplish here at Syracuse.

Then I help lay out a game plan. I talk to them about how valuable their time is right now, how college will lay the foundation for their life journey ahead, and why it's important to make the right choice, and the sacrifices you'll have to make to reach your goals.

I also want to know what's in their heads, what they think about. I ask, "What does teamwork mean to you? What's your definition of hard work?" My interpretation may be different than theirs. If they think hard work is studying two hours a night, I ask if they think that's enough. Hard work isn't always staying up until 4:00 AM studying. It also means working smart. Maybe if you're having trouble in a particular subject you need to ask for help, ask for a tutor. So many people are afraid to ask for help. I know I was one of those kids. Think of it this way—it's your life, your future. So put your pride aside and ask for help if you need it. I always say if you want to be the best, hang out with athletes who are better than you. The same goes with school. Study with students who are smarter than you.

You have to decide to make your dreams and goals happen for you. No one else is going to do that. Be responsible for your own actions. Never say, "Well, he did this so I couldn't..." No. Take responsibility. Don't let someone take your dream from you. Stay focused every day. You're only going to be here a few years and leave here when you're in your early twenties. You have a long journey ahead of you, 50 years or more. But the commitment, the sacrifice to be great starts here and now. Own your future so you won't become a victim.

I know I can get carried away even when I'm writing. But I want young people to know that I'm as passionate about their futures as they are. Coming home to Syracuse has been one of the greatest times of my life. It's a dream job. In fact, it's not a job when you love what you do. I wake up each morning with a big shit-eating grin on my face because I'm so happy I've been given this opportunity.

We have a lot of fun with the students, too. One of the administrators I work with is Herm Frazier. He won a gold medal in the 1976 Olympics in the 4 x 400 meter relay. When I was in high school I had the state record in the 100-yard dash. Somehow the students have convinced us to race each other in a 40-yard dash. Let's face it, there's no way I could even jog 400 meters, and I'd probably pull up limp in the 100. So 40 yards is plenty for me. We're having a great time joking with the students over this impending event. Even Daryl Gross, the AD, wants to race, too.

I will be sure to update everyone on the outcome. Unless, of course, I lose—then no one will ever hear about it!

My First Day on the Job

Of course, being a former Syracuse football star, a lot of football players visit me, too. Sometimes they just want to meet me, shake my hand. They tell me their dads or even their grandparents used to watch me play. But I'm not here to be congratulated and put on a pedestal. I always turn the subject to them. "What can I do for you today?" I say.

I had the opportunity to make a difference with the first player who ever walked into my office. Cameron Lynch, a freshman linebacker, came by and introduced himself, "Hello, I just wanted to meet you. I'm a freshman linebacker, but I don't think I can make the team." I sat back in my chair and asked him why. "Well, I'm too small, not big enough." So I asked him his height and weight. "I'm only 5'11", 225 pounds."

I shook my head. I played with a linebacker his size who should be considered for the Hall of Fame. "Let me ask you something, have you ever heard of Tom Jackson? The guy who's been sitting next to Chris Berman the past 25 years doing NFL countdown on ESPN?" Of course, he had heard of him. "Well, Tommy was a teammate of mine with the Broncos. He was all of 5'11", 218 pounds when we drafted him out of

Louisville. You know what Tommy did? He became a Pro Bowl linebacker. He played 14 seasons and started on two Super Bowl teams. Are you bigger than him?"

He said, "Yes."

"Look, they can measure your height, speed, and strength. But your heart, they can't measure. You can accomplish anything if you have enough fight in your heart." I told him to leave and think about whether he really wanted to make the commitment to play at Syracuse. "If you really want to play, come back tomorrow, and I'll tell you how to do it."

Here's a kid who was looking for some empathy and understanding. But he wasn't going to get it from me. That may be what he wanted, but that's not what he needed.

The next day he was standing, not sitting, when I got to my office. As we sat and talked, he told me all the things standing in his way. I knew he had too many things swimming around in his head. So I simplified things.

"Think of life this way," I began. "You only get 100 plays in life. You can't afford to take a play off because that could be your touchdown play, your interception play, or your game-changing play. If you think that way and believe that way, you will never go through life saying these two things: 'I wish I had,' or 'I should have.' If you find yourself saying either, it means you didn't give it your all. You left something in the tank."

I told him about the importance of leaving everything on the field. You can't take it with you. If you approach life that way, you will be successful.

It's like that famous quote by Grantland Rice: "For when the One Great Scorer comes to mark against your name, He writes—not that you won or lost—But how you played the Game." Some people get confused by that. It may be a quote about football, but it's really about life. In the end, no one cares if you won but how you lived your life.

So I made a deal with Cameron. I would come watch him at practice to make sure he was giving it his all. I told him, "If I give you a thumbs up after a play, then you gave it your all. If I lean my thumb sideways, it means you could have done more."

This seemed to excite and motivate the young man. I could see him getting better at every practice. If he made a great play, he would look over at me with a grin while I gave him the thumbs up. When he made a bad play, he tried not to look over. But he knew my thumb wasn't pointing up. I'm proud to say Cameron played with a high intensity all season. Not only did he make the team, by the end of the season he had become a starting linebacker!

When I talk to young athletes I stress the importance of playing hard. You may not always play your best. But if you play hard you can often make up for mistakes or lack of talent.

My Philosophy

Over the years I've developed into quite the philosopher. It started at Bordentown when I was given a chance to make something of my life. I was already motivated by then because my guidance counselor at Hillhouse High told me I wasn't college material. I set out to prove her wrong in everything I did. Once at a track meet at Bordentown, I ran against Rick Spooner, the New Jersey high school champion in the 220-yard dash. Before the race I memorized the poem, "Don't Quit." I repeated these lines to myself during the race:

> When things go wrong, as they sometimes will,
> When the road you're trudging seems all uphill,
> When the funds are low and the debts are high,
> And you want to smile, but you have to sigh,
> When care is pressing you down a bit,
> Rest, if you must, but don't you quit.
> Life is queer with its twists and turns,
> As every one of us sometimes learns,
> And many a failure turns about,
> When he might have won had he stuck it out;
> Don't give up though the pace seems slow—
> You may succeed with another blow.
> Often the goal is nearer than,
> It seems to a faint and faltering man,
> Often the struggler has given up,
> When he might have captured the victor's cup,
> And he learned too late when the night slipped down,
> How close he was to the golden crown.

Success is failure turned inside out—
The silver tint of the clouds of doubt,
And you never can tell how close you are,
It may be near when it seems so far,
So stick to the fight when you're hardest hit—
It's when things seem worst that you must not quit.

When I crossed the line I not only beat Rick, I set a new record. By the time I left Bordentown, I had 47 college scholarship offers. And the one I accepted at Syracuse was an academic scholarship.

I was a history major at Syracuse and continued to study different philosophies, as well. I memorized many different poems, and they've been the inspiration behind everything I've achieved in life. My favorite is a line from a poem by Dean Alfange that I'd like to have on my epitaph. It's become my creed:

I do not choose to be a common man. It is my right to be uncommon...
if I can.

I tried to instill these ideas in my children. My oldest daughter, Christy, used to bring home boys from school for me to counsel. I'd come in the house, and there'd be boys from her class sitting in a chair, waiting for me. She'd see them struggling in school and say, "You need to talk to my dad." A lot of them needed direction. I would tell them about the importance of education and surrounding yourself with positive people so you can plant yourself and grow. I'd say, "You need foresight and a commitment to win. You can't hang with people who procrastinate." I'd repeat famous Lombardi quotes like, "Winning is not a sometime thing, it's an all-the-time thing." I'd talk on their level and bring them up a notch.

People had a lot of wrong opinions about me growing up. So I tell kids, "Someone else's label or opinion of you should not become your reality. You have to be willing to shoot for the moon, because even if you miss, you'll land amongst the stars."

Since I was at Syracuse, I've spent a lot of my free time as a public speaker. I tell people there are seven basic principles for success:

Drive, Determination, Dedication, Desire, Commitment, Sacrifice, and Attitude. They're not just words to put on your bulletin board they're words to inspire you every day. Analyze and adopt each one. I couldn't have achieved anything in life without them.

I also tell people, there are three kinds of people, "Those who make things happen; those who watch things happen; and those don't know what just happened." Which one are you?

I was told I was too old and too small to make it in the NFL. I wanted to prove the doubters wrong. So I adopted the mantra that I was auditioning for life every day. I had to prove myself over and over again. No one could tell me what I could or could not do. It was up to me to decide. When I retired in 1975, every back from that '67 class was already gone. I was the last running back standing. Imagine that. The 25-year-old bow-legged rookie with the short frame who played on a losing team had somehow retired as the NFL's seventh all-time rusher and eventually became a member of the Pro Football Hall of Fame. That's significant.

Seven Principles for Success

Through the years I've had the opportunity to look at success. I've studied what makes someone more successful than other people. I've looked at the traits that make Donald Trump a success, as well as Oprah Winfrey. I've also looked at myself and what made me an overachiever. As I mentioned, I came up with seven ingredients for success. These are not easy to achieve. They require incredible focus. If you fall short on just one of these, you may fall short on fulfilling your dreams.

1. Drive

You gotta have drive. It's an internal mechanism that starts your day. Drive is the fuel that gets you up in the morning. If you don't have that, you're going to stay in bed.

Do you know how I start my day? The first thing I do each morning when I wake up is drop and do 50 pushups. For some that might not seem like a lot, but I'm 70 years old. A lot of people say I don't look that old. But believe me, in the morning when I wake up, my body feels like that of a 70-year-old man. I hate to do pushups. Some days I don't feel well, but I do them every day. I never miss a day. Why? Because this is a commitment I made to myself to help me stay in shape. Doing the push-ups is the drive that gets me up and ready to face the day with a smile on my face.

It's the same drive I had during my playing days with the Broncos. In the off-season I would get up each morning and head to Mile High Stadium to run the 112 steps in the South stands wearing army boots. Did that for an hour, up and down, down and up. Sometimes I would stop and hurl, but still kept going. Nemiah Wilson, a teammate of mine with the Broncos who later played with the Oakland Raiders, would join me. I stopped every day to pick up Nemiah on the way to the stadium.

Nemiah hated running those steps more than I did. It got so bad for him that he stopped speaking to me on the ride over. He used to pray that I wouldn't show up, but I always did. I'd say, "We're here. Let's get it done." This was pure drive. I knew this was what I had to do to have a successful season. I never put it off because I knew if I let one day go, then it would just make it easier for me to say, f— it tomorrow.

You've got to have that kind of drive to be successful. To get up and do something every day even if it's the last thing you feel like doing. Once you do it for a while, it becomes a habit. Then you no longer dwell on the task, you just do it.

2. Determination

This is your will. Or what I like to call your uncommon will, which I adapted from a line in my favorite poem, "An American's Creed" by Dean Alfange, an American politician. It's always instilled in me the idea of self-reliance and determination that has motivated me throughout my life.

> I do not choose to be a common man. It is my right to be uncommon—if I can.
>
> I seek opportunity—not security. I do not wish to be a kept citizen, humbled and dulled by having the state look after me.
>
> I want to take the calculated risk; to dream and to build, to fail and to succeed.

*I refuse to barter incentive for a dole. I prefer the challenges
of life to the guaranteed existence; the thrill of fulfillment to the
still calm of utopia.*

*I will not trade freedom for beneficence nor my dignity for
a handout. I will never cower before any master nor bend to
any threat.*

*It is my heritage to stand erect, proud and unafraid; to
think and act for myself, enjoy the benefit of my creations and
face the world boldly and say, this I have done.*

I've channeled this thinking when it comes to determination. I believe
in an uncommon will—a determination that I will not let you beat me. I
will always outwork you and not be denied. Tim Tebow shares this uncommon will, that indefatigable determination. No one will outwork him.
Some of my teammates, such as Billy Thompson, Rich Jackson, and Tom
Jackson, and a few others shared that same uncommon will.

One of my favorite movies is *Seabiscuit*, the true story of a small, heroic
horse that beat Triple Crown winner War Admiral during the Depression.
There's a great scene in that movie that illustrates determination. Seabiscuit's
jockey, Red Pollard (played by Tobey McGuire), fractures his leg during a
practice run and is unable to ride Seabiscuit against War Admiral. Another
jockey named George Woolf is brought in to ride against the big horse.

Pollard tells Woolf the ins and outs about racing Seabiscuit. Then
Pollard looks around and leads Woolf behind closed doors. "Here's the
key," Pollard says. "When you break first and you're setting the pace, lay
up near the end." Woolf looks incredulous. Pollard looks him straight in
the eyes. "Let War Admiral break even so Seabiscuit gets a good look at
him, then just let him go," Pollard said. "See, it's the heart in Seabiscuit
that will win the race. It's not in his head, not in his legs, but in his heart."

I get goosebumps when I think of that scene. That's determination.
Heart. Your uncommon will.

Determination is what's inside you. You're ability to shut out all the
distractions, all the pressure, to give everything you got.

3. Dedication

This is your ability to do the things necessary to achieve your goals. First, you have to know what you want to do. Then you have to be dedicated to doing the right things to reach your goal. You can't put it off until tomorrow. It's a mindset you have to develop, whether it's reading a book or doing laundry. If you're not dedicated to seeing something through, then you won't reach the highest level of success.

When I owned my Ford dealerships, I had some of the greatest sales people in the business. Most of them worked extremely hard. They put in the hours necessary to be successful and always tried to do the best for our customers. I also had a few who didn't understand the dedication required to be successful.

I remember one sales guy complained that selling cars was too hard. He said he was trying his best but just couldn't make a sale. I told him that was nonsense. Sales are all about giving yourself enough opportunities to be successful. So I called him into my office and asked, "What time do you get to work?"

"Early," he said, "a good 15–20 minutes before the store opens at 10:00 AM."

"Oh, really," I replied. "Did it ever occur to you to get here at 7:00 AM?"

"Why? That's when service opens, not sales."

"Yes, and what does our service department do?"

He looked at me like I was crazy. "You know. They fix cars."

"Right," I said. "Did it ever occur to you that people who bring their cars in to get fixed might be thinking about buying a new car?"

He looked at me like I had just discovered the first hybrid race car. His eyes were as big as headlights. "Wow, you're right," he exclaimed. "What a great idea!"

To me, that's the essence of dedication—having the discipline to do what's necessary to succeed. Even if that means coming in three hours before work instead of right before you have to be there. In today's world, that's the kind of dedication you need to be successful.

4. Desire

If you don't have desire, you won't achieve anything. You might as well stay in bed, wrinkle up, and die. Desire is your purpose, your interest. What do you want to do with your life? What do you want to accomplish? Do you want to be a school teacher, a singer, an athlete? Desire is the thing that keeps you going. The fuel that motivates you to be somebody, to accomplish something.

Some people have no desire, no interest in advancing their life. They're content to just exist, to be bland. They don't care about taking full advantage of what life has to offer. They don't want to leave a legacy for their family to cherish or to be inspired by.

Don't be one of those people. If you don't have a desire to do anything, do me a favor and at least start reading more. Whether it's books, magazines, or newspapers, try to read something substantial every day. Reading what other people are doing may spark an interest in you. It might give you a moment where you say, "That's what I want to do. I want to be just like this person!" Whatever your age, there's still time to find your desire, your purpose in life.

5. Commitment

This is huge with me. Commitment is your word. I grew up in a generation where your word meant everything. I still feel that way. Although for me the world has changed a lot when it comes to commitment. Fewer and fewer people these days say they're going to do something and actually follow through.

When I was elected to the Pro Football Hall of Fame, I was told my speech could not be longer than nine minutes. In prior years some of the speeches were so long, the ceremony lasted for more than four hours. I was not happy that our speeches had to be cut considerably shorter because of what happened in the past. I had a lot of things to say and a lot of people to thank, but those were the rules. And I always follow the rules. So I worked for months on my speech, making sure I thanked the people who impacted my life the most and still leaving enough room to impart my message. When I was finished, it ran nine minutes flat.

If you saw the Hall of Fame induction ceremony, you know mine was the shortest speech. That means everyone else went over nine minutes.

Some went way over. I'm not saying this to find fault with them at all. I understand if they decided, "To hell with keeping my speech under nine minutes. This is my moment." But I gave my word. I followed the rules because that's always been my mindset since I was in the eighth grade.

At the Super Bowl last year I was scheduled to talk to the Hall of Fame Class of 2012. The meeting was at 4:00 PM, and I was there to welcome the new class and to give them an overview of what the next six months were going to be like leading up to their induction in Canton.

Five of the six new enshrines were there right at 4:00. But one of the guys didn't show up until 4:25. He just sauntered in, no apologies, no explanation, no nothing. That really bothered me. I mean, asking some-one to be at a meeting at 4:00 PM is hardly a tough request. When I played, we got fined $1,000 for every minute we were late. Back then no one could afford to lose that kind of bread. We were always on time. Commitment is all about your word. What you say you're going to do, you're committed to getting it done. Your word is your bond. If you can't be there, you call up and say you're going to be late.

Tell you what, if I'm ever 25 minutes late for anything like that new Hall of Famer was, call up the highway patrol because I'm dead on the road somewhere.

I just wish your word still meant something today like it did when I was growing up.

6. Sacrifice

It's the sacrifices in life that truly make us successful. It's doing what you know you have to do, not doing what you want to do. If you're willing to hang out with friends and procrastinate instead of studying, you only have yourself to blame. Don't get me wrong. It's fine to hang out with friends. But make sure you put the necessary time in to reach your goal. It's impor-tant to distance yourself from procrastination.

When I got into college I was older. I had been held back a year in high school, then went to Bordentown Military Institute for two years before attending Syracuse. I was a 21-year-old freshman. I looked at it this way, I was already behind. I knew what I wanted, so I didn't fool around. My life consisted of football and studying. That's it. If I had free time, I was either working out, studying with tutors, or sleeping.

I didn't know if I would have the opportunity to play professional football, so my goal was a college degree—something that no one in my family had achieved. I woke up each morning with my father's voice in my head, asking me if I was fulfilling his promise of becoming successful. I didn't need an alarm. My father's voice was my morning wake-up call.

I did meet a lovely girl named Joyce Green at Syracuse. But she was a straight-A student and a Phi Beta Kappa. She actually helped me with my studies. She wasn't a procrastinator. I later married her, and we had two beautiful daughters together. I was even serious about dating.

Believe me, there were plenty of opportunities for me to have fun at Syracuse. I was a three-time All-American, the first since Doak Walker of SMU who played in the 1940s. I could have taken advantage of being a big man on campus. I'd go somewhere like the Varsity restaurant, and fellow students would ask for my autograph. But acting like a big shot wasn't me. I wasn't a lady's man like Joe Namath. I was more like Roger Staubach, an intense competitor, but a serious student, far from a playboy.

I looked at my college years this way—if I can make sacrifices and do the things necessary to get a college degree, I will have laid the foundation to be successful for the next 50 years. I wasn't smart, so I tried to hang out with smart people. Mirror their study habits. Be like them. Always try to hang with people who want to be better than they are.

7. Attitude

This is the most important of my seven ingredients to success because it's the only one that you have 100 percent control over—your attitude. Every morning when you wake up, you need to do a checkup from the neck up. Stand up, breathe in this glorious life that you've been given, and say, "I'm going to make something happen today." It's not always the person with the high IQ who is successful. It's the person with the most positive attitude. Employers can tell right away if they want to hire you just by the way you carry yourself. Bosses are the same way once you're hired. "This person is always upbeat. He always shows up. He's enthusiastic. He's always ready to work."

What do you think Tim Tebow's coaches and teammates love about him the most? It's his attitude. They know every day Tim will show up with a smile on his face and be ready to work. They know when the game is on the line, he's going to be as relaxed and confident on the inside as he is during the week. Attitudes like that are infectious. People can smell it. I'm not kidding. I do a weekly radio show here in Syracuse, and people tell me the one thing they like about the show is my positive attitude. They can hear the enthusiasm in my voice. I'm the same way when I come into my office every morning. I say, "Good morning. How are you?" So many people don't say anything when they get to work. They might mumble, "Mornin'" barely enunciating the word.

I'm not being phony when I greet people. I'm truly happy about another day to help someone. I know I may face some difficult situations and be asked some tough questions, but my attitude helps me face whatever comes my way that day. Seriously, what can go wrong? I'm the one who will determine if it's a good day or a bad one. Today is the best day of my life, and tomorrow will be better. I'm alive. I'm going to make someone feel good about themselves.

Try this sometime. Next time you're at work try to make two people feel good about themselves. Go up to them and say, "How are you doing? I just want to tell you how much I enjoy working with you." Or ask them about their son or grandson. There's one lady at work who sits down the hallway from me. She tells me, "You make my day every morning." She says she knows when I'm here and when I'm not here just by the attitude I bring. Now that's her positive attitude rubbing off on me.

Just think of the impact positive thinking has on athletics. I believe the all-time great NFL quarterbacks all had gobs of confidence. I think what made Roger Staubach a great clutch player was that he wanted the ball in his hands when the game was on the line. It was exciting to him. Absolutely, he had the will to win. There was nowhere else he wanted to be than with 2:00 left and 80 yards to go for a win. Quarterbacks who throw the interception on the last play instead of the touchdown probably have more demons of doubt in their heads than anything else.

You see that in golf. How else do you explain PGA pros missing 3' putts on the 18th hole to lose a tournament? They're battling the demons of doubt. As a result their knees begin to knock, and deep down they know they're going to miss the putt. Golf more than any other sport is mental. I know. I play a lot of golf. It's the one field where I have my doubts. I kid people that my handicap is my swing. But I'm a pretty good putter because I have the positive attitude that I'm going to make that putt.

People with positive attitudes live longer than those with negative attitudes. Each morning I have a choice when I wake up. I choose to have a great day and make a difference in some way.

GPS

Everyone knows about GPS. It stands for Global Positioning System, and it's finally made those awkward paper maps a thing of the past. Yet for me, GPS stands for Grace, Passion, Skill. This is something I've adopted as my own, thanks to my daughter Christy's pastor, Reverend Donnell Jones, of Grace Covenant Church in Washington, D.C. Reverend Donnell came up with this alternative meaning for GPS to illustrate how we can determine the direction we should go in our lives.

First there's Grace. Your grace is life. God has blessed you with this gift. But part of your grace is determining your talent—your blessing. That's where the second part—Passion—comes in. What are you passionate about? What's the thing that really piques your interest, that gets your juices flowing?

We are all passionate about something but may not know what our grace is, our talent. Figuring out what you're really passionate about can help you find your grace. Here's an example. A student I've been talking to a lot about careers came into my office last year and told me she had figured out what she wanted to do with her life.

"I want to help people!" she beamed. "I've always loved helping people."

I said, "Okay, what does that mean?"

She looked confused. "It means, you know, I want to help people."

I smiled, "Help people do what, get on the bus or help people get off the bus?"

She laughed. "I want to be a social worker."

So I sat back in my chair, "Okay, we're getting somewhere. Do you mean a counselor or a social worker?"

The student shrugged her shoulders, "Well, the thing is you can't make a lot of money doing social work. I guess what I really want to do is get into the communications school."

"You mean, Newhouse? You need a 3.4 GPA to get in. Do you have that?" Her GPA was several points lower. "Well, then you might need another plan. Let me ask you something," I said, leaning forward. "Is your passion to make money or do you want to fulfill your grace and help people?"

Of course, she wanted to do both. "Well, that's great," I said. "Then you need to find a career that allows you to help people and make money."

I told her if she wanted to make a lot of money and help people, then she should think about becoming a doctor or a lawyer. Or she could earn a nice middle-class salary as a teacher or a coach. "There are a lot of occupations that help people," I said. "Once you figure out your grace, then you need to develop the third part—the Skill—to fulfill your blessing." A doctor's skillset must include graduating from medical school. A lawyer must graduate from law school and pass the bar exam.

So what's my GPS? I didn't know I wanted to be a professional football player until my junior year at Syracuse when I was named All-American for the second consecutive time. I discovered that the talent to play professional football was my grace. My passion was my drive to be the best. And my skill set was becoming fundamentally sound in running, blocking, and receiving. I still had a backup plan that included graduating with a degree to make sure if I blew out my knee getting off the bus at my first training camp, I would still have my education.

Now that I can no longer score touchdowns and I've retired from the auto business, my blessing is also helping people. I'm able to do that in many different ways. But my job as the special assistant to the Syracuse athletic director allows me to do this every day.

Fantastic Outpouring

One of the things that has been so great about my induction into the Hall of Fame is the outpouring of letters and emails, handshakes and hugs from fans across the country. Many of the letters sent after the *Sports Illustrated* article brought kind sentiments from this new generation of fans. Yet since I retired more than 35 years ago, most of these fans are older now. For them to take the time to reach out to me, it makes me well up.

I read a letter recently that said, "You came to my junior high school in 1968 and talked about the importance of education and surrounding yourself with good people. You challenged us to set goals, and told us anything's possible through hard work and sacrifice. We raised our kids instilling these same values that you instilled in me all those years ago. I just want to say thank you."

Last February I was at an event at Syracuse celebrating Dr. Martin Luther King and Black History Month. A woman came up to me and said, "Many years ago you spoke at our high school and implored us to 'Shoot for the moon because even if you miss you'll land among the stars.' I have to be honest—I used to have trouble with those words. I used to think that if you shoot for the moon and don't reach it, then you've failed. It doesn't matter if you land among the stars. But as I matured I realized what shooting for the moon is all about. It means it's better to attempt to do something great and fail than to attempt to do nothing and succeed. If you never stop trying, you never fail. You only fail when you stop trying."

Astonished at her incredible introspection, I began to beam with pride. "Wow, that's better than I could have said it. You are so right!"

A couple weeks later I was forwarded a letter via email from a longtime fan, Ken Wagoner. He apologized for what he thought could be perceived as a "disposition" to my time. He didn't want to bother me. But he had lost his older brother recently, and they were as close as wingmen. He never had the chance to tell his brother how much he meant, and he said he wanted to be sure he never let an opportunity to express his gratitude pass by again.

The letter explained how his older brother taught him about football in the mid-1960s. His brother also said that I was the most exciting player in college football. He said they used to chart my games to see how many yards I gained. In the 1966 Gator Bowl against Tennessee, they thought they had miscalculated my rushing yards because it was more than 200. The next day in the paper they discovered they were right. I had gained 216 yards. Because the brothers lived in Colorado and were already Broncos fans, they were ecstatic when I was drafted by Denver.

He told me he was grateful that I had come to the Broncos and gave the team an identity and respectability during those lean years. The letter dripped with so much emotion and admiration I was sobbing at the end.

After I collected myself, I decided that merely replying by email wasn't enough. So I picked up the phone and called him.

"Ken," I said, "this is Floyd Little." There was dead silence. Then he blurted out, "Oh my God! Wait, wait, wait. I'm driving on the freeway. Please wait while I pull over!" After he pulled over we talked for 10 minutes. I could hear him fighting back the tears. He was very respectful and said that I had just made his life. Can you believe that?

Sometimes as a professional athlete you forget the impact you can have on people's lives.

You never know who you're going to influence. I've been told by fans that watching me play gave them great joy. Yet many fans said that it was my civic work in the community that made me an even bigger person in their eyes. That means the world to me. Football is just a game. Don't get me wrong, it's a heck of a game. But it's not your whole life. What you do off the football field for other people is what really counts.

Role Models

There are two sides to every argument. This is especially true when it comes to the age-old question, "Should athletes be role models?" It can be a very polarizing subject. There's no middle ground.

I know Charles Barkley has said time and again, "I'm not a role model." Knowing how much I value being a role model, some think I should be upset at what Charles said and want me to vehemently challenge that premise. But I understand his point of view. He means, "Don't look at athletes as role models. Your parents should be role models."

But from my perspective, not everyone is fortunate enough to grow up with two parents that a kid wants to emulate. Not all parents are good role models. My father had a hard life, and he was often a difficult man to understand. I was only six years old when he died, and I needed someone to look up to. My older brother, Ranger, was a great athlete, a tremendous basketball player. But he was always in trouble, and I never saw him as a role model. When I got older, Jim Brown became my idol. I looked at him as a role model, and I've been blessed to have the chance to know him. I also felt the same way when I met the great Ernie Davis. The first time I carried the ball at Syracuse it was surreal. I thought, *I can't believe I am being given the opportunity to try and continue the proud legacy of wearing No. 44 at Syracuse.*

With my difficult upbringing, it was only natural for me to want to become a role model. I was thrown out of school in junior high and had to fight and claw my way back in. Somehow, I was given a second chance. I made sure I did everything in my power to do right—to keep my promise and become the person my father asked me to be.

When I go around the country and speak to junior high schools and youth groups, I can see myself in those students. I want to show them that if I can do it, they can do it. I wasn't special, just determined. Mr. Schreck believed in me all those years ago. Now it's my turn to believe in kids who want to change. In my new position at Syracuse, I have been blessed with the opportunity to influence a lot of young people's lives. There are those I haven't been able to help—young people who don't want to listen to me. It bothers me that I haven't been able to turn them around. But I never stop trying. Every time I stand in front of group of young people, I'm determined to make a difference.

Tim Tebow

Speaking of role models, Timothy Richard Tebow has become one of my favorite subjects since the day he was drafted in the first round by the Denver Broncos. Heck, he's been the talk of the country—and even parts of the world—ever since he brought the Broncos back from a 15-0 shutout last season with 2:00 left in Week 7 for a stunning 18–15 overtime victory. That introduced Tebowing, Tebow Time, and Tebowmania. The NFL hasn't been the same since.

After taking over as the starting quarterback when the team was 1–4, Tim led Denver to seven wins in eight games, six of them in a row and most of them in last-second, jaw-dropping fashion. With Tim leading the way, the Broncos won the AFC West for the first time in six seasons.

Still, the critics, or what I like to call the haters, still don't think Tebow can be a starting NFL quarterback. They point to his mechanics and how he's not a pocket passer. Well, mechanics don't win games, people do. The haters have made up their mind about this young man after just 16 starts, even though he's already won as many playoff games as the Cowboys' Tony Romo and the Falcons' Matt Ryan combined.

Well, I'm a believer. Not only do I think he can become a great NFL quarterback, I believed he could have led the Broncos to an NFL championship. Now I still think he can if the Jets give him an opportunity to start. I know he's there to be second string to Mark Sanchez. But believe me—that young man is going to do everything he can to start. I think Tim's a better quarterback than Sanchez. He's got the intangibles, the confidence, determination, and will to win that Sanchez seems to be lacking. But even if Tim does continue to prove critics wrong, the haters will still be out there. They will always have their opinion, and there's no use trying to change it. If he wins a Super Bowl, they will say it was because of the defense or the running game. They will never give him his due, just like they refused to give it to him after he led the Broncos past the Chargers, Jets, Bears, and then the Steelers in the playoffs last season. But that's okay. The guys who played the game know whether or not a guy is any good—not the media who never strapped on a helmet.

When it comes to being a great NFL quarterback, it's not about mechanics. It's about results—winning. To be a winner you need to have the will to win ingrained in you. Tim has it. There are some NFL quarterbacks who throw the prettiest passes you ever saw. But how do they perform under pressure when the game is on the line? How many playoff victories do they have? To me, that's the true mark of a great NFL quarterback. Do you win when the game is on the line, or do you fold? I know critics talk about Tim's low completion percentage, but to me the most important completions are the ones you make to win the game. Did Tim complete that clutch 80-yard touchdown pass to Demaryius Thomas to beat the Steelers in overtime, or did he misfire? Those are the completions that matter.

Tim's been winning games like this since Pop Warner. It's nothing new for him. I saw Tim's incredible will to win years ago in college. After his undefeated Gators lost to Mississippi his junior year, the kid was so upset. He had tears in his eyes as he addressed the media. The tears were not of sadness, but of anger and remorse. With the cameras rolling, Tim spoke from the heart:

"To the fans and everybody in Gator Nation, I'm sorry. I'm extremely sorry. We were hoping for an undefeated season. That was my goal, something Florida has never done here. I promise you one thing—a lot of good will come out of this. You will never see any player in the entire country play as hard as I will play the rest of the season. You will never see someone push the rest of the team as hard as I will push everybody the rest of the season. You will never see a team play harder than we will the rest of the season. God bless."

I thought, *Wow. This is my guy. Do you see that passion, that will to win?* I knew at that moment they would not lose another game that season.

His speech was dubbed "The Promise." And as I predicted, Tim and his Florida teammates won the rest of their games, including the National Championship over heavily favored Oklahoma. Now his speech is on a plaque at Florida to inspire new generations of Florida Gators.

Somehow that one loss turned on a switch inside, motivating him with this tremendous desire to take his already sublime game to an even higher level. After that, Tim became my man. I just love his attitude. I would have loved to have him as a teammate. He could have played in my era or any era for that matter. When the Broncos drafted him in the first round in 2010, I was at the NFL Draft in New York, sitting with Jim Brown. When Commissioner Roger Goodell made the announcement, we both looked at each other and smiled.

"Nice pick," Jim said.

"You got that right," I beamed.

I think Tim will play even better this season with the Jets. You will see a big improvement in his passing and field awareness. He's got the desire to be great, and his work ethic is second to none. I see a lot of him in me. You can measure a lot of things, but you can't measure heart. Just like the naysayers told me in college and in the pros, Tim's been told on every level from Pop Warner to the NFL that he can't play quarterback. Well, he's already playing quarterback and winning big games. Haters are just adding motivation for the kid.

Just think about his comebacks against the Dolphins, the Raiders, the

Jets, the Chargers, the Vikings, the Bears, and the Steelers. Even after seven victories, the haters still said Tim couldn't pass. So he played Pittsburgh and its No. 1 defense in the playoffs and ripped them for more than 300 yards in the air, including that incredible winning score. I've never seen a string of come-from-behind victories like that in all my years. This guy finds a way to win. Tim has this natural leadership ability to rally everyone around him and raise the team's level of play.

Hey, I understand the Broncos signing Peyton Manning, but I don't agree with it. You give a 36-year-old quarterback who hasn't played in year and has undergone four surgeries $96 million?

The biggest problem I have with signing Manning is that the team isn't building for the future. What are the chances that Manning will be able to win an NFL championship in that small three-year window he probably has left? I don't believe it's ever been done before. Tell me just one 36-year-old (or older) quarterback who has ever signed with a new team and went on to win an NFL championship? I know Joe Montana, Joe Namath, and others couldn't do it, and they were younger. Johnny Unitas was older and lasted just one year in San Diego. I think the Broncos should have tried to build a team around Tebow. That's all. I believe he's that special.

Jets fans will see that Tebow will give you everything he's got on every down in every game. That's all you can ask of anyone.

How About Some Accountability?

As an athlete, I've had my battle with sportswriters. I had a lot of naysayers before I even got to the pros, writers saying I was too small and too old to make it in the NFL. Until this book, I rarely said a word. I preferred to let my actions on the playing field speak for me. But I don't play anymore, and now I have a platform as a Pro Football Hall of Famer. I can say whatever I want because they can can't cut me, they can't fire me, and they can't trade me.

Writers have to understand that they are not experts. They can watch practice and watch tape all they want. They can talk to as many GMs and personnel guys as they want. But what they write in columns or debate on TV and radio is just their opinion. It's the same with the Mel Kipers and

Todd McShays of the world. I realize they study prospects, but they are not experts, either.

As a former professional athlete, I can tell you better than a media person whether a guy is good or not. Guys who played the game and who coached the game simply know more than the media. It's just the way it is. I believe that Hall of Famers should have a vote in Canton. There has been a lot of debate over the years. Although I respect the job that Hall of Fame writers try to do, they should not be given 100 percent *carte blanche* to choose who should be immortalized in Canton. Voting should be expanded so that Hall of Famers, coaches, and GMs also have a voice.

When Peter King was making uninformed statements about my career, I just looked at an email from someone whose opinion matters. Shortly after I was nominated, Tom Mackie contacted Steelers owner Dan Rooney via email about whether I was worthy of the Hall of Fame. Here's what Dan wrote: "I believe Floyd Little should be selected to the Hall of Fame. I also believe Dick LeBeau should be selected in some category."

I believe writers provide a perspective, but you need real football people to truly evaluate someone, especially when it comes to the Hall of Fame. It's like having only writers choose the best military leaders based on video and a stats sheet instead of letting the actual military people decide. It doesn't make sense.

I say this because I'm tired of the media taking shots at football players before they actually play a down in the NFL. I remember last year before the 2011 NFL Draft, countless draftniks were bashing Cam Newton, saying he was a one-year wonder and he was another JaMarcus Russell, saying his style of play couldn't translate to the NFL. Are you kidding me? A 6'5", 248 pound Superman who ran a 4.59 40-yard dash; who led his team to an undefeated season and the National Championship; who threw 30 touchdown passes and just seven interceptions; who rushed for 1,473 yards and 20 touchdowns in a season; who even caught a touchdown pass; who won the Heisman in a landslide? You're telling me this kid can't play?

The worst slam was from Nolan Nawrocki at *Pro Football Weekly*. Before the draft, Nawrocki attacked Newton's character, saying he was, "Very disingenuous—has a fake smile, comes off as very scripted, and has a selfish me-first makeup. Always knows where the cameras are and plays to them. Has an enormous ego with a sense of entitlement that continually invites trouble and makes him believe he is above the law—does not command respect from teammates and will always struggle to win a locker room."

To make matters worse, when pressed, Nawrocki admitted that he had never talked to Newton. Never met the guy but felt compelled to destroy his character based on someone else's opinion. And this kind of journalism is deemed acceptable by his editors?

I saw Newton play last year, and he never came close to being the guy this Nawrocki fellow claims he was. Cam tossed 21 touchdowns while completing 60 percent of his passes for more than 4,000 yards. He also led all quarterbacks with 706 yards rushing and an NFL record 14 touchdowns on the ground. His coaches and teammates loved and respected him. No rookie quarterback in NFL history has come close to putting up the numbers that Cam did. But where's the accountability from these scribes? They can make outrageous comments about a player, assessing talent and deciding who's going to make it and who's not before they ever lace up their cleats in an actual game. Where's the apology? There is none, and I have a problem with that.

RGIII

This past year I saw some of the same negativity about the 2011 Heisman Trophy winner, Robert Griffin III. The year before his breakout season, so-called NFL draft expert Todd McShay said that Griffin should probably switch from quarterback to receiver.

This from a draft expert? I'm glad to see that Robert used that to his advantage by making comments like those his motivation during his off-the-charts season.

I met this young man and spent time with him and his parents at the Heisman Trophy ceremony last year. I was totally impressed by him and not because he told me he grew up a Broncos fan. I believe RGIII has the arm, legs, and focus to be a great player. His parents were both in the military, and they have instilled a strong sense of duty, responsibility, and hard work in this young man. He's a leader. RG III asked me if he should forego his last year of college for the pros, and I told him yes. "You have already graduated with a degree. You have nothing left to prove on the college level. You are a talented mature young man. I believe you are ready for the next level."

The thing that bothered me before the draft was that most experts decided that as great as RGIII was, it was an afterthought that he was still not worthy of the No. 1 overall pick. Based on what?

I know RGIII will surprise as many people in the NFL as Cam Newton did the year before. Keep using those naysayers as motivation, young man!

The Movie *The Express*

For anyone who has not seen *The Express*, I implore you to rent it. This is a story that had been long overdue. With all due respect to one of my all-time favorite tearjerkers, *Brian's Song*, *The Express* should have been made before that. The story of Ernie Davis is incredible. The first African American to win the Heisman Trophy 50 years ago, Ernie died tragically of leukemia at the age of 23.

DeBorah and I went to all three premieres at Syracuse, New York, and Los Angeles. I would have gone to 50 premieres if they had asked me. To see someone playing me on the big screen is one of the great thrills of my life. Of course, the movie was not completely accurate. They had Ernie Davis coming to watch me play at my high school in New Haven, which he never did. They also had me wearing No. 77 in high school. My number was 33 at Hillhouse High. It was 77 at Bordentown Military Institute. And as I mentioned earlier, I only met Ernie the one time when he and Ben Schwartzwalder came to my house on a snowy December night when I was home for winter break from Bordentown. He also had already passed by the time I told Ben I was coming to Syracuse.

Still, the movie was superb. I remember my grand-niece, Lynette, went to see the movie with some friends and had no idea I knew Ernie Davis. When she saw the character playing me in the movie, she freaked out and called me from the theatre screaming—during the movie! Needless to say, I got lots of calls from people who had no idea I was part of the famed Syracuse Trilogy.

Without Sacrifice, There's No Reward

In my previous book, I talked about my nephew, Mike Sturdivant, who is like another son to me.

One of my proudest moments was when Mike got a tryout with the Seattle Seahawks. He's my sister Rosa's child and went to Hillhouse High like me before becoming a terrific receiver at Virginia Tech. He was a Michael Irvin–type, 6'2", 215 pounds and could run a sub-4.4 40-yard dash. He played with Antonio Freeman, the former Packers great.

But what I didn't mention the first time around is how Mike almost didn't get the chance for that tryout. Mike's older brother, Brian, was a bad influence growing up. He was always trying to get Mike to hang with the wrong people. This went on for a few years. Then in the middle of Mike's senior year at Virginia Tech, Mike decided to quit school and go home to Connecticut. One night he and Brian got into a terrible fight with some other kids and were both thrown in jail. My sister got them out and decided to separate them. She sent Mike to Seattle to live with me, while she tried to get Brian some help.

While Mike was out in Seattle, he got a tryout with the Seahawks. Although he impressed a lot of people in training camp including former Chicago Bears coach Abe Gibron, who was an assistant with Tom Flores, Mike never got into a preseason game and was cut. After that I decided Mike needed some direction and discipline, so I made him a salesperson at my Ford dealership. I demanded more out of him than any of my other salespeople. There was no way I was going to cut my nephew any slack. After a couple months, Mike started to really apply himself and began making sales. So what did I do next? I told him, "So you can apply your-self! You're going back to Virginia Tech to get your degree."

He told me he wasn't going back and that he was finished with school. I told him, "Your mother has made too many sacrifices for you to deny her your college degree. You are going back to school." He still refused. So I told him he had a choice. "I'm going to work. When I come home, if you think you can whip me, then we can go at it. If you beat me, then you can quit school. But if you don't think you can whip me, then you better have your bags packed because I'm driving you to the airport to send you back to school."

When I got home, Mike's bags were packed. That night after I dropped him off, I was climbing into bed and there was a card under my pillow. It was from Mike. His words were so emotional, I lost it. He told me how grateful he was to me for trying to give him direction. He told me I was like a father to him, and he appreciated all that I had done. He also said he was going to get his degree and make something of his life.

Mike went on to get his degree, and he got a job with Enterprise Rent-a-Car. He's been with them for more than 15 years now and is an executive there. He must be doing well because whenever we golf, he plays with Titleist ProV1s.

Mike had made so many bad choices that he didn't know what it was like to make good choices. I talked to him about true sacrifice and hard work, what that meant and how to set goals and achieve them. After getting his degree, Mike was able to turn around his life. He now lives in Kansas with his beautiful wife, Melody, and three precious children.

While Brian did some jail time and took a while to straighten himself out, he is turning his life around, too. He is now working full-time, and he and Mike still talk. Brian was actually the best athlete in my family, better than Mike and me. But he was never serious about sports and didn't make the sacrifices necessary to be successful. But there's always still time and I'm proud of both of my nephews for never giving up.

Taking Uncle Floyd's Crazy Advice?

Of course, I believe my nephew, Mike, would have made it in the NFL if he had taken his Uncle Floyd's crazy advice.

When he signed with the Seahawks as an undrafted free agent, I told him a free agent has to work 10 times harder than a draft pick to get noticed. It was 1992, and Tom Flores was the Seahawks coach. During the preseason the Seahawks lost their first two games, and Mike hadn't played a down yet. The heat was on Flores to win. With two losses and the regular season fast approaching, I knew Mike would never get an opportunity to play. The roster would be paired down to 65 after the next game. I had been around long enough to know that if you haven't played yet, there's a 1,000 percent chance you're going to get cut.

So relying on my past experience from my first game at Hillhouse High when I changed the play and ran for a touchdown, and the Buffalo game when I refused to leave the huddle, I devised a plan so Mike would get noticed.

I told him, "Sometime during the game you have to run out onto the field, get in the huddle, and pull someone out. Tell the quarterback to call your play, and goddamn you better catch it. Here's what will happen— they will either call your play, or someone will have to physically carry you off the field. But whatever happens, you have to refuse to leave. You can bet the coaches will be mad, and they'll holler at you. But you tell them you're entitled to one play. Everyone deserves one play. If they drag you off the field, I'll be there to speak on your behalf. There will be a lot of commotion, and wherever there's commotion that's where the media will be. Even if you get booted from the team, the whole country will hear about your stand, and some NFL team will give you a second chance."

Mike wasn't sure. He didn't want to make a scene. But I told him he had nothing to lose. "They're going to cut you anyway. Why not give it a shot?" Mike told me he'd think about it. But in the end he never went through with it. Just as I predicted, he was cut the next day.

Sometimes you have to be crazy like a fox to seize your opportunity in life. I think that was one of those times when you take matters into your own hands. I'm convinced if Mike had been given a chance, he not only would have made the Seahawks, he would have enjoyed a nice career. He was that good.

His old Virginia Tech schoolmate, Antonio Freeman, agreed. "Sturdy was bad!" he said. I'm pretty sure that's bad in a good way!

One of the Greatest Men I've Ever Known

Every NFL player develops great relationships on and off the field with teammates and other players. You also get to know great people within the organization. For me the one guy who stood out and became my good friend was Val Pinchbeck. Val was the PR director for the Broncos from 1967–70. After leaving the Broncos, he became an executive with the NFL and was responsible for many things, including developing the NFL schedule each year.

Before coming to Denver, Val also was the PR director at Syracuse. He not only became a trusted friend and advisor, he was responsible for my becoming a Denver Bronco.

After my playing days, we remained good friends for years. A few years ago he finally retired from the NFL and moved to Florida with his companion, Joanne Parker, years after his wife, Panzie, passed. Of course, someone with Val's knowledge and instincts was hard to come by. So the NFL office called Val frequently for advice to help with schedules and brainstorm ideas. In March 2004, Val was in New York doing just that when he suffered a heart attack while crossing Park Avenue. It was a huge personal loss for me, his family, and many people throughout the NFL.

A memorial service was held for Val a month later in New York at St. Bart's Church. There must have been 1,000 people in attendance. It was a who's who of the NFL, including media members like Dave Anderson of the *New York Times*. Commissioner Paul Tagliabue, Wellington Mara, and other NFL executives were also there including NFLPA president Gene Upshaw. Giants great Frank Gifford, a good friend, spoke at the service. I took my son, Marc, because I wanted him to know about one of the great people who had influenced my life.

I think about Val a lot now and how proud he would have been that I was elected to the Pro Football Hall of Fame. Val was friends with a number of the writers like Dave Goldberg and Edwin Pope. When I met Tom Mackie in March 2003, he felt so strongly that I deserved to be in Canton that I introduced him to Val because he understood how the Hall of Fame worked and helped show Tom the ropes. They talked on the phone numerous times and emailed back and forth quite a bit during the next year. When Val died, Tom knew the ball was fully in his court. The baton had been passed. It was up to Tom to try to make my Hall of Fame quest happen.

Now that I'm a Hall of Famer and I'm back at Syracuse, Val comes to mind frequently. His spirit and his way with people often guide me. I miss him dearly.

Jim Brown

As much as I admire and love Jerry Rice, Jim Brown is still the greatest football player who ever lived. He was my hero when I was a kid just learning the game of football. To be able to share his No. 44 at Syracuse along with the great Ernie Davis, and to be known together as the Legend of 44 always brings a stream of emotions to me.

Jim has always been a man of few words. For many people he's an imposing person to meet, even now as an older gentleman. But he has always been extremely kind and supportive of me.

In 2005 when Syracuse retired No. 44, Jim made a point to tell everyone that I had rushed for more yards than him and Ernie. He also told everyone that I was the only three-time All-American, too. I've seen him a lot in the past few years. He came to the unveiling of the Ernie Davis statue in Syracuse and to the movie premiere of *The Express*. He was also there with me at the premieres in New York and Los Angeles.

When I wrote my first book in 2006, I was overwhelmed when Jim wrote the preface. He wrote, "I've said for years that Floyd deserves to be in the Hall of Fame. There's no question in my mind that he's one of the game's greatest players. Just ask anyone who ever played with Floyd. They'll tell you he was a pro's pro and a true legend who probably did more for the team he played for, the Denver Broncos, than any single player did for his own team."

Now that I am a Hall of Famer, Jim likes to say, "It's about time. You are where you belong, my friend." To me, receiving validation like that from Jim, a man Gary Smith calls the King of Kings, that's everything to me.

Today's Broncos

I have been very critical of the Broncos organization of late. But in no way does that reflect how I feel about the men in charge of bringing the Broncos back to prominence. I'm talking, of course, about John Elway and John Fox.

I think John Elway is proving quickly that he's going to bring a championship back to Denver. He made a lot of strides in his first season. He took over a 4–12 team and brought it to the playoffs in his first year. I'm not surprised. I got to know John years ago, and he's as competitive as a businessman as he was a quarterback on the field. He earned his stripes after his football career by taking the Colorado Crush arena football team to a championship. I think taking linebacker Von Miller in his first draft was a great move. Obviously, he remembered all those times the Chiefs' Derrick Thomas created havoc and the impact that kind of player can have on a team.

I'm also glad the Broncos hired John Fox last year. I've known John since he was an assistant with the Giants through his friendship with Tom Coughlin. When the Broncos hired John, I called and left a congratulatory message on his voicemail. John called me back five minutes later, thanking me for the phone call. We talked for several minutes. That just shows you what kind of guy John is. He's someone players will rally around because he's real. I think he did an incredible coaching job last year by changing the offense to fit the talents of his young quarterback. Not a lot of coaches would do that. And it paid off with an AFC West crown, the first one in six seasons!

The key for the 2012 season, is what are they going to do next? Build up the defense, provide more weapons on offense? Hopefully, it will be both.

The 2012 Hall of Fame Class

Once you're in the Hall of Fame, you are part of an exclusive family. When you consider that there are less than 300 members in Canton and more than 10,000 players have suited up in the NFL, it's extremely humbling. Like any family, if a member of yours asks you to do something, you don't even ask questions. You do it.

That's how I feel about the folks who run Canton. Whenever they ask me to do something, I feel like it's an honor. During Super Bowl XLVI, the day after the 2012 class was announced, the Hall of Fame asked me to address the new members.

First I congratulated everyone and told them what an honor it is to be elected. I explained what the next six months would be like as they progressed to their August enshrinement in Canton. I talked about the fun stuff, being measured for your gold jacket, having your bust created, preparing your speech. Then I really hit home about their duties and responsibilities. How when they go out in public they have a duty to their fellow

Hall of Fame brothers to do the right thing—to show respect for us, the Hall, and themselves.

"You now have a platform that allows you to give back to the community even more than you did before," I told them. "You were game-changers, now be life-changers."

After my short speech, we went around and talked about ourselves so we all got to know each other beyond the stats and Pro Bowls. When we got to Curtis Martin, the great running back for the Patriots and Jets, he stood up and said that he didn't think he deserved to be here. He confessed that he never loved playing football, that he did it because he was good at it and he could make a great living to support his family. Curtis was really humbled and blown away by being elected.

So I listened to what Curtis had to say. Finally, I stood up and said, "Curtis, thank you for sharing this with us. But I must disagree. You do deserve to be here. You were one of the most talented and consistent running backs to ever play the game. You rushed for 1,000 yards in 10 straight seasons. You scored 100 touchdowns. You led the NFL in rushing when you were 31 years old. And you retired as the fourth-leading rusher in NFL history. Only Emmitt Smith, Walter Payton, and Barry Sanders rushed for more yards than you. Most of all, you were a great teammate who respected the game and always did right off the field. Curtis, you most certainly deserve to be here."

Everyone cheered. I could tell it meant a lot to Curtis to feel validated by a fellow Hall of Famer. I remember when I was elected, I felt elated but also very humbled and appreciative of everything.

I also told the class of 2012 that their lives have changed forever. They now have a legacy that can't be touched. No one can fire you, cut you, or trade you from the Hall of Fame. "If you're ever having a bad day or feel sorry for yourself, do me a favor. Get up and put on your gold jacket and walk around wearing it," I said. "Believe me, your attitude will change. This is the highest honor in sports. Wear your jacket proudly, knowing you are now part of an exclusive club. No one can ever take that away from you."

I'm the 257th member of the Pro Football Hall of Fame. It's even stitched on the inside of my jacket so I don't forget—not that I ever will.

My Reason for Being

Of all my accomplishments on the field, nothing means more than my family. I'm still close to teammates Billy Thompson, Jerry Simmons, Rich Jackson, the fans in Denver, and people from Syracuse, New Haven, and the city I called home for more than 20 years, Seattle. But my growing family continues to be my heart and soul—my wife, siblings, cousins, and especially my four grandchildren.

Christy Little Jones

My oldest daughter, Christy Jones, went to Syracuse like her old man. She also got a Master's degree at American University. Christy and her husband, Adrian, are the parents to my four beautiful grandchildren: A.J., Skye, Blaze, and Hayes. Christy is the one who keeps us together. We would not be a tight family without her. Christy organizes all get-togethers, and she's one of the most giving, selfless people I know. When she's not raising her four children or organizing family reunions and get-togethers for our family, she somehow has the energy to run an amazing business, Relationship Revolution, where she serves as a coach, educator, and mentor.

Relationship Revolution is a three-tiered program that encourages women to revolutionize their marriages, revolutionize their parenting, and revolutionize other powerful and committed female relationships so you can all attain your dreams. A number of years ago, Christy started Mommy-in-Training to help other moms become better and more confident. Since then she's created an incredible, one-of-a-kind network of resources for women who want to do better for their children, spouses, and each other. I am so proud of Christy and her huge heart, which seems to grow bigger every day. She is beautiful inside and out, and I couldn't be more proud of her.

Kyra Little DaCosta

My youngest daughter, Kyra Little DaCosta, is the most talented of my kids. She's a triple threat. A Broadway performer who has toured with Bette Midler, Kyra can sing, dance, and act with equal aplomb. When it comes to singing, my baby girl is an alto-soprano. She also sings jazz and

R&B, plus musical theatre tunes. She's an unbelievable dancer who loves salsa, jazz, modern, the cha cha, and Broadway.

Kyra is as sweet as she is tough. She's a black belt in Shotokan Karate. I think she could probably take me in two out of three falls! But what I love and respect most about her is her incredible will and mental toughness. Making it in show business is an extremely difficult life. There are many ups and downs. But Kyra has not only endured, she has shined. She's appeared in five Broadway productions, including playing the lead role as Beverly in *Baby It's You*, and starred in *Dreamgirls* and *Unchain My Heart*, the story of Ray Charles. She's performed with legendary stars like Patty LaBelle and Morgan Freeman.

Kyra has appeared in countless commercial and TV shows, including *House*. To know Kyra is to read her two favorite quotes: "Laughter is the best medicine," and, "Success is the best revenge." I am so proud of Kyra and love her for her drive to be the best.

Marc Little

I've talked a lot of about Marc. I'll only add that he's a lawyer in Los Angeles and my best friend. He has a great wife in Tigra, and he and I talk almost every day. If we miss a day, we notice it. When I grow up I want to be like him.

I believe the true success of a parent is never having to get your kids out of jail or having to pay for drug or alcohol rehabilitation. All three of my children graduated from college and are extremely successful and happy.

DeBorah Little

Many years after my divorce, I met a beautiful woman named DeBorah Green at a Syracuse function, and we married in April 2003. She is so stunning that friends kid me that I've "out-kicked my coverage." DeBorah is a godsend who is even more beautiful on the inside. She's very supportive and loving. And she's one of the most positive people I've ever met. She travels the country as a motivational speaker. If you think I can inspire people, you should listen to her! She's made my life very enjoyable, and we laugh about something every day. Buddies nudge me and say, "Where can I get me a DeBorah?"

I've already told you all that she's done for me during those exciting but draining Hall of Fame months. The thing I love about her is that she always has my back, and she's always ready to fight the good fight for what's right. She cares deeply for me, and I appreciate everything she does for me every day. I wouldn't be the man I am today without her or my incredible children.

Final Thoughts

I've had a great time putting together this book. I didn't realize how much I had to say until I started talking about my life's journey and the commitment and sacrifice I had to put forth to attain my dreams. It made putting everything down on paper very emotional for me. Reliving your past isn't always easy. There were some really difficult, painful times. But I always kept that promise to my father in my head and in my heart. I never wanted another vision to appear with him upset or angry at me. Looking back, I feel I have done right by him. I also hope that I have fulfilled my promise to Ernie Davis in the way I performed and carried myself all these years.

In life, just remember that someone's label or opinion of you should never become your reality. What someone says about you is just one opinion. That's it. Move on and let them deal with it.

When I got to the pros, the driving force for me was the *Sports Illustrated* article that came out before the 1967 draft that said I was too small and too old to make it. That got my nostrils flaring and my antenna up. How could someone tell you that? How do they know that? You know by now that it's not about your height, your weight, your speed, or your age. It's about your heart. That's what gets you to the next level. It's your will, your fight, your strength to overcome obstacles. That's how you attain your dreams—by never saying never. Never saying you had enough. It's not up to the critics or the naysayers. It's up to you. It's not over until you say it's over. That's how you measure someone's will—by how much gas you still have in the tank.

What made the game great for me was the love of the fans and the respect players had for the way I played. The great Broncos fans never forgot me. My teammates and I didn't win a lot of games, but we played a full 60 minutes. Even when we were losing bad, guys on the Chiefs and Raiders would say to me, "Why are you still out here? Why are you still playing? It's over!" I would say, "It's not over. There's still time on the clock. This may be the play where we break a long one and score to make it closer. C'mon, let's play!" The truth is I wanted to be out there. We all get just so many plays in football and in life. I wanted to be out there as much as I could. You never know when it's going to be your last play. That's why I played every down like it was my last and volunteered to play special teams when I didn't have to.

That's why I played with torn cartilage in my knees, broken hands and fingers, broken vertebras, collarbones, concussions, and all. I never wanted to say, "I wish I had," or, "I should have." Sure, maybe I shouldn't have played with injuries, but I didn't want to second-guess myself later in life. I would tell coaches, "If you don't want me to play, then don't put my jersey in my locker. Because I'm going to play whether I can or not. Hiding my uniform is the only way to keep me from playing." I was committed to doing everything I could to help our team win. I was fortunate that I never got injured too badly. Sure, my memory could be better. Occasionally, I forget what I had for breakfast and I piss in a trash can and throw my keys in the toilet, but I'm better off than most.

I played at a pace and a position where I got hit every play whether I carried the ball or not. I don't recommend it to other players. Management didn't appreciate that kind of effort then, and they don't appreciate it now. It's still a business, pure and simple. In my day, guys fought for their jobs every week. We had to play hurt. Today guys are protected by rules, which is good. We didn't make a lot of money. We all worked in the offseason. I signed for $10,000. I told that to a young player recently and he said, "I wouldn't go to the bathroom for 10 grand."

But I wouldn't change a thing. I played for the greatest fans in the world at Syracuse and for the Denver Broncos. That made it all worth it for me. Certain things I won't ever forget—being carried off the field after my final game at Mile High; Willie Lanier following me everywhere on the field and along the sideline; Mike Curtis knocking me cold; leading the league in rushing in back-to-back seasons on a last-place team; being honored with Floyd Little Day by the great Broncos fans; and finally slipping on my gold jacket as a member of the Pro Football Hall of Fame.

In the end, I think I left the game better than when I started. But I'm nowhere near ready to start circling the drain. I still have more promises to keep and miles to go before I sleep.

SOURCES

Books

Carroll, Bob, Michael Gershman, David Neft, and John Thorn. *Total Football II: The Official Encyclopedia of the NFL.* New York: William Morrow, 1999.

Connor, Dick. *The Denver Broncos.* New York: Prentice-Hall, 1974.

Gordon, Larry. *Barely Audible: A History of the Denver Broncos.* Graphic Impressions, 1975.

Gutman, Bill. *Morris, Johnson, Hill, Little.* Tempo Books. 1974.

King, Peter. *Sports Illustrated: Greatest Quarterbacks.* New York: Time, Inc., 2000.

Libby, Bill. *Star Running Backs of the NFL.* New York: Random House, 1972.

Miller, Jeff. *Going Long: The Wild Ten Year Saga of the Renegade American Football League in the Words of Those Who Lived It.* New York: McGraw-Hill, 2004.

Rubin, Bob. *Little Men of the NFL.* New York: Random House, 1974.

The Denver Broncos Media Guide

Magazines

Sports Illustrated archives

Newspapers

Denver Post

Websites

Pro-Football-Reference.com

INDEX